The Aztec Kings

The Aztec Kings

The Construction of Rulership
in Mexica History

Susan D. Gillespie

THE UNIVERSITY OF ARIZONA PRESS

TUCSON & LONDON

THE UNIVERSITY OF ARIZONA PRESS

Copyright © 1989
The Arizona Board of Regents
All Rights Reserved

This book was set in 10/13 Linotron 202 Trump Mediaevel.
Manufactured in the United States of America
♾ This book is printed on acid-free, archival-quality paper.
93   92   5   4   3   2
Library of Congress Cataloging-in-Publication Data
Gillespie, Susan D., 1952–
The Aztec kings : the construction of rulership in Mexica history /
Susan D. Gillespie.
p.   cm.
Bibliography: p.
Includes index.
ISBN 0-8165-1095-4
ISBN 0-8165-1339-2 (pbk.)
1. Aztecs—History.   2. Aztecs—Kings and rulers.   3. Indians of
Mexico—History.   4. Indians of Mexico—Kings and rulers.
1. Title.
F1219.73.G55   1989
972'.01–dc19   89-4760
CIP
British Cataloguing-in-Publication Data
A catalogue record for this book is available from the British Library.

Contents

Figures

Tables

Preface

This book represents a departure from the usual approach to the study of the historical traditions of the pre-Hispanic people known as the Aztecs. It deemphasizes the search for some historical accuracy in these traditions and instead utilizes a hermeneutical methodology to determine the symbolic meanings embedded within them. It has therefore been written with two sometimes different audiences in mind: readers familiar with Aztec history and those interested in the symbolic interpretation of text. As both a Mesoamerican archaeologist and a symbolic anthropologist, my intention is to demonstrate that a hermeneutical approach can complement ethnohistorical analyses of Aztec historical traditions and increase our knowledge of Aztec society, since additional information can be obtained from the traditions by using more than one methodology. The Aztecs themselves understood history as a narrative form of social charter, and in particular, Aztec conceptions of the nature of rulership were made manifest in the creation and retelling of the historical traditions. Because those conceptions were not unique, neither were the historical narratives; thus they cannot automatically be assumed to have some literal accuracy, for the same stories were told in other complex societies for the same reasons.

Since the analysis focuses on Aztec traditions recounting the pre-

Hispanic past that have been preserved since the time of the Spanish
conquest in 1521, the data take the form of stories whose narrative
quality has been maintained in order for their structure and function
to be understood. Readers may often be challenged by the necessity
to comprehend the many disparate versions of episodes in Aztec history, keeping track of names and relationships that are quite flexible.
Other important historical information has been preserved not in
prose but in pictures, both the native pictographs and Europeanized
illustrations, which were also scrutinized as another kind of "text."

It may be helpful in understanding both the content and organization of this book and its major objectives to know why I came
to write it. The research was an attempt to solve an archaeological
problem. I had become fascinated by the story of Ce Acatl Topiltzin
Quetzalcoatl given in books on Mesoamerican archaeology. Topiltzin Quetzalcoatl was a ruler of the Toltecs, a pre-Aztec civilization,
the events of whose life were recorded in Aztec historical traditions
written after the Spanish conquest. Forced to leave his capital city of
Tula in central Mexico, he and a loyal band of Toltec followers made
a long journey to the Yucatan peninsula, where he rebuilt the Maya
city of Chichen Itza into a "new Tula," a copy of the Toltec "mother
center" (to use Nicholson's terminology; 1971a:109).

I began to read about the archaeology of both Tula and Chichen
Itza, looking for evidence of this migration. Clearly, the two sites
are related to one another in the similarities of their architectural
decoration and use of three-dimensional and bas-relief sculpture,
although in other ways their material remains are quite different.
What I determined from the published reports, however, was that
the archaeological evidence as then known did not actually fit the
Toltec migration story as it had been interpreted from the preserved
historical traditions of both the Aztecs and the Maya. Nevertheless,
archaeologists working in the period of the Toltec and later Aztec
civilizations (the Postclassic, A.D. 900–1500), consistently deferred
to the ethnohistorical evidence for their interpretations (Diehl 1981:
293), which they believed to be superior to the archaeological data.
One scholar summed up this position with the statement that, based
on the material remains, "one might think that Toltec elements
spread from Chichen toward distant Tula," but in fact, "the documentary sources show without doubt that the influence went in the
opposite direction" (Margain 1971:75).

I concluded from these observations that I would also have to read the ethnohistorical documents in order fully to comprehend the nature of the interaction between Tula and Chichen Itza, because all the interpretations were biased toward the story of a Toltec migration out of Tula. Upon examining the written accounts, however, I discovered that none of them told the same story, and more to the point, none of them actually said that Topiltzin Quetzalcoatl went to Chichen Itza. The narratives did reveal patterns in their contradictions and inconsistencies, however, which indicated that they held a deeper meaning that could be explicated using the methodologies of structuralist and symbolic analysis. To explain what these patterns meant first required an understanding of who was telling these stories, and when.

All the documents were written much later by people who were reflecting on their past after the Spanish conquest and even well into the colonial period. Because I was dealing with the stories told by the Aztecs, the historical traditions must have had some meaning for Aztec society. That meaning became apparent in the similarities between the stories about the Toltec king Topiltzin Quetzalcoatl and those concerning the two kings named Motecuhzoma who ruled the most important Aztec capital, Tenochtitlan, which was inhabited by the Mexica ethnic group. The Aztecs, like other peoples, used history to construct and communicate their ideas on the origin and nature of rulership, and thus the historical episodes of Topiltzin Quetzalcoatl and the two Motecuhzomas had been manipulated to fit those ideas, which accounts for their similarity. Further research into the historical traditions of the Tenochtitlan genealogy revealed that it had a cyclical form, which determined why only the kings named Motecuhzoma were singled out to be equated with Topiltzin Quetzalcoatl as endpoints of dynastic cycles. Logic then demanded an investigation of the impact of the Spanish conquest on the rewriting of history, since that event rendered Motecuhzoma II a dynastic endpoint as the last Tenochtitlan king.

In the end, I have come to a number of conclusions that are at odds with what Diehl calls the "orthodox view" of Toltec history (1981: 277), although they are derived from the same documents. Some readers may reject these ideas because they seem to be based on a selective singling out of elements from diverse sources to support my hypotheses, but then, the original Topiltzin Quetzalcoatl story was constructed in the same selective way, as are all of our reconstructions of the past. I have applied a well-known method of analysis to the Aztec historical traditions which can incorporate many historical details otherwise ignored or misunderstood because they are contradictory or supernatural. One aim of this study is to stimulate a rethinking of some old interpretations and a formulation of alternative explanations for the striking similarities between Tula de Allende and Chichen Itza. The abandonment of the as yet unproved "Tula-centric" paradigm for Postclassic Mesoamerica should also allow for further investigations of the true nature of Aztec culture, which had a strong Gulf Coast component, especially in its religion and art (see, e.g., Grove 1983; Sullivan 1982; and Townsend 1979).

This book is organized somewhat in reverse of the sequence of the research. It begins with an analysis of the dynastic history of Tenochtitlan and then moves on to other episodes in Mexica history that reveal the nature and qualities of rulership—its origin, cyclicity, and transfer—conceptions that are clearly related to worldwide notions of divine kingship. The Introduction sets the stage for the book, briefly outlining the form and function of the Aztec historical traditions and examining how they were changed by the conquest and subsequent colonial rule under the Spanish. The case study begins with Chapter 1 and is divided into two parts. The first deals with the role that certain royal females—the "women of discord"—played in the histories, and the second deals with the role played by certain royal males, the "recycled kings." These are the two key players in the construction of rulership conceptions that are dynamically related to both the cosmos and the state. The final chapter is more like a coda than a summary; more than the earlier chapters, it deals abstractly and comparatively with the kinds of information embedded in Aztec sacred history and presents avenues for further research.

Certain conventions I have followed in this book need to be explained. The spelling of personal and place names is always a problem in Aztec studies because they vary greatly from text to text and among the different ethnic groups known as the Aztec people. I have chosen to standardize the variant orthographies to simplify the reading, using spellings that seem to be preferred by modern scholars. In addition, I have restricted the name Tollan to references to the sacred city that appear in Aztec and Maya historical traditions, using its synonym Tula to refer to the archaeological site. Because it is important for the reader to be able to distinguish males from females easily, non-European names of women are preceded

by the biological symbol ♀. The illustrations were copied from facsimiles of varying quality and in some cases represent a selection
of pictographs, with other pictures and glosses deleted. Quotations
from non-English sources have been translated into English. For the
reader's convenience, citations to the published historical traditions
have been somewhat simplified.

This work is an outgrowth of my doctoral dissertation, entitled
"Aztec Prehistory as Postconquest Dialogue: A Structural Analysis of the Royal Dynasty of Tenochtitlan" (University of Illinois
at Urbana-Champaign, 1983). I would like to acknowledge the advice and support of my faculty committee: David C. Grove, the late
Douglas Butterworth, Claire R. Farrer, Norman E. Whitten, Jr., and
Rudolph Troike. The current revised and enlarged manuscript was
greatly improved by the helpful advice and criticism of R. Tom Zuidema, John K. Chance, Jonathan E. Reyman, and several anonymous
reviewers. I also acknowledge with thanks the staff of the Library of
the National Museum of Anthropology in Mexico City for the opportunity to examine the original *Codex García Granados*, and Manual
Alvarado Guinchard, who loaned me a microfilm copy of the *Codex
de Huichapan*.

An Introduction to the Analysis of Aztec Historical Traditions

History, in the sense of written record-keeping, began in the New World only after the arrival of Europeans in the late fifteenth century, with one notable exception: the culture area known as Mesoamerica. In this region, which extends from southern Mexico into northern Central America, several high civilizations flourished in the pre-Columbian era. Among their many accomplishments was the development of writing systems tied to a calendar. In addition, the different peoples maintained oral historical traditions of great antiquity, which were written down after the Spanish conquest in the early sixteenth century.

One of these civilizations, which has since been given the name "Aztec," was still thriving in central Mexico when the Spanish came in 1519. Aztec history and society are thus particularly well known because of the extensive contact between the indigenous peoples and European colonizers following their surrender in 1521 to the Spanish conquistadores led by Hernán Cortés. The term *Aztec* is a generic one, referring to a number of culturally related agrarian city-states around Lake Texcoco in the Valley of Mexico. From this base they controlled an extensive tribute-paying empire that covered much of non-Maya Mesoamerica. Unlike the Maya of southern Mesoamerica, the Aztecs never developed true writing, but they did have a

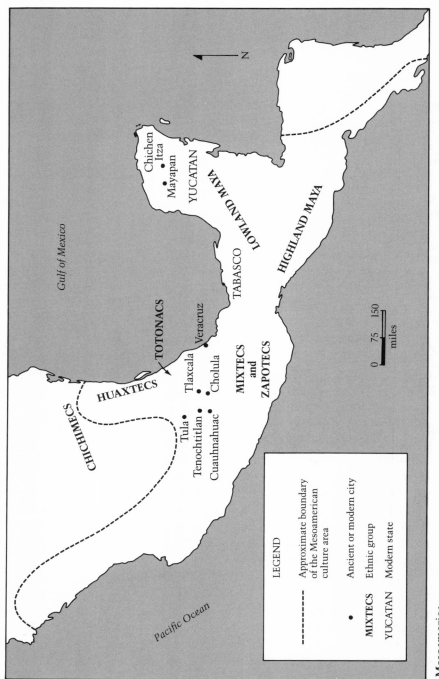

Mesoamerica

LEGEND

Approximate boundary
of the Mesoamerican
culture area

Ancient or modern city

MIXTECS   Ethnic group

YUCATAN   Modern state

Gulf of Mexico

Pacific Ocean

N

0   75   150
miles

CHICHIMECS

Tula

Tenochtitlan

Cuauhnahuac

HUAXTECS

TOTONACS

Tlaxcala

Veracruz

Cholula

MIXTECS
and
ZAPOTECS

TABASCO

LOWLAND MAYA

HIGHLAND MAYA

Chichen
Itza

Mayapan

YUCATAN

record-keeping system using pictographic symbols written on paper "books," and they maintained historical traditions based on a solar year calendar.

While none of the native "books" of the Aztecs survived the conquest (Glass 1975:11), the record of their history and culture was not immediately destroyed. Instead, it was preserved in later texts written by both the indigenous elite and the early Spanish residents (particularly the clergy) in what became known as New Spain. Many of these documents refer to events that took place prior to the arrival of the Spanish, and thus they are considered to have preserved the "native historical tradition" (Cline 1972:6–7). They include both pictographic renderings (a continuation of the original record-keeping system) and prose texts in Latin letters, written in either Spanish or a native language, usually Nahuatl, the dominant language in the Valley of Mexico. Often the postconquest documents are a combination of the two systems, either prose texts with illustrations in the pictographic style or pictographic texts with added glosses and commentaries in prose.

All these documents are often called codices (singular: codex), although this term actually refers to a particular manuscript form, one in which individual leaves are bound on a side (Glass 1975:7–8), and this form was not pre-Hispanic. The basic indigenous format for the Aztec "books" was the *tira*, a painting on a long, narrow strip of bark paper (*amatl*) or animal hide. This form is amenable to uninterrupted sequences of events tied to the Aztec calendar, a 52-solar-year cycle recorded as a continuous line of year glyphs. Tied to the year glyphs were pictographs representing the major events that occurred in that year. This type of book was called the *cexiuhamatl*, or year-count history. Another type of pictorial document was the *mapa*, in which various towns and natural features were arranged in the drawing to represent their actual geographical relationships, as on a map, and the associated actors and events were shown near the places where the events happened.

The prose manuscripts in the native historical tradition have been classified into two types: annals and chronicles (Gibson 1975:317–318). The annal type is a document that lists each year in the native calendar in sequence and describes any important events that took place in that year. The annals are clearly associated with the pictorial year-count (*cexiuhamatl*) documents and are believed by some to be prose renderings of the pictorial accounts (*Codex en Cruz* 1981:I:4).

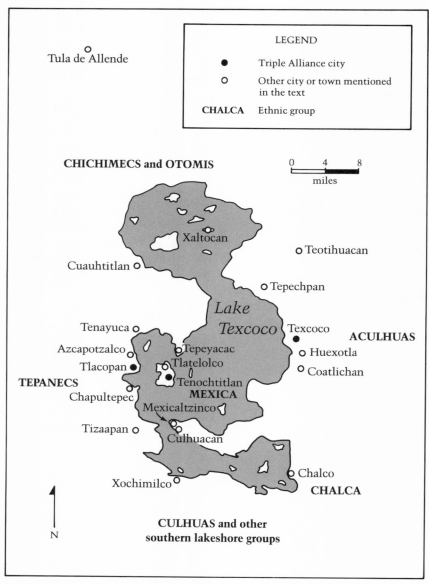

Inside the figure:

LEGEND

●   Triple Alliance city

○   Other city or town mentioned in the text

CHALCA   Ethnic group

○ Tula de Allende

CHICHIMECS and OTOMIS

0   4   8
miles

Xaltocan

○ Teotihuacan

Cuauhtitlan ○

○ Tepechpan

Lake Texcoco

Tenayuca ○

Texcoco ●

ACULHUAS

Azcapotzalco ○

Tepeyacac

○ Huexotla

Tlacopan ●

Tlatelolco

○ Coatlichan

TEPANECS

Tenochtitlan

Chapultepec

MEXICA

Mexicaltzinco

Tizaapan ○

Culhuacan

○ Chalco

Xochimilco ○

CHALCA

N

CULHUAS and other southern lakeshore groups

Cities in the Valley of Mexico and in Nearby Areas

The chronicle type presents historical events in a narrative form more familiar to Westerners, relating in a story what happened to the different peoples in the past. It is considered to be a postconquest introduction (Gibson 1975:318).

The current focus of research on these early colonial-period documents in the native historical tradition has been precisely a "historical" one. The major objective has been to glean "historical truth" from the Indian- and Spanish-authored texts in order to reconstruct an accurate chronology of the events in Aztec history prior to the coming of the Spanish. The analysis has proved to be difficult, however, because the various extant traditions do not tell a single story.

In fact, modern scholars have had to confront many problems in dealing with the documents, including the presence of mythical or supernatural elements, idiosyncratic and regional biases of the different authors, the use of slightly variant calendars among the major Aztec cities, Spanish misunderstandings, ambiguities in the native pictographic writing system, and simple error (for discussions of these problems see, e.g., Borah 1984; Davies 1977; and Nicholson 1975). Furthermore, European influences rapidly and profoundly penetrated Aztec culture and affected the form and content of the historical documents (Anderson 1960:40; D. Carrasco 1982:12; Kubler 1972b:II:417; Thompson 1970:33; also, see below). In addition, the surviving documents from this period represent only a fraction of the extant historical traditions, and they reflect narrowly selected viewpoints, whether written by natives or Spaniards (Broda 1975: 123–124; D. Carrasco 1982:15). Nevertheless, these degradations of the historical truth and the acknowledged "mythicization" (Nicholson 1979:39) in the accounts of Aztec history are generally viewed as aberrations that can be eliminated by utilizing a critical methodology developed by ethnohistorians for distinguishing the truly historical elements from the fictional or erroneous details (P. Carrasco 1966a:110; Cline 1972:4; Harvey and Prem 1984:8; Hudson 1966:53; López Austin 1973:10–11; Nicholson 1975:504; Sturtevant 1966:44).

In the process of reconstructing the most likely sequence of past events, it has been necessary to discredit some of the versions of Aztec history—namely, those at variance with the single chronology thought to be the most correct. Otherwise, the analysis could not proceed: "To deny the right to adopt at times a selective approach is really to deny the right to contemporary scholars to seek any re-

construction at all of Mesoamerican history" (Davies 1987:37). At
times, whole documents are labeled as suspect, but more frequently
only part of an account is considered erroneous or distorted (Nicholson 1957:106) and the remainder accepted as likely to be accurate. It
is also recognized that the analyst must often arrange events and persons differently from the way they are presented in the original texts
in order to make "better sense" of them (Davies 1984:207), especially since scholars believe that their original authors "juggled and
rearranged" the facts themselves when they wrote them (Nicholson
1957:190; also Davies 1977:12; Prem 1984a). Thus a consequence
of this methodology is the rejection of many details in the various historical accounts (Davies 1982:106), especially those that are
"unacceptable or improbable" (Davies 1987:4). There is left, then, a
residue, a discarded hodgepodge that includes the "mythological ex-
crescence" (Heusch 1982:8), the contradictory passages, the suspect
documents, the Spanish influence, and the errors and biases.

History in the Aztec Worldview

There are other "truths" to be found in these documents, and they
deal less with "history" than with how the natives (and even the
Spanish) conceived of and used the Aztec past to comprehend their
present world, a world that at that time included not only a memory
of past glories but also an alien—and for the Aztecs an overbear-
ing—"other." Despite assertions that the Aztecs were a "historical"
people because they kept a calendar and certain historical-looking
records (Feldman 1966:167; Prem 1984b:6; Radin 1920:6), they, like
other preliterate peoples, did not conceive of history as the unchanging, absolutely linear process that Europeans generally suppose history to be. Thus there is more to be learned from their historical
traditions than simple chronology, and the objective of the analysis
presented here is to determine what other kinds of information they
may contain.

The native traditions that survive from this period are not merely
the static remembrance of a pre-Hispanic past. Instead, they reveal
a dynamic attitude toward history, and traditions in a state of flux:
"Throughout the first 50 years of the colonial period the Indians
of the Valley of Mexico continued to develop [their] historical con-

sciousness both for the establishment of their own historical legitimacy and claims and for the edification of the curious Spaniard" (Glass 1975:16). During this time, as they had before, the Aztecs actively manipulated "history"—their understanding of the past—to explicate their sociopolitical situation, just as many other cultures have done: "pre-literate peoples only take pains to preserve versions of their historic past which explain their existing social groupings and institutions, although these versions of the past may have scant relation to the actual sequence of events in the case of the tribe concerned" (Richards 1960:177).

The active and often conscious use of "history" by the Aztecs becomes apparent when the function, form, and context of their historical record-keeping are examined. Analyzing the past of another culture as told by its representatives requires a familiarity with that culture's view of the past and of time itself. Mesoamerican conceptions of time were both linear and cyclical. With linear time, timekeeping begins at a "zero" reference point in the past and progresses at whatever rate it is being measured into the present and the future. Since it is nonreversible and nonrepeating, it provides an absolute and unique point in time for any event. In contrast, cyclical time is measured in infinitely repeating cycles so that it continually returns to its "zero" point, and a single event therefore recurs every time the cycle repeats. Concepts of cyclical time, which predominated in Mesoamerican cultures, are based in part on the endless natural cycles of the seasons and movements of the heavenly bodies. Aztec temporal cycles included the notion of a 260-day ritual cycle, a 365-day solar year, a 52-year "century," and the cycling of 5 world ages or "suns," as well as more mundane cycles, such as the rotation of offices and public duties (P. Carrasco 1976).

Since cyclical time is reversible and repeatable, in the Aztec worldview, history belonged to the past and also to the future. It explained that which had happened as well as that which would be (López Austin 1973:97). This is "prophetic history" (Gibson 1975:319), in which current events are considered to have been set in motion by past events such that the present and future are also known and explainable (D. Carrasco 1980:302–303). The advantage of this concept is that "the present becomes intelligible and at the same time less inadmissible, the moment one can see it already announced in the past" (Todorov 1984:74). Consequently, the past cannot be considered immutable or irreversible. Instead, it has to be amenable to change as required by later events—it is the past that is altered to conform to, and to be continuous with, the present.

In keeping with this prophetic function of history, the Aztec calendar was primarily used not for linear time-keeping but for divination (Dibble 1971:323). Certain good, evil, or ambiguous influences were associated with each of the days of the 260-day cycle, and these influences were interpreted by a diviner who could read the pictographs in the books or who had memorized them. The same sense of fate predicated on the influences of a single day applied as well to the different years in the repeating 52-year cycle. For instance, the year 1 Rabbit (*ce tochtli*), which recurred once every 52 years, was dreaded as a famine year, while 1 Flint (*ce tecpatl*) was a year of departures from, and the founding of, cities (López Austin 1973: 101).

Because of the cosmological associations of temporal periods, particular days and years thus possessed inherent meanings that influenced how the Aztecs perceived which events would necessarily have occurred in the past and in what order. The prophetic and divinatory concepts of time came into full play when the surviving historical accounts were written. It must be remembered that these documents are books about history, recounting events that took place centuries ago in the Aztec past, although all were actually written during the colonial period. Moreover, even if the Aztecs, like the Maya, had made permanent records of events when they happened (which a few of the late Aztec prehistoric stone monuments are), these should not necessarily be interpreted as primary historical sources in the European sense. Among the Maya, the calendar was quite consciously manipulated to yield contrived dates for the events on many monumental inscriptions. Although a true date was easily within their ability to determine, the desire was "not to record history but to provide a cosmic sanction or mandate for the ruler and his dynastic lineage and to insure a positive prognostication for the future" (Carlson 1980:203). The other Mesoamerican societies similarly manipulated their past so that certain types of events were always thought to occur on specific types of days or years for ideological purposes, which far outweighed any desire for historical accuracy (Davies 1987:25; Umberger 1982 for the Aztecs; Furst 1978b:98–102 for the Mixtecs).

The reason for such contrivances was that to the Aztecs, history was not something separated from religion or cosmology but was a manifestation of their worldview in narrative form. It explained the origins and functioning of the cosmos, to which were inextricably linked social, political, economic, and religious institutions whose nature and justification were necessarily grounded in the past. For the Aztecs, like many other peoples, the purpose of history was to explain the organization of society within the framework of the development of their world:

> Some version of historical events gives the privileged the right to enjoy political authority—some myth however fantastic, some legend of migration, conquest or the occupation of new territory, however ill-attested, some line of descent however truncated—versions of the past which social anthropologists now group loosely under the heading "historical charters" . . . (Richards 1960:176)

The use of competing historical traditions for such purposes was particularly acute among the Aztecs because they were not ethnically homogeneous, but instead encompassed different groups who were political rivals. In such a situation, "since myths and legends are used to support political claims it follows that they are most numerous and complex where the claims are contested or the population mixed" (Richards 1960:177).

As has been noted for many African cultures (e.g., Richards 1960: 176, 178), the creation of "history" is not ad hoc or arbitrary but must conform to certain principles, and it must be transmitted to later generations to be useful. Among preliterate peoples, the transmission of historical knowledge requires a number of mnemonic mechanisms to aid in the process of remembering and reproducing the past. These may include classificatory kinship terms; positional succession, such that a man succeeds to the name and kin status of a predecessor; formal recitation of ancestral names at special rites, often as part of a song in order to remember them better; possession by different groups in society of their particular version of the past and a responsibility for maintaining it; and a special group of "charter keepers," people whose job it was to remember and transmit the historical traditions (Richards 1960:179–180).

All of these mechanisms were used in Aztec historical record-keeping, for despite the presence of a rudimentary pictographic and even phonetic notational system, the primary means of preserving the past was an oral one. The pictographic "books" are very sketchy in content, lacking the detail found in the European-influenced prose documents. The diversity and ambiguity of the symbols in the aboriginal glyphic system resulted in numerous disagreements about their interpretation even among the literate Aztecs themselves, to the frustration of the Spaniards (not to mention modern epigraphers) who wished to know their meaning (D. Carrasco 1982:23). It is not a question of an inability among the Aztecs to devise a better writing system—which some scholars find difficult to understand, considering that their "historical consciousness puts so much emphasis on chronological information" (Prem 1984b:6)—but more likely the lack of any desire to fix or standardize their traditions, which would make the past less amenable to necessary variation and modification.

Thus the historical traditions were actually handed down from generation to generation by memorization, only aided or reified by the written pictographs. Teaching this memorized history was an important function of the Aztec schools, particularly the schools for elite boys and priestly novitiates. These students of history did not memorize a simple list of kings, conquests, and dates to be recited on command: "One cannot assume that only tales and fictional data will be performed in the sense of 'acted out' while somehow historical accounts would be recited *recto tono* in measured cadenza and in religious silence" (Vansina 1985:36). Instead, the historical information was incorporated into songs, discourses, hymns, prayers, and other types of verbal art (León-Portilla 1961:64; see also Acosta 1940:642), which were performed on special occasions, including the enactment of rituals.

The transmission of historical traditions was thus subordinated to the demands of the form and context of these performances. To "read" the original "books" was actually to perform the oral tradition (Dibble 1971:323), literally to "sing the paintings" (León-Portilla 1961:64). Thus, even given the Aztecs' stated emphasis on the importance of rote memorization, the texts of these histories cannot have been fixed, because verbal art is recreated every time it is performed (Lord 1964:29; Maranda 1972:56; Vansina 1973:54). The books themselves were highly sacred, and the position of the scribe in society was extremely favored (Davies 1977:9). Both the Aztecs and the Maya were deeply grieved when the Spaniards burned their native writings (Acosta 1940:461; Landa 1978:82). Rather than being the principal source of chronological records, these documents func-

tioned more as symbolic devices that kept the control of knowledge
—that is, of the "history" that explained the cosmos and legitimated
societal institutions—in the hands of the elite, who were the only
ones allowed to own and read them (D. Carrasco 1982:20).

Not only were there no fixed texts, but there is evidence that
the various city-states purposely maintained their own distinct versions of history, fully realizing that they were all different from one
another (Zantwijk 1985:9). The literati themselves did not attempt
to reconcile their traditions and construct from them a single historical sequence (which the Spanish began to do), for such was not
their purpose. The Aztec attitude toward history was the same as
that of the Kachin of Burma, among whom "each version (of the
past) was the property of one particular group and . . . there was
tacit recognition that rival groups were entitled to own other stories"
(Leach 1965:98–99). The telling of different versions of history, of
how each group had come to live and settle in central Mexico, was a
way of explaining the ethnic diversity there (for a similar situation
in Hawaii, see Linnekin 1983:241–242). The variations in the stories
justified current antagonisms and alliances, and maintained the individual identities of the various city-states in the Valley of Mexico
and beyond.

Dialogue and Dialectic

For the analysis presented here, the historical traditions of the early
colonial period are regarded as sixteenth-century narratives in which
the past was the preeminent model for interpreting present circumstances. Hence the present became the model for reconstructing the
past, because whenever the present situation changed to the point
where it was no longer perceived to be continuous with the known
past, then the past had to be created anew. Furthermore, there must
have been as many versions of the past as there were understandings of the present. The first question to be asked of these documents, then, is an anthropological one: What reality is symbolized
in each account? rather than a historical one: What really happened
in the past? (after Middleton 1967:x; on this dichotomy, see also
Dorson 1961:13–14; Hudson 1966; and Sturtevant 1966:22–24). A
more basic concern that follows from this question focuses not so
much on the content of the histories as symbolized "reality" as on

the organizing principles, the underlying structure, that governed their creation.

The preserved historical traditions provide important insights not just into pre-Hispanic Aztec history but also into the colonial period itself. Because they were written by both Spaniards and natives, they are a window into the minds of representatives of two cultures that had come into abrupt, violent, and eventually sustained contact. Indian and European perceptions of this encounter, and of each other, can be obtained by examining how they construed the events that led up to the conquest and colonial subjugation.

The worldview and cumulative experience of neither the Spaniards nor the Aztecs prepared them for the conquest. In other words, the events that occurred came to be perceived as not conforming to the known categories and relationships by which these peoples constructed and structured their worlds, and in such a case the categories and relationships had to be redefined (Sahlins 1981:67). The Aztecs especially (but also the Spanish) looked to their past to find an explanation for what had transpired, for history was the principal means of explaining the origin and nature of reality. To continue in that function, Aztec history was transformed so that it could accommodate the events of the conquest and colonization.

This process of transformation of cultural categories so that they conform to actual events as they are interpreted is the "dialectic between structure and event" (Bucher 1981:167; see also Sahlins 1985). Although it is a continual process, it becomes most prominent in situations of culture contact, when a society is confronted by the novel and unanticipated behavior of an alien people (Sahlins 1981:68). The Aztecs in particular had to deal with the profound problem of maintaining the continuity between past and present which ordered their world in the face of totally unexpected and hence inexplicable occurrences.

The meeting between the conquistador and the Indian gave rise to a similar problem for the Spaniards—namely, how to explain the existence of the previously unknown other. The strangeness of the New World societies challenged European conceptions of the world (Bucher 1981:164). It was especially difficult for Europeans to cope with the fact that the Indians were not mentioned in the Bible, the ultimate authority. The deep philosophical questions this omission provoked concerning the nature of the Indians and Indian culture, the proper relationship between Indians and Europeans, and the justification of the conquest and subsequent subjugation, all stimulated a flurry of debate on both sides of the Atlantic that continued for several centuries (Keen 1971:71; for detailed studies of this European literature, see especially Keen 1971, Lafaye 1976, and Phelan 1970, and for an iconographic analysis of European perceptions of the New World, see Bucher 1981).

Thus, both groups had to begin to try to understand each other, but there were immediate misconceptions and misinterpretations. For the Aztecs, the devastating destruction of their paramount city, Tenochtitlan, capital of the Mexica ethnic group, which had been regarded as an unthinkable event, came to be perceived as miraculous, an act obviously requiring supernatural intervention (Uchmany 1980:10). The Aztecs considered their loss to be the defeat of their gods by the gods of the Spaniards, since this was the orienting belief of the preconquest period, when the power of various tutelary deities was thought to be tested in the battles between their adherents (1980:10). The defeated group was obligated to take on the worship of the god of their conquerors by assimilating the new deity into their pantheon. By accepting the god of the Spaniards, the Aztecs signaled their submission to him (1980:46).

The Spaniards also believed that the power of one's god determined the outcome of a conflict; however, they required in addition the abolition of the preexisting indigenous pantheon. The imposition of a new religion to replace completely the existing one was totally alien to the indigenous peoples, especially considering that so much of Aztec life was governed by the ritual/solar calendar of ceremonies and the notions of deified time and space. To the Indian, conquest did not mean absolute conversion, but to the Spaniard the two went hand in hand (Gibson 1952:28–29), a view strengthened by events in Spain's own recent history, including the Reconquest—the expulsion of Jews and Moors—and the ongoing religious struggles in Europe between Catholics and Protestants.

The Spaniards thus interpreted the conquest as a god-given opportunity to create a new Catholic society in which they would be dominant. The Aztecs—thoroughly, and to them inexplicably, crushed—were left to comprehend and hence adapt to the new order. For both sides to realize their differing objectives, they needed to know each other, but they could only begin to do so on their own terms, using familiar concepts and relationships. For example, the early European accounts describe the indigenous political system using such terms as *king, empire, aristocracy, slave, confederation,* and *republic*—words with which they and their audience were familiar (Muría 1973:103; Keen 1971:56) but which really did not pertain to Aztec society. The native histories provided an important bridge between the two cultures, something that both groups recognized as potentially capable of providing explanations for events. The historical traditions became an important part of the dialogue between the two groups (Lafaye 1976:301). The transformation of Aztec history was therefore not solely a native undertaking but was the product of both Spanish and Indian input.

The surviving historical texts represent the fragments of this Aztec-Spanish dialogue frozen in time. They contain within them attempts by both groups to reconcile the events of the conquest with their separate worldviews, neither side able either fully to reject their own categories and principles or fully to incorporate those of the other. As the different authors singled out various portions of the past to be expanded and reshaped where necessary, the dialogue took the form of a dialectic, resulting in new syntheses that were themselves further modified as the colonial period progressed and changes continued to occur.

The dialogue—and it was literally such—between the European, to whom biblical teachings revealed all things, and the Indian, whose present represented a continuity with the past and future, began with the discussions held between native elites and the conquistadores as the latter group began their march into the Valley of Mexico in 1519. Contemporary records of those encounters are virtually nonexistent, the sole exception being Cortés's letters to the king of Spain (Cortés 1971), which were one-sided and colored with his own biases, intentions, and miscomprehensions (see Chapter 6). More prolonged and profound discussions took place between the Aztecs and the Franciscan missionaries. This religious order was the first to travel to New Spain, in 1523–24. A group of twelve, known as the Twelve Apostles in conscious imitation of the proselytizing mission of the early church, arrived in 1524. It was primarily the clergy who sought information about Aztec history and culture, information that they hoped to use to convert the Indians to the Christian religion as well as to European culture.

At this time the Aztecs had just been subdued, and the native priests and other religious and secular elites were being exterminated. The loss of the educated class of Aztec society, those in fullest

possession of the "great tradition" (D. Carrasco 1982:3), is incalcu-
lable. Nevertheless, a surviving group of representative individuals
was gathered together to be interviewed by the Twelve, who asked
them many questions. Some of their responses have been preserved
as the *Coloquios de los Doce Primeros Misioneros de México*, a
manuscript that was lost until 1924, although some parts of it are
also found in the sixteenth-century writings of Fr. Bernardino de
Sahagún, a Franciscan who arrived in 1529 (León-Portilla 1974a:18–
19).

Conversations between Indians and Spaniards intensified in the
schools founded by the Franciscans and other clergy to educate the
sons of Aztec nobles, including the Franciscan Colegio de Santa
Cruz, located in Tlatelolco, Tenochtitlan's sister city. Here Sahagún,
Molina, Mendieta, Motolinía, Torquemada, and other friars taught
contemporary European literary culture to an eager and bright group
of young men anxious to learn what they could (Robertson 1959:
155). From their students the clergy learned the Nahuatl language;
native views of history, religion, and folklore (1959:155–156); and
the native pictographic writing system. Some of the clergy used
the pre-Hispanic pictographs in their Christian religious teachings
(Dibble 1960:174; Dibble 1974).

The students in these schools rapidly adopted the knowledge and
conventions of their teachers, whose almost immediate influence is
manifested most clearly in the use of European literary style and
artistic forms in their writing and illustration (Anderson 1960:40;
Dibble 1960:174; for the rapidity of influence on native art, see especially Dibble 1960, Kubler 1972b:II:417–424, and Robertson 1959
and 1974). Fr. Sahagún was particularly concerned by how quickly
native culture was changing (Nicolau d'Olwer and Cline 1973:188).
European methods, terms, and conventions were accepted "as if they
had always been in Aztec culture" (Anderson 1960:40). In addition to
the adoption of European conventions in prose writing and illustration, the Nahuatl language became more simplified and standardized
(1960:40), and the native pictographic record-keeping system, still
used in the colonial period, underwent a change toward increased
phoneticism. This was due not only to the presence of a Spanish
phonetic alphabet but also to a change in the content of the native
texts. Instead of being primarily ritual, the indigenous-style documents began to concentrate on history, genealogy, and land claims
and other legal proceedings. This shift in content necessitated the

ability to express personal and place names, stimulating the increase
in homonyms and syllabic phonetics (Dibble 1960:174).

The friars' students were praised for their learning abilities as well
as their skill in rendering exact duplicates of European illustrative
styles (Robertson 1959:156). But the early-colonial-period pictorial
manuscripts they and others produced were more than a grafting of
Spanish art and writing onto a basically native format. They were a
fusion of two traditions, a new synthesis (1959:34). For the Indians,
the greatest impetus for this fusion was the "will to become Christian, so strong among the younger generation of natives, and along
with it the desire to take over European technical knowledge as well
as the religious aspects of European culture" (1959:156). If defeat for
the Aztecs meant the vanquishing of their gods by the god of the vic-
tors, then their own pre-Hispanic beliefs required that they accept
the new god as quickly as possible in order to join with the side of
their conquerors. Thus it was "social compulsion" rather than military coercion that was responsible for this tremendous changeover
from Aztec to Spanish practices (Kubler 1972b:II:418). Furthermore,
the collapse of Aztec culture meant a loss of the Aztecs' religious/
calendrical structure, institutions, and rituals, which the European
clergy replaced with their own religious guidance and calendar, and
with required labor on public works, a requirement the Aztec priests
had enforced before (1972b:II:420).

For their part, the friars had a lot to learn from their students.
They sought a knowledge of Aztec culture, however, not for the sake
of preserving a rapidly disappearing way of life, but specifically to
aid in the conversion of the Indians and the eradication of their aboriginal beliefs and practices, which was the primary purpose of the
Franciscan presence in New Spain. Fr. Sahagún wrote that his su-
periors wanted him to record in Nahuatl (which he had learned and
which could now be written in European letters) "that which seemed
to me useful for the indoctrination, development, and maintenance
of the christianization of these natives of this New Spain, to aid
workers and ministers who indoctrinate them" (Cline 1971:242).

The exact form of the Spanish-Aztec conversations on native religion and history is also known in some detail because the Spanish
friars used a particular interview methodology to elicit information (Cline 1971; López Austin 1974; Robertson 1959:46). It was
being utilized by the Franciscans by at least the 1530s, beginning

with Frs. Motolinía and Olmos (Gibson 1975:320), and the details of how it operated were recorded by Fr. Sahagún. Sahagún was based in Tepepolco, a town northeast of and peripheral to the Valley of Mexico (Nicholson 1974:145–147), and there he assembled ten or twelve elderly important men to serve as primary informants for what would eventually become his *General History*. Sahagún asked them questions based on a questionnaire he had drawn up, so the interview process was fairly narrowly focused. After he had asked his questions, the elderly men were given several days to discuss them among themselves and settle on an answer (Sahagún 1950–82:Bk. 2:Prologue), a method that has been called "interview/round table agreement" (Nicolau d'Olwer and Cline 1973:189). Some of the students from the Colegio de Santa Cruz in Tlatelolco who had learned the Latin language functioned as translators of the informants' pictographic responses.

The nature of the questions asked, the negotiation for a suitable answer, and the desire to please the friars must certainly have influenced the information obtained (Sotomayor 1979:100). The work by Sahagún in particular, in which he was assisted by Hispanicized natives and which went through many reviews and rewritings, is Spanish as much as it is Aztec (Frankl 1966:14). In fact, little of the early original Tepepolco material survived this process (Nicholson 1974:146). Sahagún continued to edit and revise his manuscript for some time: "for three years alone, I examined and re-examined all my writings. And I again amended them and divided them into Books, into twelve Books, and each Book by chapters, and some Books by chapters and paragraphs" (Sahagún 1950–82:Bk. 2:Prologue). He then gave the manuscript to the Colegio graduates for recopying, and they changed and added sections in the process (Cline 1971:243). Thus a tremendous mingling of concepts and interpretations from both sides of the Atlantic is reflected in the final product, the *General History*, which is often considered a source very representative of aboriginal Aztec culture.

Skepticism as to what extent the untouched indigenous view is present has also been directed toward the early *Coloquios de los Doce*, the record of the first meeting of friars and natives in 1524, in which even at this early date the objective of the Christians to convert and edify influenced both the questions asked and the Spanish interpretation of the responses given (Frankl 1966:16). Because this document refers to a conversation held in 1524, only three years after the fall of Tenochtitlan, it is often considered to be a faithful recording of the religious knowledge of the Aztec elite; yet this notion is suspect, for several reasons (Garibay K. 1954:II:240–241). It is doubtful that any priests or secular leaders were still around to be questioned, and nothing is known of a possible bilingual scribe at this early date, especially one who could have adequately transcribed the lengthy discourses. Instead, the direct transcription of the original encounter must have been composed first in Spanish or Latin, making use of available oral translators. Only much later (c. 1564) was it transcribed back into Nahuatl by Fr. Sahagún, who was not present at the meeting.

It is therefore difficult to distinguish the indigenous, untouched concepts of the pre-Hispanic Aztecs amid their interplay with Spanish beliefs and categories in the dialectical process, because of the nonegalitarian nature of the interaction between the two cultures, the rapidity with which the Aztecs internalized many European conventions, and the heavy influence Spanish authors exerted in their recording of native information. The indigenous conceptions simply may not have been preserved in the documents in an uninfluenced form, and conceivably many cultural categories and relationships believed to be pre-Hispanic were actually the result of a very rapid synthesis. (For the better-known Spanish viewpoint in the dialectical process, see especially Keen 1971 and Bucher 1981.) Furthermore, even discerning the post-Hispanic, transformed conceptions is made more problematical by the fact that the Aztecs and the Spaniards shared a number of religious beliefs and practices that existed independently in both cultures (Litvak King 1972:26). When such similarities appear, it can be difficult to decide whether they actually resulted from a fusion of cultures or reflect independently held ideas. On the other hand, the presence of such serendipitous parallels may have facilitated the dialogue and the cultures' attempts to understand each other, even as they may also have resulted in some confusion and misunderstanding of phenomena because they looked vaguely familiar.

An example of a fundamental principle shared by the Aztecs and Spaniards was the cyclization of time. With the conquest and the defeat of their gods, the world had ended for the Aztecs, and representatives of that vanquished society asked to be allowed to die with it. They told the Franciscans to "allow us then to die, let us perish now, since our gods are already dead" (León-Portilla 1963:63). Such was their belief in the cycle of world ages. However, this view was not theirs alone, although the pessimism surely was. The idea of cyclical time, generally regarded as the antithesis of the European lineal concept, was part of the cultural baggage the Franciscans brought to New Spain.

A world had ended for the Franciscans as well, but they looked forward to the change. For them, the discovery and conquest of the New World were part of God's plan for a new church in a new society that they believed they were to have a strong hand in making (Elliott 1967:54–55). The Church in Europe was failing, as seen by the rise of the Antichrist, Luther (Phelan 1970:24), and the loss of early Eastern centers of Christianity to the Moslems. As the Catholic church lost ground to the east, the Franciscans saw the discovery of the new land in the west as a sign of the resurgence of the Church and new prominence for their countrymen. In their eyes Cortés became the principal agent of God's divine plan to place into Spanish hands the duty and privilege of converting millions of new souls to the faith and thereby bringing about the long-desired millennium (Elliott 1967:55). This would pave the way for the Second Coming, which for the Franciscans was the third and final world age (Lafaye 1976:30–31). These messianic ideas were most fully expressed in the writings of the mystic Franciscan Fray Gerónimo de Mendieta (Phelan 1970), although their influence can be seen in the works of his contemporaries as well.

The conquest was thus the decisive event for both the defeated Aztecs, whose world had come to a gloomy and uncertain end, akin to the destruction of the fifth and last "sun," or world era, in the pre-Hispanic belief system, and the victorious Spanish friars, who saw in it the end of the Old World and the beginning of the New. In this basic underlying conception, it appears that the two cultures were as one (Lafaye 1972:19), although their outlooks were diametrically opposed. Where they differ is in the fact that for the millenarian Franciscans, this was to be the last in a series of world ages prior to the final judgment. The Aztecs' cyclical conceptions never fully waned, however, and if they saw the new era as a time of great despair and degradation, they also came to hope that with the passage of time, this cycle, too, would be ended and a new one would take its place.

History as Symbol

Among the Aztecs, the impact of the conquest on the historical traditions, as part of the dialectical process, may be elicitable from the surviving documents of the early colonial period. As already noted, a number of problems must be confronted in undertaking such an analysis: (1) only a few voices in the "dialogue" have been preserved; (2) no purely pre-Hispanic versions of Aztec narrative history survive, making it difficult to discern which elements they originally brought to the dialogue; (3) distinguishing preconquest Aztec concepts from postconquest syntheses is complicated by the presence of independently developed similarities in the Spanish and Aztec worldviews; (4) specific events, dates, and personages can and do recur in the histories because of Aztec conceptions of time as cyclical and as under the influence of supernatural forces; and (5) there are contradictions among the different accounts because of competing claims and varying understandings.

Despite these concerns, because the traditions have been preserved in texts written over a century's time, a reconstruction of the process of their transformation is conceivable, especially where the focus is on isolating the organizing categories and their syntagmatic relations (Valeri 1985:193) that underlay the creation of the historical narratives. In other words, an examination of the structure of the narratives and how that structure was transformed to accommodate events should prove fruitful. The structuralist approach contrasts with the more usual critical historical methodology in several ways and has been promoted as complementary to it: "The advantage of the structuralist analysis is that it is not selective [like the historical approach], but respects the need to conserve *all* the details of a given story as part of the process of decoding, regardless of whether they make immediate sense" (Davies 1987:12).

Because it is nonselective, this approach posits that all the contradictory accounts of the past may be equally legitimate; that is, there is no single correct version or more reliable text (Lévi-Strauss 1963:218). Instead, "each version must be considered insofar as they document . . . a system of possibilities, each of which can be 'transformed' into all the others" (Valeri 1985:194). The objective, therefore, is not to reconcile the contradictions posed by the varying traditions but to explain them in a way that allows not only for contradiction but also for the incorporation of supernatural or implausible elements.

A basic axiom of the analysis, then, is that the narratives are simply accepted "as they are" (Lévi-Strauss 1973:121). They are symbolic texts to be "read" in the sense of "interpreted" (following Geertz 1973).

Because the historical accounts are narrative in format, many events and persons that seem to be similar to one another are separated by chronological time and therefore appear to be distinct. These details, however, are simply different manifestations of a single episode (see Lévi-Strauss 1979:190), part of the repetition that renders the structure of the texts more apparent (Lévi-Strauss 1963:229). In addition, these retellings of the same story over and over reflect Aztec conceptions of cyclical time, of prophetic history, of the past repeating itself. Cyclical time therefore increases the number of different accounts of the same event, which, far from being a hindrance, is absolutely necessary to the analysis. Such repetition is required because the competing versions of a story collectively express ideas that cannot be expressed by any one of them (Leach 1970:72) concerning fundamental problems of the nature of the cosmos and society. It is in this totality of surface expressions that the underlying rules that govern the creation and recreation of text are revealed.

By examining the transformation of Aztec history after the conquest, one can begin to elicit these rules and categories of Aztec thought. Many of the elements of the Aztec historical narratives are linked to one another by such means as "similarity, opposition, parallelism, transmutation, juxtaposition, the use of *pars-pro-toto*, or other mechanisms . . . operators, in the logical sense, which create the mythical codes and develop their relationships" (Hunt 1977:43). These linkages reveal that the elements are at once the same and different. Thus from the variant historical episodes are reconstructed the "recurrent patterns that establish relations of substitution and combination" (Valeri 1985:193).

Whereas a historian would prefer to deal with those events that take a consistent form from one text to another, with such consistency implying a historical accuracy (Calnek 1973), from the perspective pursued here the contradictions take on greater significance than the consistencies (Leach 1965:267; Leach 1983:24). This is because the contradictions indicate the points in the different accounts which are alternative surface manifestations of an underlying principle, retellings of basically the same episode linked to one another by various means. The mutability of these points is an indication of the complexity of their multiple meanings, and understanding them provides the clues to the cultural categories and relationships that generated the different accounts.

The approach adopted here is similar in some ways to R. Tom Zuidema's studies of the postconquest Andean traditional histories (Zuidema 1962, 1978) which, rather than being simply chronologies, reveal Inca conceptions of rulership and their experience with the Spanish conquest. From the other side of the world, comparisons may be drawn to Sir Edmund Leach's structuralist analyses of biblical stories (Leach 1967, 1969, 1976, 1983), which demonstrate some of the basic models on which Old and New Testament episodes were constructed. With regard to the dialectical processes evident in the clash of cultures, similarities are also noted with Marshall Sahlins's work in the "anthropology of history" (Sahlins 1981, 1982, 1985), which investigates the transformation of Polynesian conceptions due to the impact of the English presence in the islands beginning in the eighteenth century. In addition, the relationships linking Aztec divine kingship to history and cosmology are shown to be quite comparable to African conceptions, drawing especially on Luc de Heusch's (1982) study of the historical traditions of Bantu peoples of central Africa.

Objections have been raised that the structuralist orientation is more appropriate to the study of myth or folklore, whereas the Aztec documents in the native historical tradition are history, and any symbolic or achronological treatment of them would deny them this inherent quality (Davies 1982). It is true that some anthropologists have gone too far in treating oral historical traditions as nothing more than social charters, ignoring their potential for recording actual historical events (Richards 1960:177), but the practice of fragmenting these documents into different parts, which are then labeled true or false, does a disservice to the Aztec histories if it fails to deal with why so much patterned contradiction and so many supernatural elements exist within the historical records. Moreover, the Aztecs made no such distinction between history and myth (P. Carrasco 1976:247; but see Calnek 1978:241), so in interpreting their viewpoint, this argument becomes irrelevant.

In fact, the idea of an opposition between history and myth is itself an artificial construct of Western culture, for both are endpoints of the same processes (Brady 1982:185; Gossen 1977:250; Leach 1970:8). To assert, as we tend to do, that our history is true while myths are false by definition (Bricker 1981:3; Leach 1970:54) is to ignore the reality that both are symbolic narratives. "Myth and history are bundles of meaningful experience about the past—symbols, in a word—which are conditioned by utility for and relevance to the present, as it is experienced by a particular cultural tradition" (Gossen 1977:250).

Furthermore, as the analysis in this book demonstrates, structuralist studies are wrongly labeled ahistorical or synchronic, for "structure is processual" (Sahlins 1985:77). The incorporation of actual historical events, as they were interpreted against a background of underlying cultural categories and relationships, is crucial to understanding how and why these traditions were created to communicate a social reality. Finally, these documents can and should be analyzed using a variety of approaches in order to elicit from them all the information about Aztec society and history that they may contain. The Aztec historical traditions, like those of other preliterate peoples, even those with highly developed sociopolitical systems, reveal themselves to be quite amenable to this type of analysis.

The study of the Aztec historical traditions presented here is restricted to available documents written by both Aztecs and Spaniards and dating from approximately the first century after the conquest (see Appendix). This was the period when most of the surviving historical accounts were composed, and more important, these texts preserve the greatest variability and creativity, reflecting the native view that history is conceived and used for certain ends, and therefore there will be many competing versions of the past. Excluded were works by Spanish authors who attempted to synthesize the different traditions into a single, consistent chronology, thus obscuring the variety and separateness of the different traditions, many of which were suppressed. This category includes the writings of Bartolomé de las Casas, Joseph de Acosta, Antonio de Herrera, and Juan de Torquemada (León-Portilla 1980:97), as well as later histories, such as the works of Francisco Clavijero and Mariano Veytia.

The analysis focuses on one small portion of the Aztec past: the genealogy of the ruling dynasty of Tenochtitlan, the principal city of the Mexica people and virtually the capital of the empire at the time of Spanish contact. It is fairly short, since Motecuhzoma II, who met with Cortés in 1519, was only the ninth Mexica king. Modern scholars have attempted to derive a single accurate dynastic history for Tenochtitlan from the different accounts; nevertheless, this genealogy suffers from perhaps the least consistency from one account to another of any segment of the Aztec past. The high degree of discordance among the different versions is a clue to the significance of dynastic history in Aztec thought. Its importance is not surprising, since genealogies, a very compact form of historical narrative, function in other cultures to validate sociopolitical and economic relationships (Bohannan 1952; Goody and Watt 1962–63:308–309). When the relationships change, the genealogies must change. Disputes concerning social relationships are therefore often manifested in differing versions of the genealogy, since each party to the dispute maintains a version that corresponds to his view of the current situation.

The variations in the accounts of the Tenochtitlan dynasty, however, reveal much more than arguments and rivalries among different pre-Hispanic ethnic groups. They reflect profound questions about the nature of rulership which many societies have posed, as well as major elements of the Aztec worldview. They also reveal the strong Spanish influence as part of the dialectical conversation between the two cultures. Interestingly, most of this variation concerns not the nine kings themselves but the women who were their wives and mothers. The Aztec "queens" provide a key to understanding how history in the form of genealogy was manipulated to communicate basic ideas about man, society, and cosmology in pre- and post-Hispanic Mexico.

The first part of the book deals with these women in detail, showing how their structural positioning within the Tenochtitlan dynasty reveals an important aspect of the genealogy—namely, that it took the form of a repeating cycle, like other Aztec temporal cycles. Three queens in particular reappear in the dynasty at certain critical junctures, precisely at the points where one dynastic cycle of kings is ending and the next is about to begin. Similarities in the historical accounts concerning these women reveal that they are repeating manifestations of one another and that they are also linked to other women in the Mexica past, prior to the founding of the city of Tenochtitlan. An examination of these earlier historical episodes indicates that these key women are all aspects of the Aztec mother-earth goddess (by which is meant a complex of goddesses with earth and fertility associations), and they function in the histories to generate the next temporal cycle, an act that often requires their sacrificial death. Thus they are linked to a well-known event in the Mexica past, the sacrifice of the "woman of discord."

The second part of the book focuses on the two kings who appear at the endpoints of the repeating dynastic cycle, both of whom are linked by the sharing of the name Motecuhzoma, as well as by other details. The patterning revealed by the two Motecuhzomas further illuminates how historical events were replicated back in time to the period before the Aztecs, to the era of their predecessors, the Toltecs. The cyclically repeating Tenochtitlan kings are firmly tied to the historical episodes of the Toltec king Topiltzin Quetzalcoatl, who appeared in the same structural position in the cycles of Toltec dynastic history. The postconquest shaping of Toltec history was part of a continuing process of rewriting Aztec history to explain the defeat at the hands of the Spaniards by referring to the downfall of an earlier empire, that of the Toltecs, who were the cultural forebears of the Aztecs. This rendered the Aztecs' fate inevitable, but it also held out the hope that their descendants would rise again, just as the Aztecs believed that they had risen out of the ashes of the Toltec civilization.

Finally, in the last chapter the discussion turns to an examination of Aztec history as "sacred" history. It investigates how the historical time of the past was integrated with the annual calendrical cycle, which served as a "map" or spatiotemporal model for the organization of the people of Tenochtitlan. It also deals more generally and comparatively with how the Aztecs constructed and embedded their concepts of divine kingship within their own historical principles in ways that are almost identical to those of other complex societies.

Part I

The Woman of Discord

Chapter 1

A Model of the
Tenochtitlan Dynasty

The Aztec histories, like history books elsewhere, are concerned with the activities of the rulers, especially their conquests. Although the historical traditions of many of the different city-states of the Valley of Mexico have been preserved, it is clear from these documents that the city of Tenochtitlan was of paramount importance. This city headed the tribute empire often referred to as the Aztec empire and known more formally after the Spanish conquest as the Triple Alliance of Tenochtitlan, Texcoco, and Tlacopan (Gibson 1971:389). The rulers of Tenochtitlan were credited with the conquest of many of the peoples the Triple Alliance subjugated and forced to pay tribute, and thus their exploits are found in the historical traditions of many cities in the Valley of Mexico as well as those in neighboring regions.

The people of Tenochtitlan shared the same basic cultural patterns and language (Nahuatl) with most of the other cities in the Valley of Mexico, but all the cities thought of themselves as belonging to several diverse ethnic groups. Their differences were especially emphasized in their traditional histories, which related how each of the groups had come into the valley at separate times or had settled in various areas. According to the sacred tales told by the literati of Tenochtitlan, the people of this city were known as the Mexica and later took the name Tenochca after the founding of their city. They

Figure 1.1. Chichimecs emerging from their place of origin, Chicomoztoc ("Seven Caves"), to start their migration to the Valley of Mexico area. The cave opening is drawn as the mouth of an earth monster. They are dressed in animal skins and equipped with hunting gear as befitted their occupation (Durán 1967:II:Fig. 3).

considered themselves to be intruders into the valley, one of the many Chichimec peoples, who were originally nomadic hunters and gatherers and whose homeland was somewhere in northwest Mexico. They left their place of origin (Fig. 1.1), which was known variously as Chicomoztoc, Aztlan, and Culhuacan or Teoculhuacan, and undertook the long migration to the Valley of Mexico. They were led by their tutelary deity, the man-god Huitzilopochtli ("Hummingbird on the Left"), who was born under miraculous circumstances, and by a series of secular chiefs. The Mexica and the other Chichimec groups who eventually settled around Lake Texcoco, the major lake in the Valley of Mexico, quickly adopted the trappings of civilization from the sedentary agriculturalists already living on the southern edge of the lake.

The Mexica believed that they were the last people to leave the homeland and wander into the valley, by which time all of the land there had been claimed by other groups. The major powers in the valley at that time were the Tepanecs west of the lake, the Aculhua on the eastern side, and the Culhua to the south. Led by a chief named Huitzilihuitl the Elder, the Mexica settled at Chapultepec on the western lakeshore, a territory claimed by previously established groups. The other cities conspired to drive the Mexica out of Chapultepec, and they were forced to seek refuge in Tizaapan, a

Figure 1.2. The founding of the city of Tenochtitlan at a place in Lake Texcoco where an eagle perches on a prickly pear cactus, which grows from a stone. The eagle grasps a snake in its mouth. To the right, the central individual is named by a glyph on his clothing—the prickly pear cactus on a stone—indicating that he is Tenoch, a leader of the Mexica at the time of the founding of their city, Tenochtitlan (Durán 1967:II:Fig. 6).

part of the territory of Culhuacan, the Culhua capital. Eventually they were able to build their own city, Tenochtitlan, on an island in the lake. They were directed to this spot by a vision, an eagle on a prickly pear cactus, produced by their god. This vision incorporated the place glyph for Tenochtitlan, a rock (= *tetl*) from which a cactus (= *nochtli*) is growing, giving the sounds in the name Tenochtitlan. In some accounts, the leader of the Mexica at the time was named Tenoch, and the city was thus named for him (Fig. 1.2). Some of the Mexica people split off to form another city just north of Tenochtitlan, Tlatelolco. By the time of the Spanish conquest, Tlatelolco had essentially merged with Tenochtitlan, the result of the violent takeover of Tlatelolco by Tenochtitlan.

With the founding of their own city, the Mexica-Tenochca desired to establish a true royal dynasty to replace their military chiefs. Their first "king" (*tlatoani*, meaning "speaker") was Acamapichtli. Even though the city now had a king, Tenochtitlan was not an independent polity but was instead tributary to Azcapotzalco, the Tepanec capital on the western edge of the lake. According to tradition, Tepanec hegemony was finally overthrown by the Tenochca under their fourth king, Itzcoatl, with the help of the city of Texcoco, capital of the Aculhua ethnic group. At the conclusion of this war, Itzcoatl reorganized the sociopolitical and economic structure of his city. A powerful alliance was created among Tenochtitlan, Texcoco, and Tlacopan (the new Tepanec capital) to rule the Valley of Mexico, exacting tribute from other cities. Tenochtitlan was at the head of this alliance. Later Tenochca rulers continued the expansion of the empire with new conquests, many of them in areas far from the Valley of Mexico. The exploits of the later kings provide the histories with much of their detail.

The form of the Aztec traditions is thus quite comparable to historical legends of other peoples, since their purpose and function were the same: to use history to comprehend the current reality. Identical patterns have been found, for example, for the Maori of New Zealand (Sahlins 1985:57), and for many African peoples:

> [African historical traditions] may consist, in fact, of a first period which is little more than a series of postulated zero-points for the origin of social groups such as tribes or clans—a geographical area or even a point of the compass; a tale of first occupation of the tribal territory; an eponymous ancestor with no other attribute than that of being first; or perhaps alternatively an ancestor who has a miraculous origin and is therefore somewhat larger than life and does things which no human being has subsequently been able to do—myths that seem to be common in chiefly society in which rulers do actually claim extraordinary powers.
>
> There follows a second period in which well-known social processes are merely repeated. Lineages grow and divide and chiefs succeed each other. Historical events are not unique in our sense of the phrase; they are, on the contrary, as identical as possible. . . . Lastly there is . . . "historical time," a period in which real events have taken place and for which real genealogies are remembered. (Richards 1960:177–178)

The dynastic history of Tenochtitlan can be found in documents recounting the traditions of many of the ethnic groups, most often in the form of a king list giving the dates of tenure of the Tenochtitlan rulers, sometimes with additional information on their conquests. These rulers sprang from a common descent line, forming a single genealogy, which is the focus of the analysis of how the Aztecs conceived and explained their world using history—in this case, history condensed and represented by the most important royal genealogy.

A number of contradictions concerning the biological relationships of the Tenochtitlan kings appear in the historical documents of the early colonial period. These contradictions are not random but are patterned in such a way as to reveal certain underlying conceptions of rulership, cosmology, and time. This chapter summarizes the extant versions of dynastic history, showing that their inconsistencies can be understood as reflecting a generational model of the succession of kings. This model revolved around certain key women who played a most important role: they endowed the attributes of kingship itself.

The Kings of Tenochtitlan

Nine kings or *tlatoque* (plural of *tlatoani*) were said to have governed Tenochtitlan from the establishment of the city, traditionally given as being in the fourteenth century, to the coming of the Spanish in 1519. After the death of the ninth king but prior to the fall of Tenochtitlan to Cortés, two more persons ruled as leaders of Tenochtitlan (Fig. 1.3). Most of the documentary sources agree on their names and the order of their rule, as follows (etymologies are from *Codex en Cruz* 1981:I):

1. Acamapichtli ("Handful of Reeds," from *acatl* = reed or arrow + *mapichtli* = grasped in the hand); his glyph is a hand holding reeds or arrows.

2. Huitzilihuitl ("Hummingbird Feather," from *huitzilin* = hummingbird + *ihuitl* = feather); his glyph frequently is a hummingbird or hummingbird head with feathers on it.

3. Chimalpopoca ("Smoking Shield," from *chimalli* = shield + *popoctli* = smoke); his glyph is a round shield with curls of smoke rising from it.

4. Itzcoatl ("Obsidian Serpent," from *itztli* = obsidian + *coatl* = snake); his glyph is a serpent with obsidian blades along its back.

5. Motecuhzoma ("Angry Lord," from *tecuhtli* = lord + *zomalli* = angry), sometimes called Huehue Motecuhzoma (Motecuhzoma the Elder); his glyph is the diadem (*xiuhuitzolli*) worn by a ruler or lord (*tecuhtli*). Motecuhzoma was also called Ilhuicamina ("Archer of the Skies," from *ilhuicatl* = sky + *mina* = piercing arrow [Chavero n.d.:552]); this glyph is an arrow entering the sky, which in the pre-Hispanic conven-

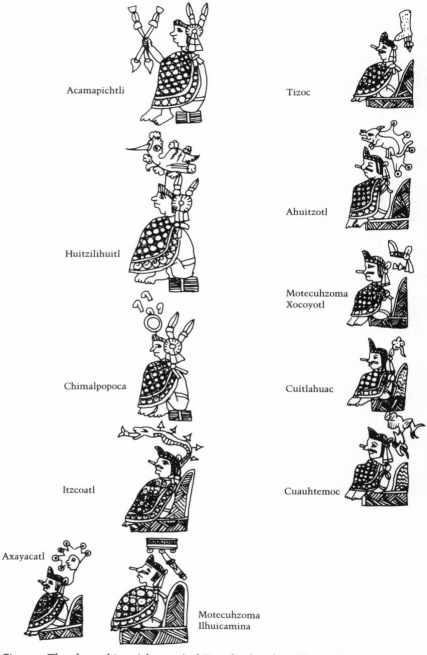

Fig. 1.3. The eleven kings (*tlatoque*) of Tenochtitlan, from the *Códices Matritenses* (Sahagún 1964:Pl. 39). Beginning with Itzcoatl, who organized the Triple Alliance, they wear the royal diadem (*xiuhuitzolli*) and are seated on thrones.

tion is drawn as a rectangle with horizontal lines representing the layers of the heavens.

6. Axayacatl ("Water-Face," from *atl* = water + *xayacatl* = face); his glyph is a human face with water coming out of it.

7. Tizoc (etymology uncertain, perhaps the "Bled One," from *zo* = to bleed); his name glyph is usually a bloody or punctured leg.

8. Ahuitzotl (the *ahuitzotl* was a mythical water animal); his glyph is the mammalian *ahuitzotl* drawn with water along its back.

9. Motecuhzoma, often called Motecuhzoma Xocoyotl or Motecuhzoma the Younger (*xocoyotl* is the nose ornament in the glyph of his name, and *xocoyotl* means younger or last child [Molina 1977]); his glyph is the lord's diadem, like that of Motecuhzoma the Elder, sometimes with a nose ornament attached. Motecuhzoma the Younger was the ruling *tlatoani* when Hernán Cortés led his men into the Valley of Mexico and is better known today by the corrupted form of his name, Montezuma.

10. Cuitlahuac (from *cuitlatl* = excrement); his glyph is often a little curl of excrement, sometimes in water.

11. Cuauhtemoc ("Descending Eagle," from *cuauhtli* = eagle); his glyph is a downturned eagle or eagle head, often with downward-pointing footprints. It was Cuauhtemoc who finally gave in to the Spanish siege of Tenochtitlan and surrendered himself and his city to the conquistadores.

The postconquest documents in the native historical tradition which preserve the dynastic history of Tenochtitlan fall into two broad categories: (1) those which merely list the rulers in order, with or without their dates of tenure; and (2) those which provide additional genealogical information linking the rulers into a family line (Table 1.1). This dichotomy is not an arbitrary one but instead conforms rather closely to the two major types of historical documents. Generally speaking, genealogical information is lacking in the annal-type prose documents and the related pictographic books in the year-count (*cexiuhamatl*) format often considered most representative of the aboriginal form of record keeping. Especially in the pictographic documents, where events are represented according to the year in which they occurred as part of a running sequence of 52-year cycles, it is difficult to indicate the kings' parents, siblings,

Table 1.1
Genealogical Information and King Lists for the Tenochtitlan Dynasty

Category	Genealogical Information	King List Only
Pictorial	*Codex Mendoza* (commentary) *Codex Mexicanus* (family tree) *Genealogía de los Príncipes* *Mexicanos* *Codex Xolotl*	*Codex Aubin* *Codex Azcatitlan* *Codex Cozcatzin* *Codex en Cruz* *Codex García Granados* *Codex de Huichapan* *Plano en Papel de Maguey* *Codex Ríos* *Codex Telleriano-Remensis* *Tira de Tepechpan* *Anales de Tula*
Native- or Mestizo- authored prose	*Crónica Mexicana* Chimalpahin's *Relaciones* *Anales de Cuauhtitlan* *Leyenda de los Soles* Ixtlilxochitl's *Relaciones* and *Historia Chichimeca* *Crónica Mexicayotl* *Carta* of Pablo Nazareo	*Anales de Tlatelolco*
Spanish- authored prose	*Relación de la Genealogía* *Origen de los Mexicanos* *Historia de los Mexicanos* *por sus Pinturas* Durán's *Historia* Tovar's *Historia* *Codex Ramirez* Mendieta's *Historia* Motolinía's *Historia* and *Memoriales*	Sahagún's *Historia General* (*Códices Matritenses* and *Florentine Codex*)

spouses, or children. Some pictographic records of the "Texcocan school" of manuscript painting (Robertson 1959), such as the *Codex Xolotl*, used the *mapa* rather than the *tira* or year-count format and did picture the wives and children of the kings, but these documents are few in number and concentrate on Aculhua history rather than the history of Tenochtitlan.

For the most part, then, genealogical information and accompanying inheritance rules must have been retained by the Aztecs as part of the oral historical tradition. These data were preserved after the conquest in the prose chronicle accounts as well as in European-introduced "family trees" drawn up to verify one's ancestry in court proceedings under the new Spanish law. Some of these non-native–style documents provide only partial genealogical information for the Tenochtitlan dynasty, leaving unclear the biological relationships among some of the kings. For instance, the family tree in the *Genealogía de los Príncipes Mexicanos* mentions only the fourth through eighth Tenochca kings. Several accounts, however, include a complete genealogy for the kings of Tenochtitlan, showing them all to have been members of a single family line. For this analysis, these genealogical data were summarized using anthropological kinship diagrams to indicate descent (by a vertical line), marriage (by an equal sign), and sibling ties (by a horizontal line).

Even the documents that do have genealogical information fail to present a clear picture of the dynastic history because they do not agree on the relationships among the kings. The frustrations the contradictions in them present are manifest in a statement by one scholar who did not even attempt to interpret the name glyphs in a dynastic family tree, because, he said, since "the traditions we possess are full of gaps, errors, and contradictions, it is impossible to undertake the details of identifying the numerous hieroglyphs which are found on these pages" (*Codex Mexicanus* 1952:414). Not only are the kings' biological ties inconsistently indicated from one account to the next, but even the order of their tenure as ruler is not always maintained. Neither are the contradictions a simple consequence of multiple authors; they exist among different works by the same author and may even be found within the pages of a single account.

A number of explanations have been put forth to account for these discrepancies (see Introduction). Reliance on imperfect human memory, error or misunderstanding, and personal or ethnic bias are the usual reasons proffered, especially when it is considered that both Spaniards and natives from different towns wrote these documents and that they were composed within a period of more than a century. Some lack of clarity is also due to the fact that the genealogical position of a newly seated king was often given only in reference to his immediate predecessor. This means that if two brothers followed their father to the throne, the second brother would not be indicated as a younger son of the father who had ruled before. Instead, he would be called the brother of his predecessor. It is left to the reader to deduce that the second brother was therefore a son of the earlier king. Building royal genealogies from these documents involves a good deal of this type of working backward.

Another explanation for the inconsistencies in the accounts concerning kinship position is that there were marriages within the royal family that "jumped" a generation. The result of these intermarriages is that certain persons ended up having more than one kinship role. For instance, the daughter of Motecuhzoma I married her father's cousin, Tezozomoc, son of Itzcoatl (Motecuhzoma's uncle). Her children therefore regarded both Motecuhzoma I and Itzcoatl as their grandfathers (two generations distant), even though Motecuhzoma was actually one generation removed from Itzcoatl (see Chapter 4).

It is also likely that in some cases the Spanish chroniclers tried to choose among variant traditions by making the historical data fit certain rules of succession. An obvious example of this practice is found in Mendieta's *Historia Eclesiástica Indiana* (1945:164), in which he first stated that some said Chimalpopoca was a son of Huitzilihuitl, while others said he was his brother. Mendieta decided this question by stating emphatically that Huitzilihuitl, Chimalpopoca, and also Itzcoatl must have been brothers because the inheritance rule was that brothers should succeed one another.

Some misunderstanding may have resulted from the Spanish chroniclers' attempts to make sense out of the indigenous kinship terminology, since Classical Nahuatl kinship categories did not correspond to the Spanish kin classification system. In particular, among the Aztecs the distinction between lineal and collateral relatives with respect to ego was not made in every generation, as it is in the European system. The only generations with terms to distinguish collateral kin from lineal kin were the first ascending and descending generations, ego's parents and children (P. Carrasco 1966b: 161; P. Carrasco 1984:51; Gardner 1981:98). This means, for example, that ego's first cousins were classed with his siblings by a term that referred to "children of the same grandparent" (P. Carrasco 1966b:151; see also Berdan 1982:67; Offner 1983:Table 5.1). Similarly, the terms for nephews and nieces also referred to the children of one's cousins, and terms for grandchildren applied to the children of nephews and nieces (P. Carrasco 1984:51). Thus, generation was a crucial component of Classical Nahuatl kinship terminology, but within the same generation the lineal-collateral differences were often obscured.

As noted above, information on the generation represented by a ruler is not found in the aboriginal-style year-count books and prose texts that simply list the kings in succession, because these documents lack the requisite genealogical details. What they do reveal is a "vertical" succession of rulers. Each king takes the office of the dead king who preceded him and thereby replaces and replicates him. The pictorial accounts illustrate this concept graphically by their lack of any desire to show portraiture; instead, each king is depicted as identical to all the others with the exception of his name glyph. With the addition of genealogical information from the other accounts, the different kings are tied together biologically, and this results in a collapsing of the vertical succession. Because of sibling relationships, some of the kings appear in the same generation, drawn together by this horizontal link. Such individuals are thereby equated in a generational sense, each representing the same generation. Other kings, however, lack collateral ties with their predecessors or successors and thus stand alone in their generation. Among the various traditions, the biological ties that vary the most refer to kings who are collateral relatives.

A pattern thus emerges as to the degree of consistency accorded to the kings depending on their generational relationships with respect to the adjacent kings, their predecessors and successors. For example, comparing information from several prose sources reveals variant relationships, especially for the three kings who followed after the very first, Acamapichtli (Fig. 1.4). The basic disagreement is whether the relationship among these three men was one of brothers, father and sons, or uncle and nephew (as already indicated in Mendieta's account). These discrepancies are more apparent than real, for these relationships (especially brother-brother and uncle-nephew) are often equivalent in Aztec texts and in the sacred tales of other cultures as well. In the stories about the Mexica tutelary deity, Huitzilopochtli, and the Toltec culture hero, Topiltzin Quetzalcoatl, their enemies are in some versions their brothers and in other versions their uncles (Chapters 3 and 5). Maya heroic epics exhibit the same patterned ambiguity, with brothers who were equated with father-son pairs (Pickands 1986:114). An example from another culture is found in the Egyptian myths of Horus and Seth, who are sometimes presented as brothers and at other times as nephew and uncle (Watts 1963:116). One plausible explanation for this equivalence is that for some purposes, sons, as "extensions" of their fathers, can be equated with them as their brothers (Pickands 1986:114).

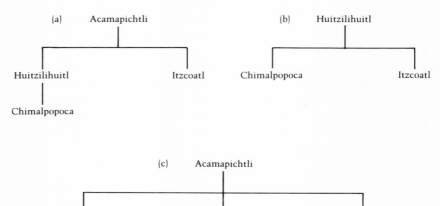

Figure 1.4. Variation in the genealogical position of the second, third, and fourth kings in the different accounts: (a) version found in Mendieta's history, Durán's history, Chimalpahin's third and seventh *relaciones*, the *Crónica Mexicayotl*, and the *Leyenda de los Soles*; (b) version found in Ixtlilxochitl's *Relaciones* and his *Historia Chichimeca*, the *Codex Xolotl*, and the *Crónica Mexicana*; (c) version found in Mendieta's history, Motolinía's history and *Memoriales*, the *Origen de los Mexicanos*, the *Relación de la Genealogía*, and the *Historia de los Mexicanos por sus Pinturas*.

Another group of three kings, the ones who followed Motecuhzoma I (Axayacatl, Tizoc, and Ahuitzotl), were also subject to a great deal of contradiction in the documents in the native historical tradition. This second group of three exhibits more variability than the first group in birth order and succession but greater consistency in biological relationships. Most frequently they are said to be brothers, sometimes grandsons of Motecuhzoma I, and other times his sons (Chapter 4). Some authors specified that they ruled in order of birth, while others emphasized that the opposite occurred, that Tizoc and Ahuitzotl were older than Axayacatl, who was nevertheless chosen to rule before them. As for order of tenure, there is more inconsistency among the documents. For example, Ahuitzotl precedes Axayacatl in the *Historia de Tlaxcala* (Muñoz Camargo 1978: 107), Tizoc precedes Axayacatl in the *Codex Ramirez* (1980:66), and Ahuitzotl even precedes Motecuhzoma Ilhuicamina in the illustrations in Tovar's history (1972), while Tizoc is left out entirely in the *Plano en Papel de Maguey* (1910).

There is much less variation concerning the biological relationships or order of tenure for the kings who rule as sole representatives of their generation. The first king, Acamapichtli, who founded the dynasty, always stands alone in his generation in the different accounts. His successor is always from a descending generation (a son). The fifth king, Motecuhzoma I, is usually indicated as the son of Huitzilihuitl, although the Texcoco area accounts, reflecting Aculhua traditions (Ixtlilxochitl 1975:409; Ixtlilxochitl 1977:80), have Chimalpopoca as his father. Thus, although there is some variation concerning his parentage, Motecuhzoma Ilhuicamina is given as the son of one of the three kings who ruled before, usually Huitzilihuitl, and he is virtually always one generation below Itzcoatl, his predecessor. Motecuhzoma is also at least one generation above his successor, Axayacatl. Thus the fifth king, like the first, Acamapichtli, stood alone in his generation.

One apparent exception to this rule is extremely revealing. The author of the *Anales de Cuauhtitlan* (1975:35) first indicated that Itzcoatl and Motecuhzoma were brothers, and therefore in the same generation, by placing both in the list of Chimalpopoca's children. Significantly, later in the text when Itzcoatl took the throne and it was decided that Motecuhzoma would be his successor, only then did Motecuhzoma refer to Itzcoatl as his uncle, putting him one generation above, since he was to precede him (1975:38). In this account it appears that order of succession determined generational position, not vice versa.

Finally, Motecuhzoma II is almost always described as the sole reigning member of his generation before the coming of the Spanish. While he had a brother, Cuitlahuac, who ruled after him in some accounts, Cuitlahuac's reign was very short (usually given as eighty days, a ceremonial span of time), and occurred only after the Spanish had entered Tenochtitlan. Cuauhtemoc, who followed Cuitlahuac, was one generation away from Motecuhzoma II. According to some sources, neither of these two last rulers was crowned as *tlatoani* but served only as a temporary leader filling in for the deposed or deceased Motecuhzoma. Therefore, for the period preceding the Spanish arrival (and it was this period that concerned later Aztec attempts to reconcile past and present), Motecuhzoma II was the last king and stood alone in his generation, as had Acamapichtli and Motecuhzoma I before him.

Thus the variations among the different accounts as to the kinship positions of the nine kings reveal a singling out of three rulers as sole representatives of their generation. The three who are so marked are the first, middle, and last kings. The other six kings often compose two sets of three, representing a single generation or uncle-nephew relationships, and they alternate with the sole representatives, as indicated by the collateral ties they possess. These six rulers can parsimoniously be represented as two groups of three brothers, which most emphasizes their horizontal links, and in fact this is the relationship often given, especially for the second set of three. This generational model of the dynasty takes the form of an alternation of one and three kings per generation (1–3–1–3–1).

This abstract form of the dynasty constructed from the different historical accounts refers not to kinship rules or to actual historical succession but to a surface manifestation of certain underlying principles, and as such it is similar to the models for royal dynasties proposed for the Maya (Joyce 1981) and Inca (Zuidema 1977). Furthermore, Rudolf van Zantwijk (1978), who has called attention to the pattern revealed in the two sets of three brothers, noted that the individual kings in these triads shared some characteristics with their positional counterparts in the other half of the dynasty, which indicates that this pattern extended beyond genealogical considerations and was instrumental in determining how the kings were viewed historically. In particular, Itzcoatl and Ahuitzotl, the last kings in each group of three brothers, were great conquerors who expanded the empire. In contrast, Tizoc and Chimalpopoca, in the middle of the two sets, are said to have been cowards with short reigns and ignominious deaths (Zantwijk 1978:95).

The similarities between the latter two rulers go beyond these brief observations. Tizoc and Chimalpopoca met identical fates in the various accounts, having been poisoned by their own people (Chimalpopoca in Motolinía 1951:78; Tizoc in Durán 1967:II:311; and *Codex Ramirez* 1980:67) or killed at the behest of an outsider who in the case of both kings had the same name, Maxtla (Chimalpopoca in *Relación de la Genealogía* 1941:252; Ixtlilxochitl 1977: 112, 119; Chimalpahin 1965:190; and Tezozomoc 1975:104; Tizoc in two later sources, Torquemada 1975:255 and Veytia 1944:I:236). As for the fifth and ninth kings, who shared in the same name, Motecuhzoma, they were both lawgivers for the empire (*Codex Mendoza* 1964:34) and were equated in the historical narratives in many other important ways (Chapter 5).

Certain Tenochtitlan rulers were thus interchangeable in Aztec history, precisely those who held the same position in the replication of the generational structure of the dynasty. For this reason, events assigned to Chimalpopoca in one source, such as his death by poison, are attributed to his positional counterpart, Tizoc, in other sources. The pattern revealed by these similarities indicates an adherence to principles governing the construction of the narratives despite an apparent disregard for consistency in the content—the historical detail—of the traditions.

The patterned repetition of the genealogy, seen in terms of biological relationships and succession, events in the reigns of the kings, and in one case their names is not unique to the Tenochtitlan dynasty but is a function of certain concepts of rulership in which the nature of the king is tied to the functioning of the cosmos; thus kingship, like the cosmos, is cyclical (Chapter 7). Exactly the same principle operated in the traditions of other peoples. The Rwanda of Africa, for example, similarly conceived of kingly succession as cyclical and expressed this principle in the names and attributes of the kings:

> One of four dynastic names is given to every king of Rwanda, depending on his position in the cycle [of succession]. They are Yuhi, Mutara, Kigeri and Mibambwe. The secret ritual code promised the king who began the cycle, as well as his immediate successor, that they would reach a ripe old age. They have specific mystical functions related to the fertility of man and cattle. On the other hand, the Kigeri and Mibambwe kings had a military vocation. Dynastic history teaches that all the sovereigns who ruled under the name Mibambwe either met with a dramatic death or, for various reasons, were graced with the title of "liberator" . . . The dynastic cycle has to end with the sacrificial death of the Mibambwe king before the Yuhi king, who is promised a ripe old age, regenerates the life forces of the universe by extinguishing and then relighting the sacred fire for four generations. (Heusch 1985:116–117)

Just like the Rwanda kings, the Aztec kings were perceived as structured in a cycle of four after the first, Acamapichtli, who in some sources is considered not to have ruled as *tlatoani* (Chapter 2), ending in a ruler named Motecuhzoma. Also, as with the kings of Rwanda, the Tenochtitlan dynasty had to be regenerated at the end of the first cycle in order for the second to begin. The principal agent at this critical juncture was a woman, a queen, who held the right to endow rulership. Thus the function of royal females in the maintenance of the dynasty was just as important as that of the ruling males.

The "Queens" of Tenochtitlan

Women, of course, are necessary in a biological sense to the maintenance of any family line, for it is through them that men are related to one another. More particularly, when certain key women are added to the Tenochtitlan royal genealogy, the abstract model of the alternation of one and three kings achieves its greatest potential for explaining the patterning of that dynasty. Three women played major roles in the founding, ennobling, and maintenance of the ruling line. Significantly, all three are said in some accounts to have been queens in their own right, or at any rate to have had a legitimate right to rule. What is more interesting is the fact that each of these women is associated with one of the three "marked" kings in the generational model: the first, middle, and last. Although these women are generally absent from the king lists, their contributions to the dynasty are crucial for discovering how the genealogy was constructed. The inconsistencies as to the very existence, names, and kinship relations of these women, which far surpass the contradictions concerning the kings (Zantwijk 1985:187), reveal major structural principles on which Aztec history was created.

The similarities shared by two of these women were briefly noted in a study by Zantwijk (1978) concerning the few versions of Tenochca history in which the son of Motecuhzoma I, rather than inheriting his father's throne, was passed over in favor of his sister. This woman, who then went on to rule as queen, is most often named ♀Atotoztli ("Water-Bird," from *atl* = water + *tototl* = bird) in the various accounts. The preference for this woman over a son of Motecuhzoma is even more extraordinary, and yet it becomes more understandable in light of the fact that the same event apparently would have occurred following the death of Motecuhzoma II according to Zantwijk's interpretation of some accounts (1978:95). The daughter of this last king, known by her baptismal name, Isabel, did not become queen, since the Spaniards had by then disrupted the dynastic succession. Still, she apparently had some right of rulership, for a few sources indicate that Cuauhtemoc, Motecuhzoma II's

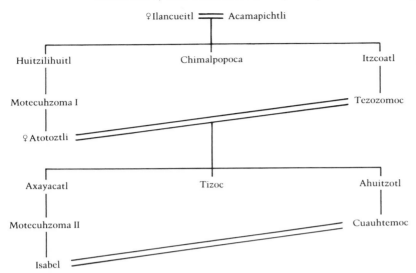

Figure 1.5. Patterned reconstruction of the Tenochtitlan royal genealogy according to Zantwijk 1978, emphasizing the fraternal ties between kings number two through four and six through eight, and the marriages of the daughters of the middle and last kings with their father's father's brother's sons.

heroic but doomed successor, legitimated his right to rule by marrying her. These two daughters of the kings named Motecuhzoma are further linked by the fact that each married a man in exactly the same kinship position, their father's father's brother's son (FFBS).

The third key woman is ♀Ilancueitl ("Old Woman-Skirt," from *ilama* = old woman + *cueitl* = skirt), who appears earlier in the dynasty in association with the first king, Acamapichtli, and she further confirms the patterning of the generational model. When she is added to the dynasty as the wife of Acamapichtli, the position she holds with respect to ♀Atotoztli (as her great-grandmother) is identical to the position the latter woman holds with respect to Isabel (Zantwijk 1978:95; see Fig. 1.5). Thus, Zantwijk's tentative suggestion that the Aztecs may have employed certain structural principles in the dynastic history of Tenochtitlan (1978:96; see also Zantwijk 1985:186–192) is supported and elaborated here by demonstrating that the "usurpation" by the daughters of the two kings named Motecuhzoma is only one aspect of an abstract model on which colonial-period versions of the pre-Hispanic dynasty were constructed.

All three key females are sometimes said to have had the right of

rulership or to have bequeathed that right to their husbands or children. This means that power, in the sense of legitimacy of rule, came
with or through these females even though only males appear in the
pictorial king lists. Their role as ennoblers of the Tenochtitlan dynasty was said to have begun at its founding in the marital union of
Acamapichtli and ♀Ilancueitl. According to the historical traditions
of Tenochtitlan, the Mexica and other Chichimec peoples, who were
barbarian hunters and wanderers, intruded into the Valley of Mexico
following the collapse of an earlier civilization, that of the Toltecs,
centered at the city of Tollan. The different Chichimec groups established their cities in the valley, but as an "uncivilized" people they
lacked a hereditary nobility. Thus they believed they had no right to
designate one of their members as king to rule over them. Only the
Toltecs, who the later Aztecs believed represented the qualities of
original civilization, had the right of kingship. By procuring a king
from among the non-Chichimec groups in the valley who claimed
Toltec ancestry, or by marrying into one of those lineages, these
foreign, intruder groups could establish their own noble houses.

The Culhua people of the southern lakeshore city of Culhuacan
were just such a "civilized" agricultural people, who maintained a
strong tradition of being the direct descendants of the Toltecs. Some
sources indicate that the Toltecs and the Culhua were in fact the
same people. According to the *Histoyre du Mechique* (1905:19–20)
the people known as the Toltecs first lived in a place far from the
Valley of Mexico called Culhuacan. Only after they moved to Tollan
were they given the derivative name Toltecs. When Tollan fell, signaling the end of Toltec hegemony, the people moved to the southern
part of the Valley of Mexico and built a new Culhuacan, where they
practiced the very productive *chinampa* (raised field) farming and
where they were held to be a "noble" people.

Other versions of Aztec history that do not mention the earlier
town of Culhuacan do indicate that the Culhuacan in the Valley of
Mexico was settled by remnant Toltec groups following the destruction of the city of Tollan. The author of the *Anales de Cuauhtitlan*
(1975:71) explained, "After the Toltecs were dispersed, their only
name was Culhua." Likewise, on the eastern shore of the lake, Aculhua tradition held that Nauhyotl, a relative of the last Toltec king,
established a new dynasty at Culhuacan. He and his descendants
were "kings of the Culhua, for thus the Toltecs were called after their
capital city became Culhuacan" (Ixtlilxochitl 1975:285). The notion
that the Culhua preserved the legitimacy of the previous civilized

era is found as well in their name, for the root of their name is the word *colli*, meaning "ancestors."

The first kings of Tenochtitlan, like some other royal families in the Valley of Mexico, were legitimated via a kinship tie with the Culhuacan dynasty. By marrying into this noble lineage, the Tenochca kings claimed descent from the Culhua and thereby ultimately from the Toltec ruling house: "From the Toltecs descended the nine [kings] who held the palace, throne and government of Mexico Tenochtitlan" (Chimalpahin 1965:62). The Tenochca-Mexica thus also referred to themselves as the Culhua-Mexica (Barlow 1945b, 1949), and one of the Tenochtitlan *tlatoani*'s titles was Culhuatecuhtli—"Lord of the Culhua." It is for this reason that Cortés (1971:47), when he wrote about the "Aztec" empire in his Second Letter to the king of Spain, used the word "Culua" for the name of their domain (see Chapter 7).

The link between the dynasties of Tenochtitlan and Culhuacan was embodied by a woman, a Culhua princess. The versions differ as to the specific relationship that tied her to the Tenochca royal line, usually portraying her as either the mother or the wife of the first king, Acamapichtli. Thus, in some sources Acamapichtli was half Mexica and half Culhua, the son of a Culhua princess and a Mexica man. In other accounts he was ethnically pure Mexica but was married to a Culhua princess, an act that rendered his children half Mexica and half Culhua. Additional accounts strengthen the female Culhua tie to the Tenochtitlan dynasty by insisting that the first king was not only the son of a Culhua princess but also the husband of a Culhua princess, thereby combining the two variations (see Chapter 2).

Women thus constituted the "Culhuacan connection" necessary for the institution of kingship at Tenochtitlan. The tie between ♀Ilancueitl, a Culhua princess, and Acamapichtli gave the Tenochca the right to claim the inheritance of the old Toltec empire. This marriage also united the two opposing categories of people, the barbarian, nomadic Chichimecs from out of the north and the civilized, sedentary agriculturalists in the southern valley (Zantwijk 1981:25). On such a basis, the most powerful of the Aztec dynasties was established. Even then, however, it was not capable of sustaining itself without the intervention of other women, who were needed to renew the legitimacy of the dynasty—that is, to regenerate it—following the fifth and ninth *tlatoque*. This was the role played by the daughters of the middle and last kings (see Chapter 4).

The ennobling power of women is not confined to the Tenochti-

tlan case but also occurs as a structuring principle for rulership in
other cultures (Chapter 7). An Old World example is found in the
succession rituals of the Pabir of Nigeria, a Chadic-speaking people
among whom it was the duty and privilege of the "Queen Mother"
(a title not referring to the king's actual mother) to ennoble the king
as the "sacred giver of royal power" (Cohen 1977:22):

> She literally legitimizes the king by providing him with the
> mystical power of the sacred objects of the state. These objects
> date back to the founder of the dynasty. They represent the
> continuity of the state as well as the king's capacity to commu-
> nicate with the royal ancestors to ensure the welfare of his land
> and people. (1977:23)

On a more abstract level, the continuity of the dynasty represented by the Tenochtitlan royal females further supports the patterned construction of the genealogical model (where they are associated with the three marked kings) by reiterating its cyclical nature.
As the wife or mother of the first king, Acamapichtli, the Culhuacan-
born queen is instrumental in the establishment of the dynasty. As
the daughter of Motecuhzoma I and mother of his successor, she
links the two halves of the dynasty and thereby maintains the ruling
line. As the daughter of Motecuhzoma II, she is the final hope for the
resurgence of indigenous culture in the face of inevitable destruction. All of these appearances at critical junctures in the genealogy
reveal that the history of the Tenochtitlan royal family, modeled on a
repeating cycle of kings, was periodically regenerated between those
cycles by the ennobling power of queens.

The cyclical nature of the dynasty is a part of Mesoamerican
conceptions of time, for genealogies are a way of measuring time
(Vansina 1973:101). As a result, the genealogy exhibits other characteristics of cycles. Cycles pose inherent contradictions that must
be dealt with on a philosophical level. They actually move through
time, and for Mesoamericans, through the cardinal directions of
space as well, the two were understood together as space-time (Elzey
1976b:315; León-Portilla 1974b:120; Soustelle 1959:97). The Mesoamerican peoples conceived this movement very graphically, as an
individual carrying the burden of a particular period of time through
a particular segment of space to which it was linked and then trans-
ferring the burden to the next burden bearer in the series.

Because of this movement, all the cycles in a repeating series exhibit a dynamic quality. However, the individual periods that make up that series, such as every day named 1 Wind or every year named 2 Reed, are ideally repetitive and unchanging from cycle to cycle, and hence are stable and timeless. Thus, cycles have simultaneous dynamic and static qualities. In the same way, any event in a single cycle has a unique identity and point in time, allowing for a chronology, even an evolutionary progression, but it also has counterpart events in the parallel cycles that occurred in the past and that will recur in the future. In this view, events and people are at once unique and recurrent.

A further problem inherent in the cyclical concept is that although its repetitive nature allows for a sense of certainty, providing knowledge about the present and future as long as one knows the past, the inescapable fact that a cycle ends and must be succeeded by another entails maximum uncertainty. Unlike the linear view of time marching onward into infinity at a steady, unstoppable pace, there is a point of instability in cyclical time at the juncture of two adjacent cycles. At this point the possibility exists that no new cycle will take over when the previous one is completed; there will be no one to assume the burden. This was the critical point (Elzey 1976a:128), for if no new cycle began, then there would be no time, no order, and the world would be plunged into chaos.

This possibility was the source of great anxiety for Mesoamerican peoples. In their belief it was the responsibility of society—the antithesis of chaos—to minimize disorder by ensuring the prompt succession of the next cycle: "The major themes of mythology and ritual [in highland central Mexico dealt] with the crises encumbent upon the termination of one cycle and the beginning of another" (Cohodas 1978:20). Among the Aztecs the fear of impending doom at the end of cyclical periods was expressed in the negative quality of the five "empty" days at the end of the solar year (which fell outside of the eighteen 20-day months comprising the first 360 days of the year), the great New Fire rituals at the juncture of adjacent 52-year "centuries," and the notorious human sacrifices to the gods said to ensure the daily cycle of the sun's movement, the continuance of Aztec hegemony, and the existence of their world age, the fifth "sun" in the series.

The dynastic history of Tenochtitlan incorporated these aspects of the cyclical principle as well. The three key royal females are both unique and recurrent. Although they are all superficially dif-

ferent, living at different times, because of the kinship positions
they assume in the genealogy (Fig. 1.5), all three can be considered
structurally identical. They are manifestations of one woman who
reappears at patterned intervals in the dynastic history. This underlying identity produced the similarities of historical detail linking
♀Ilancueitl, ♀Atotoztli, and Isabel, as will be seen in the following
chapters. Furthermore, they appear at the juncture of the repeating
dynastic cycles, which from other examples of time measurement
would be the point of greatest uncertainty and instability. This point
is thus represented by a female, the antithesis of male hegemony
expressed in masculine rule. An ambiguous creature, she represents
chaos and threatens order (i.e., the succession of male kings), but
she is also the source of power, since she legitimates her husband or
his heirs, and she is absolutely essential as the link that binds the
male rulers to one another in a descent line. Her equivocal nature is
expressed in the contradictory kinship roles she holds in the various
traditions (Chapter 2), in her multiple incarnations as other women
in Mexica history (Chapter 3), and in her structural position in the
genealogy, in which she both begins and ends the cycles of Tenochca
dynastic history (Chapter 4).

Therefore, despite the fact that Tenochtitlan was (by almost all
accounts) ruled exclusively by kings, its dynastic history, as it was
shaped after the Spanish conquest, revolved quite literally around a
few relatively unknown "queens." These women performed a crucial
function in the royal genealogy, endowing the kings with a nobility
that they would not otherwise have possessed. This nobility had to
be regenerated at certain points in the genealogy—namely, at the beginning of its successive cycles, associated in the model with the
three kings who were sole representatives of their generation. With
the commencement of each cycle, a woman endowed the succeeding kings with the right to rule, a woman who thereby merged with
her counterparts before and after her, to whom she was structurally
identical. She was one woman and many women at once, a means of
achieving union but representative of opposition, a source of power
yet also of chaos, a threat to the orderly progression of the world
but absolutely necessary to its maintenance; in short, a woman of
discord.

Chapter 2

The Founding Queen

The founding of the Tenochtitlan dynasty began with the ennobling of its first king, Acamapichtli, because he was married to, or the son of, a Culhua (Toltec) princess. The two women who played the roles of mother and wife of Acamapichtli are usually named ♀Atotoztli and ♀Ilancueitl, respectively, in the various historical accounts that mention them. Besides being related as mother-in-law and daughter-in-law, however, they were also said to be sisters. The closeness of their kinship tie is an aspect of a deeper identity that unites these two women into one. The patterned variation in their treatment in the different traditions demonstrates that they are substitutable for one another. In other words, the wife and mother of the first king, for certain conceptual purposes, were the same woman.

This act of "royal incest," the marriage of a man to his mother, is revealed in the way the historical episodes were manipulated. They deal not so much with history as with basic philosophical and cosmological issues concerning the nature of kingship and the relation of kings to gods. The historical traditions of the Aztecs, like the sacred symbolic narratives of other cultures, preserve in written form the attempts of a people to reconcile fundamental contradictions inherent in their worldview. These include: (1) the necessity of demarcating someone with the power of rulership and thereby separating him from his subjects, although he is ostensibly the same as they are; (2) the need to relate the functioning of the sociopolitical realm—the realm of the people—to the domain of the gods and cosmos, and thereby to endow it with order, legitimacy, and permanence, that is, "truth" in the Aztec view; (3) the confrontation of male hegemony with the actual impossibility of succession through the male line, since males are born of females; (4) the juxtaposition of an eternal office of king with the mortality of the individual officeholders; and (5) the clash between the dynamic and static aspects of cyclical time-space. Such contradictions are dealt with in part in these narratives by the inclusion of key characters, such as the women of discord, who embody ambiguity.

To understand how the Aztecs used the creation and telling of dynastic history as a continuing process of communicating ideas about themselves, as well as wrestling with ultimately unresolvable philosophical problems, it is necessary to examine the various accounts in some detail, especially with regard to kin relationships. This chapter begins the analysis of the critical role in the shaping of the dynasty played by the three Tenochtitlan "queens" by considering how the first of the three, the female founder of the ruling house, is represented in the different versions of the historical traditions. As a woman of Culhuacan, she gave the fledgling dynasty its nobility; in an act of "royal incest" with her husband-son, she demonstrated that the power of kings is beyond that of their subjects (Chapter 7). And as the ultimate genetrix, she was a manifestation of the mother-earth goddess, a topic explored in the next chapter.

The Founding Woman: Variations on a Theme

♀Atotoztli: Mother of Acamapichtli

There are two basic versions of Tenochtitlan dynastic history that mention the founding woman: those that state that ♀Atotoztli, a princess of Culhuacan, was the mother of Acamapichtli, and those that name ♀Ilancueitl, also a princess of Culhuacan, as his wife. Even within this simple dichotomy there is a great deal of variation concerning the kin relationships of these principal characters. For example, several of the *Relaciones* of Chimalpahin, a native from Chalco in the southern valley, refer to ♀Atotoztli as the mother of

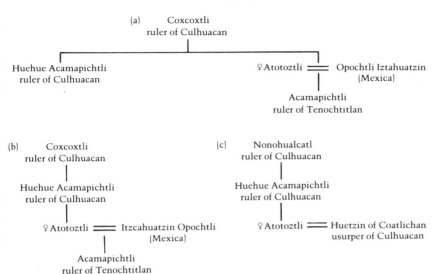

Figure 2.1. Variation in the genealogical position of ♀Atotoztli in three of Chimalpahin's accounts: (a) the founding of the Tenochtitlan dynasty according to Chimalpahin's *Seventh Relación*; (b) the founding of the Tenochtitlan dynasty according to Chimalpahin's *Fifth Relación*; (c) the relationship of ♀Atotoztli, the Culhua princess, to Huetzin of Coatlichan and usurper of Culhuacan, according to Chimalpahin's *Memorial Breve*.

Acamapichtli, emphasizing the descent of the first Tenochca king from a Culhua princess. Nevertheless, none of these versions by the same author are identical to any of the others.

In the *Seventh Relación* written by Chimalpahin (1965:182), Acamapichtli's parents are Opochtli Iztahuatzin, a man of Mexica ethnicity, and ♀Atotoztli, the daughter of Coxcoxtli, ruler of Culhuacan. The Mexica people wanted Acamapichtli to be their king since he was thus of both Mexica and royal Culhua ancestry. Acamapichtli was not living in Culhuacan at that time but resided instead in Coatlichan, an Aculhua city ruled by Acolmiztli on the eastern side of the lake. The Mexica sent a delegation to Coatlichan to secure their new king and bring him to Tenochtitlan. In this account there is also another Acamapichtli, Huehue Acamapichtli (Acamapichtli the Elder, to differentiate him from the younger Acamapichtli, king of Tenochtitlan). The text states that Huehue Acamapichtli was the uncle of Acamapichtli the Younger and successor to Coxcoxtli as king of Culhuacan. Presumably then, Huehue Acamapichtli was the son of Coxcoxtli and brother of ♀Atotoztli (Fig. 2.1a).

The shorter *Fifth Relación* of Chimalpahin (1965:151) has Aca-mapichtli's mother, ♀Atotoztli, again as the wife of the Mexica man, here Itzcahuatzin Opochtli. Unlike the *Seventh Relación* version, however, she is the daughter, not the sister, of Huehue Acamapichtli, and the granddaughter rather than daughter of Coxcoxtli of Culhua-can (Fig. 2.1b). Thus she is one generation removed from her familial relationships as indicated in the *Seventh Relación*.

In another Chimalpahin account, the *Memorial Breve* (Chimal-pahin 1958:39), quite a different story is told, and it is ultimately linked to the first two by reference to other texts. The *Memorial Breve* provides little information on the Tenochtitlan rulers since this document is concerned primarily with the early history of Cul-huacan, and the narrative ends prior to the founding of Tenochtitlan. Nevertheless, the princess ♀Atotoztli does appear as the daughter of Huehue Achitometl (not Huehue Acamapichtli), a king of Cul-huacan who was preceded by his father, Nonohualcatl (Fig. 2.1c). A further difference is that instead of marrying the father of Acama-pichtli, she married Huetzin, a native of Coatlichan. (Coatlichan is the city where Acamapichtli was living in the *Seventh Relación*, above.) Finally, all of this is said to have happened more than a hun-dred years prior to the reign of Coxcoxtli and the entry of the Mexica into the Valley of Mexico.

All of these details would lead one to believe that this ♀Atotoztli should not be associated with the events of the founding of the Tenochtitlan dynasty. It would seem that this is an entirely differ-ent woman of the same name. Her relationship to both Achitometl as his daughter and Huetzin as his wife, however, indicate that she was indeed the woman elsewhere associated with Acamapichtli de-spite her placement in time in the preceding century. This is because the Aculhua traditions of the eastern lakeshore have ♀Atotoztli, the wife of Huetzin of Coatlichan and daughter of Achitometl of Cul-huacan, as the *sister* of the Culhua princess who became the wife of Acamapichtli of Tenochtitlan. In addition, other sources link this ♀Atotoztli with the mother of Acamapichtli in contexts other than Chimalpahin's *Fifth Relación* and *Seventh Relación*.

♀Ilancueitl: Sister of ♀Atotoztli

The Aculhua tradition is preserved in the prose histories written by Ixtlilxochitl, spokesman for Texcoco, who also made the most

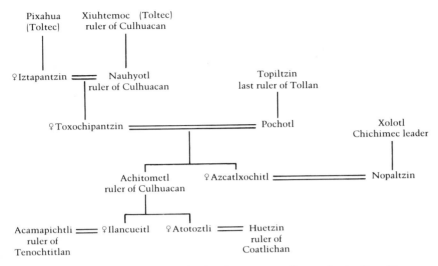

Fig. 2.2. The founding of the Tenochtitlan dynasty according to the Aculhua (Texcoco area) histories of Ixtlilxochitl.

direct genealogical link between the Culhua and Toltec dynasties. According to Ixtlilxochitl (1975:297–303), the Culhua kings were descendants not just of the Toltecs in general but of the Toltec kings. In his genealogy, Pochotl, a surviving son of Topiltzin, the last Toltec king of Tollan, married ♀Toxochipantzin, daughter of Nauhyotl, the ruler of Culhuacan (sometimes equivalent to Nonohualcatl of the other traditions, e.g., the *Memorial Breve* account, above). The son of Pochotl and ♀Toxochipantzin was Achitometl, a direct descendant of Topiltzin of Tollan, who succeeded Nauhyotl to the throne of Culhuacan (Fig. 2.2). Achitometl had two daughters: ♀Ilancueitl, who married Acamapichtli, ruler of Tenochtitlan, and ♀Atotoztli, who married Huetzin, heir to the throne of Coatlichan (as above in the *Memorial Breve* version).

The marriages of these two women are illustrated in the pictorial *Codex Xolotl*, one of the sources thought to have been used by Ixtlilxochitl to write his histories (Fig. 2.3). The women are shown first with their father, Achitometl, in Culhuacan (the place indicated by a curved hill glyph). They are named by the glyphs attached to them, ♀Atotoztli ("Water-Bird") having a bird with water down its back, while ♀Ilancueitl ("Old Woman-Skirt") is named by teeth

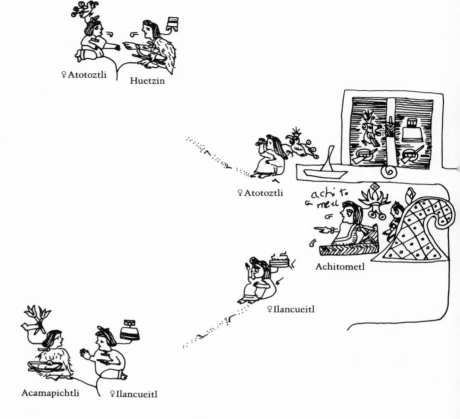

♀ Atotoztli   Huetzin

♀ Atotoztli

achi to
meil

Achitometl

♀ Ilancueitl

Acamapichtli   ♀ Ilancueitl

Fig. 2.3. ♀Ilancueitl and ♀Atotoztli, princesses of Culhuacan and daughters of Achitometl, are shown with their father in Culhuacan (right) and then with their respective spouses, ♀Atotoztli married to Huetzin of Coatlichan (above) and ♀Ilancueitl married to Acamapichtli of Tenochtitlan (below). Above the Culhuacan place glyph (the curved hill) are two tracts of irrigated chinampa land with the two women's name glyphs (selected pictographs, *Codex Xolotl* 1980:II:Pl. III).

Fig. 2.4. Huetzin is shown married to a woman who may be ♀Ilancueitl in the *Mapa Tlotzin* (1886). Only the skirt (*cueitl*) part of her name glyph remains.

(for the sound of *tlantli*) on a skirt (*cueitl*), for the combined sound of tlan-cueitl. Above them are irrigated fields (*chinampas*) with the sisters' name glyphs on them, perhaps indicating the dowries that they brought to their husbands (*Codex Xolotl* 1980:I:52) and clearly linking them with the agricultural practices of a civilized people. In contrast, their husbands wear animal skins and carry bows, identifying them as nomadic hunters, Chichimecs. The women are redrawn another time on the same page next to their respective husbands and children in their new homes.

In the Aculhua accounts, then, ♀Ilancueitl and ♀Atotoztli were sisters, daughters of Achitometl of Culhuacan. Even within this basic tradition there are several variations. In one of Ixtlilxochitl's histories (1975:303), ♀Ilancueitl is named as the older sister of ♀Atotoztli, while in another (1977:49), ♀Atotoztli is said to be older than ♀Ilancueitl. The two women are further confounded when, after first stating that ♀Ilancueitl married Acamapichtli, Ixtlilxochitl (1975: 304) then indicated that Huitzilihuitl was the son of Acamapichtli and ♀Atotoztli (rather than her sister ♀Ilancueitl).

A final variation in the Aculhua traditions comes from the *Mapa Tlotzin*, another pictographic document, which shows Huetzin of Coatlichan with his wife and descendants (Fig. 2.4). In this document Huetzin's wife's name glyph, though partly obscured, has a skirt in it for the sound of *cueitl*, giving a possible reading of ♀Ilancueitl, elsewhere named as the wife of Acamapichtli. To reconcile this read-

ing with the other Aculhua versions in which ♀Atotoztli, not her
sister ♀Ilancueitl, married Huetzin, one early scholar, J.M.A. Aubin
(in *Mapa Tlotzin* 1886:318), suggested that perhaps there was one
woman with two names, ♀Atotoztli and ♀Ilancueitl. In fact, all the
variations among these sources show that the two sisters were interchangeable in terms of birth order and in terms of which one of them
married Huetzin and Acamapichtli. The suggestion that one woman
appeared in two manifestations under two names is confirmed in
other historical traditions, as discussed below.

♀Atotoztli as Mother and ♀Ilancueitl as Wife of Acamapichtli

In Chimalpahin's *Relaciones*, discussed above, ♀Atotoztli was the
mother of Acamapichtli; in the Aculhua histories of his contemporary, Ixtlilxochitl, ♀Atotoztli was the sister of Acamapichtli's wife,
♀Ilancueitl, but not his mother. In other traditions, including those
of the Mexica themselves, both ♀Atotoztli and ♀Ilancueitl appear
again as sisters but as the mother and wife of Acamapichtli. The city
of Coatlichan, already mentioned as the residence of Acamapichtli
and the city ruled by Huetzin, plays an important part in these versions as well. It was equivalent in some respects to Culhuacan in
that both ♀Atotoztli and ♀Ilancueitl were associated with it, and like
Culhuacan it was a place of ennoblement and royal legitimacy.

The history of the Mexica-Tenochca written by Fr. Durán gives
a complete, though not unambiguous, genealogy of the Tenochtitlan kings. In his account, ♀Atotoztli and ♀Ilancueitl have the important role of "mothers of the kings of the Aztec nation" (Durán
1967:II:115). ♀Atotoztli is mentioned first as the daughter of Nauhyotl, who succeeded Achitometl as ruler of Culhuacan (see above
in the Aculhua version, where instead Nauhyotl was the predecessor
of Achitometl). ♀Atotoztli was married to a Mexica named Opochtli
or Opochiztahuatzin (as in Chimalpahin's *Seventh Relación*, above).
Their son, Acamapichtli, was sought by the Mexica to become the
first ruler of Tenochtitlan, since he was descended from both Mexica
and royal Culhua lines. The Mexica accordingly asked Nauhyotl to
give them his grandson to rule them, and also to give them another
Culhua princess, ♀Ilancueitl, to be the wife of Acamapichtli (Fig.
2.5). This marriage was fruitless, however, and Acamapichtli had to
take other wives in order to produce his heirs (Durán 1967:II:51–53,
56–57).

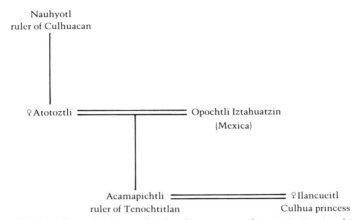

Fig. 2.5. The founding of the Tenochtitlan dynasty according to Fr. Durán's history.

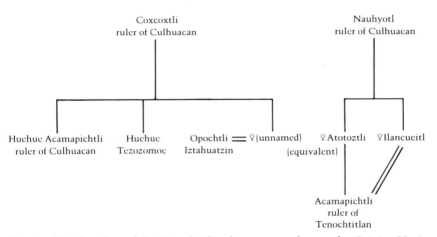

Fig. 2.6. The founding of the Tenochtitlan dynasty according to the *Crónica Mexicayotl.*

Whereas Durán did not state that the woman Acamapichtli married was his mother's sister, this relationship is found in another prose account, the *Crónica Mexicayotl* (authored in part by Chimalpahin). It is revealed only implicitly, by the failure in one instance to give the name of a woman that can be reconstructed by reference to the other accounts. First, this document mentions that Huehue Acamapichtli of Culhuacan was the son of Coxcoxtli, the king, and that his (unnamed) sister married Opochtli Iztahuatzin (Tezozomoc 1975:52). This is just like Chimalpahin's *Seventh Relación*, which means that the unnamed woman should be ♀Atotoztli (as is also given in Durán's history). However, the account continues by referring to a woman named ♀Atotoztli who was the daughter of Nauhyotl, ruler of Culhuacan (the same father given to her in Durán's version) and the mother of Acamapichtli of Tenochtitlan. Nauhyotl was approached by the Mexica, who desired that his descendant, Acamapichtli, be their first king. As in Durán's account, the Mexica also requested that the Culhua woman ♀Ilancueitl be given as the wife of Acamapichtli (Fig. 2.6).

According to this text, Acamapichtli was not living in Culhuacan but was in Coatlichan with the ruler of that city, Acolmiztli (the same detail given in Chimalpahin's *Seventh Relación*). At this point in the narrative the author "corrected" himself in a very enlightening way: "I said first that his mother was ♀Ilancueitl, but she only adopted him as a son and raised him; she was the beloved aunt of Acamapichtli" (Tezozomoc 1975:84). Actually, the first mention of Acamapichtli's mother is a reference Nauhyotl made to his daughter, ♀Atotoztli, not ♀Ilancueitl. In other words, although the author had stated that ♀Atotoztli was the mother, he indicated at this point that it was ♀Ilancueitl whom he had designated as mother, substituting the one for the other. The "correction" has Acamapichtli living in Coatlichan with his adopted mother and aunt, ♀Ilancueitl, already identified as a Culhua princess.

Reconstruction of this relationship from the other versions would make ♀Ilancueitl the sister of ♀Atotoztli, who was Acamapichtli's real mother. It was ♀Ilancueitl, however, who raised her sister's child and in that respect acted as his mother. She took on a final role with regard to Acamapichtli when he was brought to Tenochtitlan to be ruler, for at that time she became his wife. Thus, while the author of the *Crónica Mexicayotl* maintained that ♀Atotoztli was the biological mother of Acamapichtli, her sister and counterpart, ♀Ilancueitl, became his acting mother as well as his wife.

This single account thus preserves what elsewhere are three distinct versions relating to ♀Atotoztli and her kin relationships: (1) ♀Atotoztli was a daughter of Coxcoxtli of Culhuacan and sister to Huehue Acamapichtli, who married a man named Opochtli Iztahuatzin; (2) ♀Atotoztli was a daughter of Nauhyotl of Culhuacan and had a son named Acamapichtli who married another Culhua princess named ♀Ilancueitl; and (3) ♀Atotoztli was the sister of ♀Ilancueitl who married Acamapichtli of Tenochtitlan. These seemingly mutually exclusive versions can exist in the same text without real contradiction only because the author failed to give a name to the daughter of Coxcoxtli, who should be ♀Atotoztli, reserving that name for the daughter of Nauhyotl.

Since the daughter of Coxcoxtli and Nauhyotl in this account is the same woman, ♀Atotoztli, there is a question as to why there would be different names for the Culhua king who was her father. It has already been shown that in addition to the various documents that name Coxcoxtli and Nauhyotl as the father of ♀Atotoztli, he was Achitometl in the Aculhua sources and Huehue Acamapichtli in the *Fifth Relación* of Chimalpahin. All of these names occur in the Culhuacan king lists given in other documents, but there is no fixed order for their reigns (Davies 1977, 1980; Prem 1984a). Nevertheless, certain Culhua rulers' names were substitutable among the different "ethnic" traditions for the father of ♀Atotoztli and ♀Ilancueitl.

♀Ilancueitl: Wife of Acamapichtli

Just as some texts mention only ♀Atotoztli as the mother of Acamapichtli, others refer only to ♀Ilancueitl, emphasizing that the first king's link to Culhuacan was through his wife rather than his mother. For instance, the pictorial *Codex de Ixhuatepec* shows Acamapichtli as ruler of Tenochtitlan with his wife ♀Ilancueitl, named by the skirt (*cueitl*) glyph (Fig. 2.7; Zantwijk 1976:189). Another account that mentions ♀Ilancueitl but not ♀Atotoztli is the *Third Relación* of Chimalpahin (1965:82), which gives yet a different Culhuacan king as the father of ♀Ilancueitl. In this long text, ♀Ilancueitl's ancestry is presented in the greatest detail (Fig. 2.8a): Huehue Achitometl (Achitometl the Elder), ruler of Culhuacan, had a son,

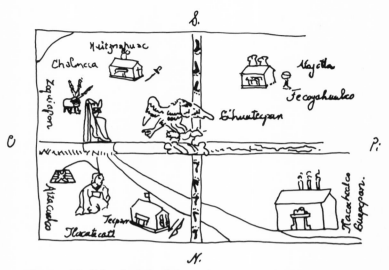

Fig. 2.7. Acamapichtli (to the left of the eagle) and his wife ♀Ilancueitl (below him, tied to him by a line) in Tenochtitlan as shown in the *Codex de Ixhuatepec* (after Zantwijk 1976:189).

Acxocuauhtli, who married ♀Azcatlxochitl, daughter of a Mexica named Huitzillatl. Huitzillatl also had a son, Teuhctlehuac, who had a daughter, ♀Ixxochitl. Acxocuauhtli and ♀Azcatlxochitl had two sons, Coxcoxtli and Xihuitl Temoc, both of whom ruled Culhuacan. Coxcoxtli had a son, Huehue Acamapichtli, and his brother Xihuitl Temoc had a daughter, ♀Ilancueitl. Huehue Acamapichtli married ♀Ixxochitl, daughter of Teuhctlehuac, and they had a son, Acamapichtli. Acamapichtli (the Younger) became the first king of Tenochtitlan and married ♀Ilancueitl of Culhuacan.

As the kinship diagram shows, both ♀Ilancueitl and Acamapichtli had the same Mexica great-grandfather as well as the same Culhua ancestry, but on the Culhua side they were one generation apart, since ♀Ilancueitl was a generation above her husband, as a mother would be. Their "generation-jumping" marriage (shown in Fig. 2.8b) has Acamapichtli marrying his father's father's brother's daughter (FFBD; see Chapter 4). In contrast to some of the previously discussed traditions, Acamapichtli was Culhua on his father's side and Mexica on his mother's side.

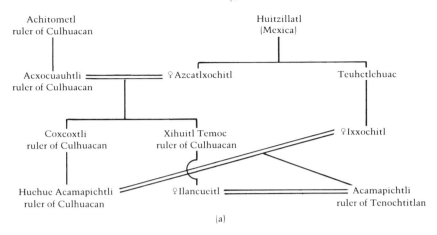

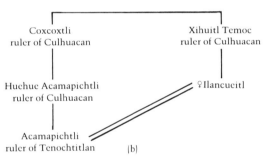

Fig. 2.8. The founding of the Tenochtitlan dynasty according to Chimalpahin's *Third Relación*: (a) all of the genealogical relationships as given in the account; (b) redrawn section from the above chart, highlighting only the "generation-jumping" marriage of ♀Ilancueitl and Acamapichtli. Acamapichtli thereby married his father's father's brother's daughter.

Most of the documents that speak of ♀Ilancueitl but not of ♀Atotoztli refer to a marriage between Acamapichtli of Tenochtitlan and his adoptive mother, ♀Ilancueitl, as well as their connection with the Aculhua town of Coatlichan, events that also appeared in the *Crónica Mexicayotl*, discussed above. While these accounts emphasize Acamapichtli's marriage to a Culhua princess but fail to mention his descent from a Culhua princess, they nevertheless place his wife in the position of an adoptive parent and therefore do imply Culhua descent through the maternal line via the creation of a fictive rather than a biological relationship. The texts that elaborate this point are four Franciscan-authored prose documents (*Origen de los Mexicanos, Relación de la Genealogía*, and the writings of Fr. Motolinía and Fr. Mendieta) and a native-authored prose text, the *Anales de Cuauhtitlan*.

These versions, like the *Third Relación* of Chimalpahin, have Acamapichtli of Tenochtitlan as the Culhua son of the elder (Huehue) Acamapichtli, the ruler of Culhuacan. An important additional detail found in the parallel texts of the *Origen de los Mexicanos* (1941:267–270) and the *Relación de la Genealogía* (1941:249–251) is that Acamapichtli the Elder was first married to ♀Ilancueitl. The couple lacked a son of their own but adopted a boy of the Culhua lineage to be their heir and renamed him Acamapichtli. While Acamapichtli was still a child, the elder Acamapichtli was killed by a usurper, Achitometl, who took the throne for himself. (Achitometl is elsewhere ♀Ilancueitl's father and Acamapichtli the Younger's father-in-law.) ♀Ilancueitl, aware of Achitometl's murderous intentions toward her and her son, the rightful heir, fled with Acamapichtli during the night. Accompanied by four other women, they went by canoe to the city of Coatlichan. After staying in Coatlichan for four days, they went to Tenochtitlan, where Acamapichtli, who was believed to be related to the Tenochca, became their leader. Acamapichtli later married his adoptive mother, ♀Ilancueitl, in order to produce children of pure Culhua blood, but he, like his father, had no children by her. Acamapichtli then married twenty other women, one of whom was a Mexica who became his principal wife and the mother of his legitimate heirs.

Here Acamapichtli seems to be of purely Culhua origin, yet the Tenochca considered him to be related to them in an unexplained way. His marriage with his adoptive mother proved to be fruitless, so his principal heirs were part Culhua (through him) and part Mexica (through their mother). It is important in this respect to note that these two accounts explicitly state that Acamapichtli was *not* the first *tlatoani* of Tenochtitlan but only a progenitor of the ruling line. Instead, his son Huitzilihuitl, half Culhua and half Mexica, is named as the first *tlatoani* (*Origen de los Mexicanos* 1941:270; *Relación de la Genealogía* 1941:252). The notion that the first male ruler should be a hybrid of Culhua and Mexica lineages is consistent with other accounts in which Acamapichtli was the first *tlatoani* and was half Culhua, half Mexica.

Two other Franciscan sources, the histories of Motolinía and Mendieta, provide less information, concentrating on the escape to the city of Coatlichan. Fr. Motolinía (1903:6–7) wavered on the questions of whether Acamapichtli was the son or nephew of the murdered king (Huehue Acamapichtli of Culhuacan) and whether the woman who rescued him was his mother or his wet nurse. In his version, Acamapichtli did not marry the woman who rescued him but did marry the daughters of twenty Mexica principal leaders in order that his children be both Mexica and Culhua. Fr. Mendieta (1945:163) gave even fewer details, although he noted a correspondence between this episode and a biblical story. He also equivocated as to whether the unnamed woman who rescued Acamapichtli was his mother or his nurse.

The *Anales de Cuauhtitlan* (1975:29–31), a prose document from the city of Cuauhtitlan in the northwest corner of the valley, also tells the story of Acamapichtli, successor to Coxcoxtli, who was killed by the usurper Achitometl. In this version, however, it was ten years after this event that a Culhua woman named ♀Ilancueitl went to Coatlichan, where a young Acamapichtli was being reared. Two years later, ♀Ilancueitl, now the wife of Acamapichtli, took him to Tenochtitlan, where he became king the next year. This account gives no relationship between the elder Acamapichtli and ♀Ilancueitl, no reason for ♀Ilancueitl's trip to Coatlichan, and no mothering role for ♀Ilancueitl with regard to the younger Acamapichtli. It is not that these facts as given in other traditions are contradicted; they are simply not included, as if the reader had to call upon knowledge of these other versions to fill in the blanks.

A significant statement made by the Cuauhtitlan chronicler in this document (*Anales de Cuauhtitlan* 1975:31) is that Acamapichtli became king because of his wife, ♀Ilancueitl, and on this basis the Tenochtitlan monarchy was begun. How ♀Ilancueitl provided the legitimacy for this dynasty is not more precisely stated. This text does stress, however, that the ennobling of the Tenochtitlan dynasty by ♀Ilancueitl's Culhua blood was further strengthened by the marriages of the later Tenochtitlan kings, for whom ♀Ilancueitl secured Culhua women as wives.

In addition to these prose texts, the pictorial *Codex Telleriano-Remensis* shows some relationship linking ♀Ilancueitl of Culhuacan, Acamapichtli of Tenochtitlan, and the city of Coatlichan. Unfortunately, this scene in the codex has not been well deciphered. This

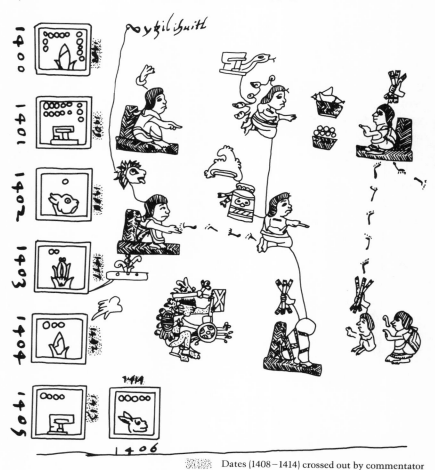

Dates (1408–1414) crossed out by commentator

Figure 2.9. Acamapichtli (bottom center) as a corpse and as a young child, tied to ♀Ilancueitl (center) of Culhuacan and a woman from Coatlichan (above) whom he is shown marrying (*Codex Telleriano-Remensis* 1899:fol. 29v; text deleted).

information comes from the pictographs themselves, since the Spanish prose commentary added to the codex gives a version of the founding of the dynasty that does not actually correspond to what the pictures relate. Acamapichtli is first shown already deceased, in the lower right corner of a page that gives the year signs for the period of his rulership of Tenochtitlan (Fig. 2.9). His corpse is linked to a woman with both the ♀Ilancueitl name glyph and the Culhuacan place glyph, indicating a relationship (either marriage or descent) between Acamapichtli and ♀Ilancueitl of Culhuacan. A line also ex-

Figure 2.10. Acamapichtli and his wife in Tenochtitlan (left center). On the top and bottom of the page are the ten founders of the city of Tenochtitlan, including Tenoch (second from the right on the bottom row). In the bottom left corner is Acamapichtli's successor, Huitzilihuitl (*Codex Telleriano-Remensis* 1899:fol. 30r; text deleted).

tends from ♀Ilancueitl to a woman with the Coatlichan place glyph (a serpent emerging from a dwelling). This second woman lacks a name glyph attached to her neck in the usual manner but does have water on her back, which is probably part of her name, giving the sound *atl* (water).

An infant Acamapichtli also appears adjacent to the corpse of Acamapichtli. This infant is shown growing up to become an adult by the addition of footprints going up the page and connecting with a third Acamapichtli, depicted in the act of marrying the Coatlichan

woman in the top right corner. The couple is redrawn on the next
page (Fig. 2.10) with Acamapichtli clearly associated with Tenochtitlan, as indicated by the Tenochtitlan place glyph (the cactus on the
rock), although he doesn't have a throne like Huitzilihuitl, seated
below him. This detail could indicate a relationship between this
pictorial version and the predominantly Franciscan prose accounts
in which Huitzilihuitl, not Acamapichtli, was the first *tlatoani*.

Because the infant Acamapichtli and the events of his adult life
follow from the picture of a corpse with the same name, the artist
may have been attempting to depict the episode of Acamapichtli the
Elder and Younger, the escape to Coatlichan with a woman, and the
marriage of Acamapichtli there, but this is uncertain. Another interpretation is that there was only one Acamapichtli, and on the page
that includes the glyphs for the years of his reign up to his death,
the artist also drew in the major events in his life. These include his
marriage and his meeting with the ten principal Mexica leaders at
the founding of Tenochtitlan, as a pictographic "flashback" (these ten
leaders are arranged at the top and bottom of the page; Fig. 2.10). Huitzilihuitl appears in the scene, off in the lower left corner, because he
succeeded Acamapichtli in the year of his death. What the pictures
unequivocally reveal is that Acamapichtli, leader of Tenochtitlan,
married a woman of Coatlichan, and both were somehow linked to
♀Ilancueitl of Culhuacan.

♀Ilancueitl of Coatlichan

In addition to the several accounts that mention ♀Ilancueitl's
flight to Coatlichan, there is a complementary version that reverses
this story and places ♀Ilancueitl originally in Coatlichan. It is preserved as an episode from Durán's history and is illustrative of the
processes involved in the creation and manipulation of these narratives. Durán mentioned that he saw a pictographic document in
which ♀Ilancueitl was married to the ruler of Coatlichan (1967:II:
115). This man was killed by a usurper, who also wanted to kill the
Coatlichan heir, ♀Ilancueitl's son. ♀Ilancueitl hid her son and fled
with him to Culhuacan, since she was a native of that town. This
account thus reverses the role of the two cities—Culhuacan and
Coatlichan—given in other versions of the usurpation and flight. In
order to make this story fit with his account of ♀Ilancueitl's mar-

riage to Acamapichtli, Durán averred that these events took place
after the death of Acamapichtli.

Other sources further emphasize ♀Ilancueitl's connection to Coatlichan by indicating that she was a native of that city rather than
of Culhuacan. Fr. Torquemada's *Monarquía Indiana* (1975:137), a
document not utilized as a primary source in this study because of its
synthetic nature, has ♀Ilancueitl as the daughter of the Coatlichan
king, Acolmiztli (who elsewhere gave the young Acamapichtli and
her sanctuary). Two additional texts provide the significant detail
that not only was ♀Ilancueitl from Coatlichan but also that she was
actually a ruler in her own right.

In the Franciscan-authored *Historia de los Mexicanos por sus Pinturas* (1941:227–228), ♀Ilancueitl was a native of Coatlichan, and her
husband is said to have been the son of a Mexica woman and a Culhua nobleman. In this version, the parentage of ♀Ilancueitl's husband
is the reverse of the more common situation, a Mexica man and a
Culhua princess. The inversion continues because her husband, Acamapichtli, did not become the first *tlatoani* of Tenochtitlan. Instead,
♀Ilancueitl, his wife, was the first ruler of that city, and her husband
succeeded to the throne only upon her death. In this account, then,
the right to rule came through a woman, as has been seen before, but
this woman was a wife who ruled first, not an ennobling mother.

The prose *Fragment de l'Histoire des Anciens Mexicains* (1981:
107) describes ♀Ilancueitl as not just of the royal house of Coatlichan but the actual ruler of that city. While holding this office, she
married Acamapichtli, who later ruled Tenochtitlan, and had a son.
Unlike the version in the *Historia de los Mexicanos por sus Pinturas*,
this account does not state that ♀Ilancueitl ruled Tenochtitlan as
well as Coatlichan. An illustration in the text depicts ♀Ilancueitl as
an elaborately dressed noblewoman, while Acamapichtli wears only
a loincloth and carries the obsidian-edged wooden sword of a warrior (Fig. 2.11). ♀Ilancueitl extends to her husband a plant—perhaps a
cultivated plant—bequeathing to Acamapichtli, the Chichimec, the
knowledge and right to begin agriculture, characteristic of a civilized
people.

The connection between ♀Ilancueitl and Coatlichan in all these
texts reveals how this Aculhua city was used interchangeably with
Culhuacan as the source of the women who ennobled the Tenochtitlan dynasty. That is, the quality of being the origin-place of legitimacy was shared among several towns in the different traditions.

Figure 2.11. ♀Ilancueitl, clothed as a civilized woman and holding a plant, stands with her husband, Acamapichtli, who is dressed as a Chichimec and who holds an obsidian-edged sword (*Fragment de l'Histoire des Anciens Mexicains* 1981:fol. 8r).

One explanation for the equation of these two towns is that Culhuacan means "Place of the Ancestors" and is the name given to the emerging place, where the first people came out of the earth (equivalent to Chicomoztoc, "Seven Caves"). Similarly, Coatlichan refers to emergence from the Underworld. Acolmiztli, the Coatlichan ruler who sheltered ♀Ilancueitl and Acamapichtli in some accounts, is the name of one of the aspects of the Underworld deity (Nicholson 1971b:Table 3). As a "Serpent-Dwelling," Coatlichan is the place where the sun emerges from the Underworld on its daily journey across the sky, just like Coatepec, "Serpent-Hill," the place where the Mexica tutelary deity, an aspect of the day sun, was born (Chapter 3).

A further example of how these two cities are substitutable for one another in the traditions is the fact that some kings, notably Huetzin and Coxcoxtli, were said to have ruled both Culhuacan and Coatlichan. Sources that list the kings of Culhuacan have a "Coatlichan" ruler, Huetzin, in the Culhuacan dynasty (e.g., *Anales de Cuauhtitlan* 1975:16; *Relación de la Genealogía* 1941:246), while the Texcocan historian, Ixtlilxochitl (1975:313; 1977:67), put a "Culhua" king, Coxcoxtli, in the Coatlichan dynasty. Coatlichan and Culhuacan were thus interchangeable as the city ruled by Huetzin and by

Coxcoxtli, as the hometown of ♀Ilancueitl, and as the city ruled by the husbands of both ♀Ilancueitl and ♀Atotoztli.

Ilancueitl the King

The connection of ♀Ilancueitl to Coatlichan explains a further variation in Aztec narrative histories. The repetition of proper names has been used thus far in a very productive manner to indicate patterns in the creation of the different versions of dynastic history (as demonstrated also by Leach for structuralist analyses of the biblical stories [1969:34]). For this analysis to be complete, all of the instances of persons named ♀Ilancueitl and ♀Atotoztli in the accounts should be examined.[1] An apparent problem arises in the fact that there is another important Ilancueitl in Aztec history, an individual who was a male rather than a female, even though ♀Ilancueitl is a feminine name (Chimalpahin 1958:104).

The male Ilancueitl was a ruler of one of the cities of the Chalco-Amaquemeca confederation (Kirchhoff 1954–55) at the southern end of the valley, and as might be expected, he is mentioned only in

---

1. Other repetitions of the names ♀Ilancueitl and ♀Atotoztli include the following: In the *Carta* of Pablo Nazareo de Xaltocan (1940:122, 124, 125), ♀Ilancueitl was the grandmother of Axayacatl (according to the Cuitlahuac traditions), ♀Atotoztli was the daughter of Tezozomoc of Azcapotzalco (see discussion below in the text on ♀Ilancueitl as the wife and mother of Huehue Tezozomoc in the *Codex García Granados*), and ♀Atotoztli was one of the names of the wife and daughter of Pablo Nazareo himself. ♀Ilancueitl was a daughter of Motecuhzoma II in the *Crónica Mexicayotl* (Tezozomoc 1975:153) (see Chapter 4; the structural position of the daughters of Motecuhzoma is the same as that of the founding women). The *Codex Xolotl* (1980:II:Pl. VI) pictures her as a daughter of Chimalpopoca who had a son, also named Chimalpopoca. The *Anales de Tlatelolco* (1948:54) has ♀Atotoztli as a daughter of Quaquauhtzin of Tlatelolco who married an important Chichimec emperor, Tochintecuhtli. In Ixtlilxochitl's histories (1975:541; 1977:73), an ♀Atotoztli appears as Acamapichtli's daughter and the wife of a ruler of Chalco. His *Historia Chichimeca* (1977:39) also has an ♀Atotoztli as the sister of Nezahualcoyotl, whose wife is ♀Azcatlxochitl (see Chapter 3 on the repetition of this name).

See the discussion of a male Ilancueitl below in the text. There were also at least three male Atotoztli's. One was a Mexica leader at the founding of Tenochtitlan (e.g., *Codex Mendoza* 1964:Pl. 1) and therefore important to the beginning of the Tenochtitlan dynasty, as was the female ♀Atotoztli, one was a ruler of Xochimilco pictured in the *Codex García Granados*, and the third was a son of Chimalpopoca in the *Codex Xolotl* (1980:II:Pl. VI), whose sister's name was ♀Ilancueitl! Thus, many of these instances of name repetition are further confirmation of a pattern of associating these names, whether for males or females, with one another and with rulers and founders of Tenochtitlan and other major cities.

the works of Chimalpahin, a native of Chalco. The presence of this
ruler in the histories might seem to undermine the patterning that
has been revealed (see Davies 1973:62–63; Davies 1980:200–201),
but this other Ilancueitl is actually a sexual inversion of his female
counterpart of the same name and thus *confirms* this pattern. His
identity as a Chalco native is explicable since Chalco was another of
the southern agricultural cities, like Culhuacan, and Chimalpahin
(1965:85) credited Chalco with the importance elsewhere given to
Culhuacan, including the right to invest rulers with the legitimacy
of the Toltecs.

The story of the male Ilancueitl appears in Chimalpahin's third,
fifth, and seventh *relaciones* and in his *Memorial Breve*. The most
complete account is in the *Fifth Relación* (Chimalpahin 1965:136–
138). Huehue Itzcuauhtzin, who ruled one of the cities of the Chalco
confederacy, Tzacualtitlan Tenanco Amaquemecan, appointed his
son, Ilancueitl, to the throne of the city of Atenco. To establish himself further as ruler, Ilancueitl married a Culhuacan noblewoman,
daughter of Huehue Tezozomoc, a prince in Culhuacan, and granddaughter of the ruler of Culhuacan, Coxcoxtli. This woman is not
named, but other information is provided about her background,
including the fact that her father's brother was Huehue Acamapichtli, whose daughter (her cousin), ♀Atotoztli, married Itzcahuatzin
Opochtli and bore him a son, Acamapichtli the Younger of Tenochtitlan (Fig. 2.12). After ruling Atenco for seventeen years, Ilancueitl
turned his throne over to his son, Itzcuauhtzin the Younger, and
went to Coatlichan.

No further information is given concerning the fate of Ilancueitl
of Atenco, but none is needed here, for the most interesting thing
about him, besides the fact that he married a Culhua princess to
strengthen his legitimacy, is that he went to Coatlichan. This otherwise meaningless detail (no reason or purpose is given for his trip)
makes sense only because this is just what the female ♀Ilancueitl
did. Thus a Chalca male Ilancueitl takes the place of the Culhua
female ♀Ilancueitl in terms of a trip to Coatlichan. Furthermore, the
male Ilancueitl is related to ♀Atotoztli of Culhuacan, as husband of
her female cousin, that is, as husband of her classificatory sister. He
thus appears as a "brother" rather than the usual sister of ♀Atotoztli.
Torquemada's history (1975:138) provides a similar detail that relates the story of the male Ilancueitl to the female ♀Ilancueitl, for
whereas the male Ilancueitl of Atenco has a son named Itzcuauhtzin

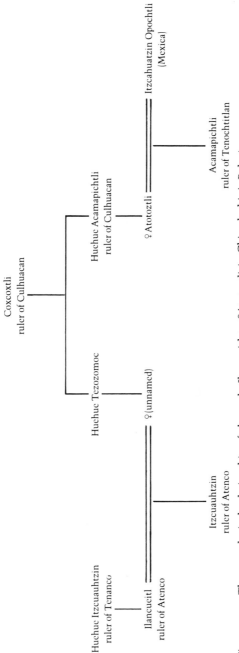

Figure 2.12. The genealogical relationship of the male Ilancueitl to ♀Atotoztli in Chimalpahin's *Relaciones*.

in Chimalpahin's *relaciones*, Torquemada gave the female ♀Ilancueitl a son named Itzcuauhtzin.

The trip to the city of Coatlichan and the kinship ties to ♀Atotoztli and Itzcuauhtzin thereby indicate an identity between the male and female persons named ♀Ilancueitl. The variation of having a male Ilancueitl in the traditional histories adds to the sexual ambiguity of the female ♀Ilancueitl already alluded to. In several accounts she has children, but in others she is sterile, and a woman who cannot have a child is for that reason equated with a man (Heusch 1982: 156).

♀Ilancueitl: Grandmother of Acamapichtli

In the *Historia de los Mexicanos por sus Pinturas*, ♀Ilancueitl was the first ruler of Tenochtitlan, and her husband succeeded her, as if she were in an ascending generation with respect to him. Thus her relationship to him as wife (the same generation) is also like the relationship of mother (one generation removed). ♀Ilancueitl has already been shown in some sources to have been the aunt or adoptive mother when she married Acamapichtli, indicating that the wife of Acamapichtli was also a relative from the first ascending generation, and a "generation jumping" marriage to Acamapichtli is given in Chimalpahin's *Third Relación* (Fig. 2.8).

Another document puts her even further back in Acamapichtli's ancestry, as his grandmother. In the dynastic histories of the major Aztec royal houses provided in the *Carta* (Letter) by Don Pablo Nazareo de Xaltocan to the king of Spain (1940:121), ♀Ilancueitl appears as the wife of the Culhuacan king, Coxcoxtli (whereas ♀Atotoztli is more usually associated with Coxcoxtli, as his descendant; see Fig. 2.1). The product of the marriage of ♀Ilancueitl and Coxcoxtli was a son named Cuauhtzin, who married the (unnamed) daughter of Iztahuatzin, a Mexica. They were the parents of Acamapichtli of Tenochtitlan, whose Culhua grandmother was ♀Ilancueitl (Fig. 2.13).

The movement of ♀Ilancueitl up the ancestral tree is not the only variation provided by this document, for the father of the unnamed mother (♀Atotoztli) of Acamapichtli is given as Iztahuatzin. This is the same name provided by Chimalpahin and Durán for the *husband* of ♀Atotoztli and father of Acamapichtli; here he appears as the *father* of ♀Atotoztli and grandfather of Acamapichtli, one generation removed from his more usual position (as is ♀Ilancueitl). So a hus-

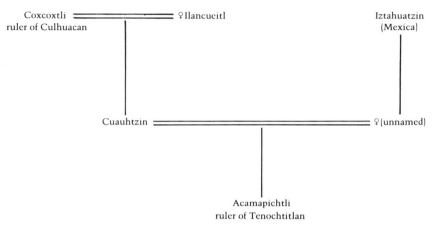

Figure 2.13. The founding of the Tenochtitlan dynasty according to the *Carta* of Pablo Nazareo of Xaltocan.

band in some versions becomes a father in this one, just as the various accounts of ♀Ilancueitl have her as wife and mother of the same man. Furthermore, ♀Ilancueitl and ♀Atotoztli have reversed their more usual roles: ♀Ilancueitl becomes the Culhua mother-in-law to ♀Atotoztli, just as in other versions ♀Atotoztli was the mother-in-law of ♀Ilancueitl. This is another indication of the equivalence of these two women in the historical traditions.

The Genealogical Model and the Merging of Kinship Roles

When all the versions involving the founding females of the Tenochtitlan dynasty are summarized, the following roles prove to have been assigned to ♀Ilancueitl and ♀Atotoztli with respect to the first Tenochca king, Acamapichtli: ♀Ilancueitl appears as his wife, his adoptive mother, his grandmother, his aunt, and possibly his sister-in-law (from Aubin's interpretation of the *Mapa Tlotzin*). ♀Atotoztli is his natural mother, his wife, and his sister-in-law. In addition, ♀Ilancueitl and ♀Atotoztli were sisters, mothers- and daughters-in-law, and princesses of Culhuacan who were also associated with the town of Coatlichan. Both women ennobled Acamapichtli and his heirs, providing them with the right of rulership, which distinguished them as legitimate kings, in contrast to the earlier leaders of the Mexica-Tenochca, who were only military chiefs.

The conclusion to be drawn from these variations is that ♀Atotoztli and ♀Ilancueitl functioned interchangeably as the wife and mother (as well as other important kinship roles) of the male founder of the Tenochtitlan dynasty, Acamapichtli. This is because these two women were manifestations of a single individual, for to be the wife of the first king was to fill the same structural position as his mother. The *Crónica Mexicayotl* comes closest to expressing what none of these accounts fully articulates, since it would go against both Aztec and Spanish incest taboos for Acamapichtli to have married his mother. In this document, the woman who plays wife/mother is split into two persons, whose equivalence appears in her manifestation as two sisters, so that one can be the biological mother and the other can take on the kinship role of mother, but as a surrogate mother who can therefore marry her son.

The effect of the interchangeability of ♀Ilancueitl and ♀Atotoztli at the founding of the Tenochtitlan dynasty is thus the following scenario: Acamapichtli married his mother and thus became like his father (which helps to explain why in some versions he has the same name as his father). Or, working back the other way, since Acamapichtli was to begin the dynasty, Acamapichtli's wife became like his mother so that he would be her descendant (Chapter 7), for it was she who was noble, and it was from her that he derived the right to rule, as some accounts explicitly state.

Moreover, the role of ♀Ilancueitl/♀Atotoztli as noble ancestress is not confined to the royal house of Tenochtitlan. She appears as well at the head of the royal houses of the other two great powers in the Valley of Mexico, the Tepanecs of Azcapotzalco and the Aculhua of Texcoco. The *Codex García Granados* depicts ♀Ilancueitl as the wife of Tezozomoc the Elder, founder of the Azcapotzalco dynasty, and as the mother of Tezozomoc the Younger, its most powerful king (Fig. 2.14). In this pictorial document, the Tenochtitlan rulers appear as descendants of the ruling lineage of Azcapotzalco. Thus ♀Ilancueitl here retains her position as genetrix of the Tenochtitlan rulers but is placed much farther back in time.

Similarly, according to Muñoz Camargo's *Historia de Tlaxcala*

Figure 2.14. ♀Ilan-
cueitl (below) is
shown as the wife of
Huehue Tezozomoc of
Azcapotzalco in the
*Codex García Gra-
nados* (Anonymous
1979:cover).

(1978:42), the Aculhua of Texcoco had a woman of this name in their
ancestry. She was the grandmother of Nezahualcoyotl, the most famous ruler of Texcoco. Significantly, this account gives her name
not as ♀Ilancueitl or ♀Atotoztli but as a combination of the two—
♀Ilancueitl Atotoztli—indicating that these two names indeed refer
to a single personage, a woman who appears again and again as royal
genetrix.

The merging of the wife and the mother of the founder of the
Tenochtitlan dynasty into a single personage is only one aspect of

a more general pattern of "royal incest" found in other ruling families around the world, especially in cultures with conceptions of divine or sacred kingship. This custom has been described as a sort of "Oedipal drama" in which the act of succession becomes "a defeat of the father by the son," who then takes his father's wife or a substitute for her (Cohen 1977:15). Even among societies well known for this practice—the Incas, Hawaiians, and Egyptians—actual cases of incestuous marriages in the ruling line, particularly mother-son, were rare (Bixler 1982). Nevertheless, it was part of the political ideology in many cultures for the wife of the king to represent the king's mother. In some African societies a half sister may have been considered an appropriate substitute spouse for the queen mother (Cohen 1977:15), while in Hawaii, either a sister or a woman of the same royal rank could serve as a "replica" of the king and a suitable spouse (Valeri 1985:149). This discrepancy between an ideal and actual practice was also true for the Aztecs. No account ever mentions a marriage between son and mother or brother and sister, yet the patterning of the variations concerning the royal women of Tenochtitlan shows that they all merge into one another, that the roles of mother, wife, daughter, and sister are borne by a single woman.

What these different versions of the dynastic history reveal are attempts to deal with conceptual problems concerning the nature of kingship and the transition of power and office, problems that similar societies have had to face (Chapter 7). It is not unusual in the historical traditions of many complex societies for the ruling dynasty to be founded in an act of incest. Incest or some other "barbarous" event, such as murder, is a typical mechanism for establishing a line of rulership because kingly power "reveals and defines itself as the rupture of the people's own moral order, precisely as the greatest of crimes against kinship: fratricide, parricide, the union of mother and son, father and daughter, or brother and sister" (Sahlins 1985: 79). In this way, the king reveals that he is above the normal social order, and in particular that he is above the restraints of kinship, against which kingship collides, producing a disorder out of which he can then establish order: "Having committed his monstrous acts against society, proving he is stronger than it, the ruler proceeds to bring system out of chaos" (1985:80). Furthermore, where the king is considered divine, incestuous marriage is a sign of divinity and, in a more practical sense, the only way for the king to be provided with a divine spouse worthy of him (Valeri 1985:149).

The king's need to produce children to succeed him who have his same ennobling qualities is also a concern addressed by the practice of intrafamilial marriage. As noted in Chapter 1, the Aztec year-count histories, which give the sequence of the years and their events, show only a line of male kings, each succeeding king replacing and thereby becoming his predecessor. The notion of replacement is inherent in the institution of kingship, for the individual kings are rulers not by the force of their own personalities, but as holders of a preestablished office. As Leach notes, "One of the merits of kingship over other forms of political organisation is that it ensures continuity. Individual kings may die or abdicate or be deposed, but the kingship, as such, is immortal. The living king is simply the temporary holder of an eternal office" (1983:37).

The replacement of kings by succeeding kings ensures the perpetuation of the kingship that orders the sociopolitical system, and thus the continuity of kingship is a critical issue (Leach 1983:54). The reality of biology intrudes into this ideal order, however, for kings are descendants not only of other kings but also, and much more obviously, of queens. The king lists show only the replacement of males by males, yielding a single continuous male succession. The problem in dynastic history, then, is to maintain the unity of male succession and the purity of the descent line while still acknowledging that females produce the males. This requires some assurance that these females are endowed with qualities that fully legitimate their sons as future sovereigns, and one way to obtain this assurance is for the ruler to marry females of his own family. In the Egyptian, Hawaiian, and other cases of royal incest, the ruler was considered to be divine, and in order to produce equally divine offspring to succeed him, he had to acquire a divine mate, that is, a classificatory sister.

There is also the related question of the differentiation between rulers and ruled. For a single lineage to claim exclusively for itself the right to rule other persons, who are ostensibly the same kind of people, that lineage must distinguish itself somehow and maintain this distinction over time, guarding for itself the right of rulership. Among the Aztecs, this right was usually expressed in terms of descent from the earlier Toltec civilization. Only those descent lines with Toltec blood, which was necessarily in limited supply, had the

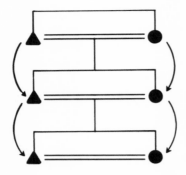

Figure 2.15. Abstract model of royal incest, in
which all the primary kinship roles are merged.
Males (triangles) are simultaneously father,
husband, brother, and son. Females (circles)
are simultaneously mother, wife, sister, and
daughter.

right to rule. Once a family acquired this right, its members would
want to keep their Toltec-derived nobility to themselves.

One way to preserve the purity of descent is for the women, like
the men, to replace one another and have their identities merge.
They thereby function as a single person being constantly replicated
by a female in the next generation. As long as the first woman has
the necessary qualities of queenship, then all the succeeding women
will also have these qualities as manifestations of the first woman.
With descent being the link between replacements and their predecessors, the implication is a positional succession rule, meaning that
as sons succeed their fathers, daughters succeed their mothers. The
"mytho-logic" of this replacement requires that the wife of a man
who "becomes" his father be the same woman his father married,
that is, his mother (Leach 1983:54). Actually, he marries the woman
who replaces his mother, namely his mother's daughter, who is his
sister (see also Cohen 1977:15). In this way, the distinctiveness of
the primary kin roles becomes blurred: the man is at once brother,
husband, father, and son to the woman who is simultaneously his
sister, wife, mother, and daughter (Fig. 2.15).

This positional replacement model is implicit in the patterned
variation of the historical accounts dealing with the Tenochtitlan
dynasty. It is best expressed in the treatment of the females in the
dynasty, both the founding genetrix and the two later princesses
(Chapter 4). Furthermore, this model corresponds to the ideology
underlying other examples of royal brother-sister incest in which
there is a desire to express the purity of the line of descent. The
mythology of ancient Egypt, for example, reveals the same concepts
in this respect as those held by the Aztecs. The Egyptian pharaoh

was conceived as the incarnation of the god Horus, son of the divine Osiris, who had married his sister, Isis. When the pharaoh died, he was equated with Osiris, moving up one generation, while his son, the new pharaoh, assumed his position as Horus. The living queen represented Isis, wife of Osiris (the dead pharaoh) and mother of Horus (the living pharaoh). In other words, the wife of pharaoh, who was supposed to be his sister, was also the incarnation of the divine aspect of his mother, the same woman who would necessarily become his daughter (Leach 1983:39).

The Aztecs thus reached the same solution to the problem of maintaining the unity of descent as did the Egyptians, by merging all the primary kinship roles in the royal dynasty. But resorting to actual and continual brother-sister marriage to maintain the royal line presents a problem for a society with incest prohibitions (see, e.g., Trautmann 1981:408 for a discussion of royal incest in Sri Lanka). The historical traditions concerning the Tenochtitlan dynasty avoid dealing with incest explicitly in two ways. One of these has already been discussed, namely, the presence of such mechanisms as the insistence on fictive kin relationships (e.g., an adoptive mother marrying her son), splitting a single person into two personalities who can hold otherwise contradictory kinship positions and maintaining variation among the different versions of history so that a single person plays all these roles but only one at a time per telling of a particular narrative (see especially Chimalpahin's variable *Relaciones*). For such contradictions in the different traditions to be understandable as variations on a theme, certain clues, such as name repetition, indicate that it is indeed the same personage who appears in the variant surface manifestations and who is simultaneously playing many roles.

The second way to deal with incest was to remove it from the realm of mortal men and project it into the realm of the supernatural. Like the Egyptians, the Aztecs replicated these conceptions on the divine plane by assigning the same role-merging behavior to their supreme deities, who were not constrained to obey the same natural or moral laws that humans do. In particular, the story of the incestuous marriage of the founders of the dynasty of Tenochtitlan was reproduced in the marriage of Tenochtitlan's tutelary deity, Huitzilopochtli, to the mother-earth goddess, ♀Toci, tutelary deity of Culhuacan.

The first Tenochtitlan king and queen were thus human representatives of these deities and shared in their divine qualities. In particular, the traditional histories emphasize that the founding queen, who
ennobled the male kings, was none other than the mother of the gods.
This identification is clear from other episodes in Mexica history,
dealing with their migration prior to the establishment of Tenochtitlan. The divine nature of this key woman, her link to the Culhua-
Toltecs, and her relationships to Mexica-Chichimec men and their
male god, which further grounded the structure of the Tenochtitlan
dynasty in general principles of Aztec cosmology, are explored in the
next chapter.

Chapter 3

Mothers of Gods
and Daughters of Chichimecs

To establish the ruling dynasty of Tenochtitlan, the first *tlatoani* married a woman who was structurally equivalent to his mother, an act of royal incest that allowed the king to "inherit" nobility from his wife and that also distinguished him from other mortals. This woman ennobled the king by virtue of being a Culhua princess and a carrier of Toltec "blue blood," thereby linking the Aztec present to the Toltec past. Other evidence associates her with even more fundamental founding roles in the traditional histories.

In addition to her appearance as ancestress of the Tenochtitlan dynasty, the same woman also existed farther back in time, even before the Toltec era, during the liminal period after the gods had created the world but before the settling of central Mexico by its various peoples. According to the account in Fr. Mendieta's history (1945: 159), all of the different ethnic groups were descended from a single primordial couple who lived in Chicomoztoc ("Seven Caves"), the legendary womb of many of the peoples in and around the Valley of Mexico (Fig. 1.1). The names of this Aztec Adam and Eve were Iztacmixcoatl and ♀Ilancueitl. ♀Ilancueitl is once again the original genetrix not just of a dynasty or an ethnic group but of the human race.

It is only one more step to cross the line that separates human and divine, placing this woman in the time that existed before humanity, in the realm that is apart from worldly space. She appears as the mother of the gods, in a role clearly related to her position as the human mother of mankind and the mother-founder of royal dynasties. The Aztec mother-earth deity, worshiped under a variety of names and aspects, appears in the Mexica histories in episodes that reveal her affinity with the mortal ♀Ilancueitl. This chapter considers the deity implications of the Tenochtitlan queen by examining events of the Mexica past prior to the establishment of Tenochtitlan, in which the mother-earth goddess played a role equivalent to the role of the founding queen.

Besides the supernatural re-creation of this woman, she is also found in the guise of mortals, in a contrasting position, as daughters of the secular Chichimec-Mexica leaders who ruled before the establishment of the dynasty of Tenochtitlan. Whereas the mother-earth goddess manifestation raises this feminine role to the highest possible level of existence—that of the gods, even the progenetrix of gods—the opposite occurs in the episodes of Mexica history that deal with females belonging to the lowest position on the perceived cultural scale, that of the barbaric Chichimecs, who were closer to the level of the animals they hunted and whose skins they wore.

The relationship of these Chichimec women to the mother goddess and to the founding woman of the Tenochtitlan dynasty (who lies in the middle of these polar oppositions as a mortal but civilized and noble [Toltec] woman), is revealed in the sacrificial deaths they suffered and in the consequences of their deaths. These events are part of the fundamental antinomy between the civilized and the noncivilized, between Toltec and Chichimec, which was eventually resolved in the marital union of the two oppositions, necessary to begin the Tenochtitlan dynasty. In all these historical episodes, which alternate the oppositions and thereby resolve them, the Aztecs constructed cosmological conceptions and relationships of which the Tenochtitlan ruling dynasty was an integral component.

Mothers of Gods

The association linking ♀Ilancueitl and ♀Atotoztli to the mother goddess is found in the person of yet another Culhuacan princess. The accounts of this woman unambiguously indicate the merging of the roles of wife, mother, grandmother, and sister in a single woman. This merging is explicit and permissible because these relationships were entirely fictive, being on a supernatural level. The woman who played these roles was a mortal who became a goddess, and thus she mediated between the human Tenochca and their tutelary deity, Huitzilopochtli.

This princess became the "woman of discord" (♀Yaocihuatl, "War-Woman," in the *Crónica Mexicayotl*) because she was the reason for the conflict between the Culhua and Mexica that led to the founding of their own city, Tenochtitlan. This episode is given in several of the surviving documents, appearing in the Mexica-based "Crónica X" tradition (Durán 1967:II:41–43; *Codex Ramirez* 1980:28–29, 120; Tovar 1972:19–20), the *Crónica Mexicayotl* (Tezozomoc 1975:54–58), and in an abbreviated form in the *Historia de los Mexicanos por sus Pinturas* (1941:226). Only the *Historia de los Mexicanos por sus Pinturas* indicates her given name, ♀Avenci.

The Crónica X versions of this story are all very similar, even word for word in some parts. The following summary is based on Durán's account: Following their ouster from Chapultepec, the Mexica went to Tizaapan, part of the territory of Culhuacan. There they established harmonious relationships with the Culhua, even intermarrying with them. Their patron deity, Huitzilopochtli, feared they would never willingly leave that place and go on to the land he had promised would be theirs. He thus decided to do something that would break the peaceful ties between the Culhua and the Mexica, and commanded his priests to search for a "woman of discord." She would be the cause of a war whereby the Mexica would be forced to leave Tizaapan and go on to create their own city, Tenochtitlan.

The woman whom Huitzilopochtli ordered the priests to seek was the daughter of Achitometl, king of Culhuacan. The Mexica were told to go to this king and ask that he give them his daughter, referred to as the "lady heir" of Culhuacan (apparently indicating a right of rulership), to be their mistress and the bride of their god, Huitzilopochtli. Achitometl agreed, pleased with the idea that his daughter would be worshiped as a living goddess. Once she was given to the Mexica, however, Huitzilopochtli ordered that she be killed and her skin flayed from her body. The Mexica had arranged for Achitometl to come to Tizaapan to make an offering to his goddess-daughter, but it was really a priest dressed in the woman's skin that Achitometl saw. Horrified by the barbarous cruelty of the Mexica,

Achitometl quickly called on his people to drive them from their land. The Mexica fled once again into the lake itself, where they would build their new city.

This woman, as Durán made clear, was none other than the goddess ♀Toci, a name that means, he said, "mother or grandmother," a deity venerated by all the Aztecs. Huitzilopochtli's words as he instructed his people were that the woman of discord was to be known as "my mother, my grandmother." Actually, ♀Toci means "our grandmother"; "our mother" would be ♀Tonan. Both of these personages, ♀Toci and ♀Tonan, were aspects of the complex mother-earth deity, and the two goddesses were almost identical in their attributes (Nicholson 1971b; Sullivan 1982).

Even though this is how Huitzilopochtli referred to her, ♀Toci was more than his mother and grandmother, in an ascending generation. She was specifically requested of the Culhuacan king to be the wife of Huitzilopochtli and the royal queen of the Mexica, who at that time still lacked a king; thus the first noble ruler would be female. In other words, the chosen Culhua *wife* of Huitzilopochtli was upon her unnatural death to become his *mother* and *grandmother*, a reigning female mortal apotheosized into a goddess. Furthermore, the *Codex Ramirez*, another Crónica X account, adds another role for ♀Toci— when she died she was to become the *sister* of Huitzilopochtli.

Here again is the story of a Culhua princess, daughter of Achitometl, who is elsewhere given as the father of ♀Ilancueitl and ♀Atotoztli (Chapter 2). She played a role in Mexica history just prior to the founding of Tenochtitlan and its royal dynasty, and therefore just prior to the entrance of ♀Ilancueitl and ♀Atotoztli into the drama of the Mexica past. That ♀Toci, ♀Ilancueitl, and ♀Atotoztli all had the same Culhua father and that they were queens in their own right are only two of the clues to their structural equivalence.

♀Toci functions in the histories as a divine role model for the composite figure that has been constructed for ♀Ilancueitl/♀Atotoztli, representing the merging of primary kinship roles with regard to the patron deity (grandmother, mother, wife, sister), which for the human genetrix of the royal dynasty is manifest only in combining the contradictions among the accounts. Whereas the female founder of the dynasty conforms to a natural, as opposed to a supernatural, reality, ♀Toci is a goddess and the wife of a god, so she is not constrained by mortal prohibitions against holding mutually contradictory kinship roles. Her relationships with Huitzilopochtli are supernatural, are fictive (since she does not really give birth to him or marry him), and are said to pertain only after her death and apotheosis. She, too, was genetrix, but the ultimate genetrix, not just of the dynasty, of mankind, or of the gods, but of all things, for she was the earth, source of all life.

A relevant detail in the story of ♀Toci is that after her death her flayed skin was worn by a male priest. In this manner she embodied the same sexual ambiguity (male inside, female outside) as that expressed by the presence of a male, a sterile being (neither fully female nor fully male), and a fertile female ♀Ilancueitl in the different accounts. Gender ambiguity is an important aspect of the Aztec mother-earth deity and pertains as well to their other major gods. The Aztec gods often appeared in male-female pairs, sometimes as husband-wife, sometimes as brother-sister (Nicholson 1971b), since the exact kinship bond was unimportant. What was at issue was the recognition that the power of creation derived from the union of the two opposing genders (León-Portilla 1963:99). The Aztec pantheon was headed by the supreme deity, Ometeotl, whose name means "Two-God" and who was such a male-female composite. This being was composed of two separate manifestations, Ometecuhtli ("Two-Lord") and ♀Omecihuatl ("Two-Lady"), father and mother of the gods, respectively. The Aztec kings identified themselves with this supreme deity, as "Father and Mother" of the people on earth (Pasztory 1983:64).

Another name for the mother goddess that further confounds her masculine and feminine aspects was ♀Ilamatecuhtli, meaning "Old Woman-Lord" (Klein 1980:159), a name that implies both genders. The mother-earth deity appeared in different aspects, corresponding to the stages of the life cycle (Nicholson 1971b:420), and the ♀Ilamatecuhtli manifestation was the old-age aspect (Hunt 1977:175), appropriate for the founder of a dynasty or ancestress of a people. The name ♀Ilamatecuhtli shares the same root, *ilama* (old woman), with ♀Ilancueitl; in fact, they are sexual opposites, ♀Ilamatecuhtli meaning "Old Woman-Lord" and ♀Ilancueitl meaning "Old Woman-Skirt," thus "Old Woman-Lady" (see also Brundage 1979:242). ♀Ilancueitl is thus equated with the elderly mother deity, and her role as wife of Iztacmixcoatl and genetrix of the Chichimec tribes is simply a manifestation of the old creator couple, Ometecuhtli and ♀Omecihuatl, who appeared many times under different names (Spranz 1973:85).

The mother goddess had many other aspects besides ♀Toci,

♀Tonan, and ♀Ilamatecuhtli. She was ♀Teteoinnan, "Gods-Their Mother"; ♀Xochiquetzal, "Flower-Quetzal Feather"; ♀Cihuacoatl, "Woman-Serpent"; ♀Quilaztli (who is also called ♀Yaocihuatl [Zantwijk 1985:41], the woman of discord); ♀Coatlicue, "Serpents-Her Skirt"; ♀Tlazolteotl, "Filth-Deity"; and ♀Chimalman, "Shield-Lying" (Nicholson 1971b; Sullivan 1982). Among her other activities, she played an important role in the ritual-divinatory cycles of time, appearing especially at the completions of those cycles. She was patroness of the twentieth (last) day name and thirteenth (last) day number in the 260-day ritual cycle (Hunt 1977: Table 3), and of the eighteenth (last) 20-day month, which concluded the solar year (Klein 1980:159). These positions at the end of temporal cycles parallel the appearance of the key Tenochtitlan royal females at the end of the genealogical cycles (Chapter 4).

Furthermore, ♀Toci was the patron deity of Culhuacan, as was ♀Xochiquetzal, another aspect of this goddess (Anales de Cuauhtitlan 1975:29; Historia de los Mexicanos por sus Pinturas 1941:225; Davies 1977:433). Similarly, in her aspects as ♀Cihuacoatl-Quilaztli, she was the patron deity of Xochimilco, another of the southern lakeshore chinampa towns, and was considered to be a sister to Huitzilopochtli (Durán 1967:I:125, 131). This means that the female patron deity of Culhuacan (as representative of the southern agricultural people) became in the Mexica histories the wife/mother/grandmother/sister of the male patron deity of Tenochtitlan, indicating a relationship on the cosmological level that is repeated in the royal genealogy by the marriage of a Culhua princess with a Mexica man to begin the dynasty. Here the merger of two opposing sets (barbarian, hunters, Chichimec, north, male vs. civilized, farming, Culhua-Toltec, south, female) was accomplished using a kinship metaphor (wife-husband, mother-son) on the supernatural plane, which further legitimated the people's view of themselves as the Culhua-Mexica.

The mother-earth goddess also appeared in Aztec society on a mundane level, for ♀Cihuacoatl (cihuatl = woman + coatl = serpent), one of the many names of this deity, was also a political title. The office of cihuacoatl was second only to the tlatoani, and its incumbent was his counterpart, in keeping with the identification of the rulers with gods who had both male and female aspects. Despite the feminine name, the cihuacoatl title was held by men, and in fact the goddess ♀Cihuacoatl has been called "a woman with a penis"

(Hunt 1977:100). In some of the pictorial representations, she has a snake coming out from under her "skirt," which is actually a man's loincloth (1977:100). It has been suggested that ♀Ilancueitl herself may have held the office of *cihuacoatl* while Acamapichtli was *tla-toani* (Davies 1980:200; Zantwijk 1963, 1976, 1985), although some texts, especially the Crónica X sources, emphasize that the office of *cihuacoatl* was not created until after the formation of the Triple Alliance. (The implications of the human *cihuacoatl* as a double for the *tlatoani* are explored further in Chapter 5.)

Another name of the mother-earth deity is ♀Coatlicue, "Serpents-Her Skirt," a name similar to ♀Cihuacoatl, "Woman-Serpent," with the meaning of "woman" represented by "skirt." She also appears in the Mexica traditions as the real mother of Huitzilopochtli (but not in the Crónica X accounts, which have the ♀Toci episode). Sahagún related the story of ♀Coatlicue and the birth of her son, Huitzilopoch-tli, in some detail (1950–82:Bk. 3:1–5). As the story begins, ♀Coa-tlicue was already the mother of the Centzonhuitznahua (*centzon* = 400 or, more figuratively, innumerable + *huitznahua* = people of the south) and of their sister, ♀Coyolxauhqui ("Bells-Painted"). ♀Coatli-cue was sweeping the temple at Coatepec (*coatl* = serpent + *tepetl* = hill) near Tollan when a ball of feathers came down from the sky. She tucked the feathers into her waist and later discovered that she had become pregnant with Huitzilopochtli by this act.

Her children were aghast at this discovery, and they decided to kill her. But as his siblings approached his mother with murder-ous intent, Huitzilopochtli emerged from the womb fully grown (Fig. 3.1). He was armed with the *xiuhcoatl* (fire-serpent) with which he dispersed all his brothers, the Centzonhuitznahua. He cut his sis-ter, ♀Coyolxauhqui, into pieces, her head remaining on top of the hill of Coatepec, while the rest of her body was scattered below (Fig. 3.2). The innumerable Huitznahua were chased four times around the ser-pent hill, and those who managed to escape fled to the south (to *huitzlampa*, the direction indicated in their name).

The *Historia de los Mexicanos por sus Pinturas* (1941:220–221) also tells in brief form the miraculous conception of Huitzilopochtli by ♀Coatlicue. Here she appears as a virgin who found some white feathers, which she placed in her bosom, thereby resulting in her pregnancy. Both this text and Sahagún's stress that Huitzilopoch-tli was conceived without a male contribution, and thus he had no father. The *Historia de los Mexicanos*, however, states that Huitzi-

Figure 3.1. Huitzilopochtli, with his deity markings and *xiuhcoatl*, is born full grown from his mother, ♀Coatlicue ("Serpents-Her Skirt"), in the *Florentine Codex* account (Sahagún 1950–82:Bk. 3:Fig. 1).

lopochtli already existed prior to this "rebirth," and he was able to reenter a womb and be born again because he was a god. This detail relates this version to other accounts of the slaughter at Coatepec in which the birth from ♀Coatlicue does not appear because Huitzilopochtli was already alive.

As mentioned above, the Crónica X versions and the *Crónica Mexicayotl*, which give the story of ♀Toci, do not relate the miraculous conception and birth of Huitzilopochtli from ♀Coatlicue. They do provide an account of the death of ♀Coyolxauhqui by Huitzilopochtli at Coatepec, but it is told in the context of Mexica history, not cosmogony. According to the Crónica X versions (*Codex Ramirez* 1980:24–25; Durán 1967:II:31–34; *Crónica Mexicana*, Tezozomoc 1980:228–229; Tovar 1972:15), the Mexica, on their journey to their promised land, arrived at Coatepec, near Tollan. Here Huitzilopochtli created an artificial lake by damming a nearby river, and the hill of Coatepec became an island within this lake. The water in the lake fed an abundance of plant and animal life, changing the landscape from a desert to a lush paradise. This was Huitzilopochtli's purpose, to show the Mexica what the promised land he was leading them to was like; hence, the resemblance to the island city of Tenochtitlan. The same idea is depicted graphically in a drawing

Figure 3.2. The defeat of the Centzonhuitznahua by Huitzilopochtli at Coatepec ("Serpent-Hill") in the *Florentine Codex* account (Sahagún 1950–82:Bk. 3:Fig. 2). A dismembered body lies at the bottom of the Coatepec glyph, while the head remains on the hill, referring to the dismemberment of ♀Coyolxauhqui (though the victim is depicted as a male).

in the *Codex Azcatitlan* (Fig. 3.3) in which water is shown as flowing out from the hill of the serpent, Coatepec. In this painting and in the illustrations in Sahagún's account, Huitzilopochtli has deity markings and is garbed in the hummingbird guise that is part of his name.

According to the Crónica X accounts, the stay at Coatepec was to be only temporary, a respite from the migration to the promised land, but there was a group among the Mexica who wished to remain at Coatepec permanently. These were the Centzonhuitznahua, and ♀Coyolxauhqui was among this group (in these versions, they are not said to be related to Huitzilopochtli). To punish the traitors and ensure the obedience of the rest of the Mexica, Huitzilopochtli killed them one night and took out their hearts and ate them (beginning the custom of heart sacrifice). ♀Coyolxauhqui was beheaded as well. Then Huitzilopochtli caused the lake to dry up, and all the plant and animal life perished. The Mexica were thereby forced to

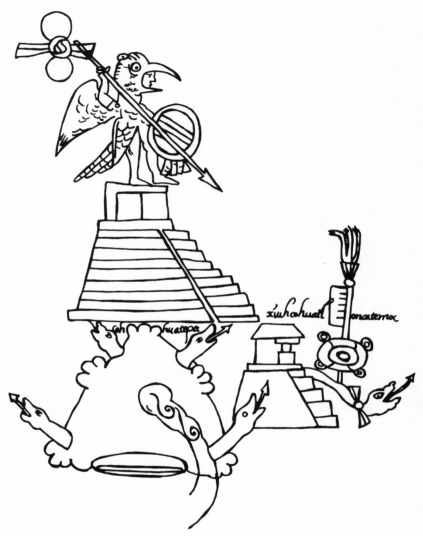

Figure 3.3. Huitzilopochtli appears at Coatepec in the *Codex Azcatitlan* (1949). The *xiuhcoatl* below him is represented by a serpent (*coatl*) with a banner marked with a turquoise symbol (*xihuitl*). Water flows out in a stream from Coatepec.

leave Coatepec and resume their peregrination toward the promised land, traveling first to nearby Tollan.

The stories about what happened at Coatepec thus take two forms: (1) the miraculous birth of Huitzilopochtli from ♀Coatlicue in a totally supernatural domain, with the subsequent slaughter of his elder siblings, who were attacking his mother; and (2) the death of ♀Coyolxauhqui in a totally historical setting because she and her co-conspirators were traitors to the promise Huitzilopochtli held out to his people. In the *Crónica Mexicayotl* (Tezozomoc 1975:31–37), these two versions come together at a certain point. Although this document tells the story of the murder of ♀Coyolxauhqui like the historical version (the second form above), it has the significant variation that she was related to Huitzilopochtli not as his sister but as his mother.

Just as ♀Coyolxauhqui is moved up a generation from Huitzilo-pochtli, so are the Centzonhuitznahua, the older brothers of Hui-tzilopochtli in Sahagún's version, who here appear as his uncles (another instance of brother-uncle identity, as noted in Chapter 1). Though ♀Coyolxauhqui takes ♀Coatlicue's place as mother, there is no miraculous birth in this account. The fate of ♀Coyolxauhqui is the same as in the other examples of the second version: at mid-night the Centzonhuitznahua and she were killed and their hearts removed. ♀Coyolxauhqui was also beheaded in the ballcourt.

The replacement in the *Crónica Mexicayotl* of ♀Coatlicue by ♀Coyolxauhqui, who is elsewhere her daughter, and other informa-tion about how both these women are related to the mother-earth deity complex (Nicholson 1971b:Table 3, pp. 413–414), indicate that ♀Coatlicue is structurally equivalent to ♀Coyolxauhqui. Thus, this woman was both mother and sister of Huitzilopochtli, brutally mur-dered by her own son/brother in order to force the Mexica to leave Coatepec, an island paradise made to look like Tenochtitlan. Her heart was torn from her body and eaten by Huitzilopochtli, and she was beheaded and cut into pieces scattered about the "Serpent-Hill."

The same sacrifice transpired at Tizaapan, as has already been dis-cussed, but there the victim was ♀Toci, another manifestation of the mother-earth deity. In addition to being mother and sister of Hui-tzilopochtli, she was also his grandmother and wife. The exact form of her sacrifice was the reverse of ♀Coyolxauhqui's. She was flayed —her outer covering (skin) removed and worn on the outside of a male priest—rather than her innermost parts (heart) consumed and thereby internalized in the body of the male god. The reason for the death of ♀Toci was the same as for the death of ♀Coyolxauhqui, to force the removal of the Mexica from a land they wished to settle permanently.

These two episodes, one at Coatepec and one at Tizaapan, separated in time and space, are thus repetitions of a single story, a rather violent event linking Huitzilopochtli with a manifestation of his mother, the mother-earth deity. In each case there is the sacrificial death of the goddess at the hands of her divine son/brother/husband as a mechanism for the continuance of the Mexica peregrination. Due to the cyclical aspects of space-time, their repetition reveals that these two events coincided cosmologically in time and therefore in space as well.

Some texts indicate that the cyclical point in time when the event occurred was in fact the critical juncture of calendrical cycles (which is where these earth women appear in other contexts, at the endpoints of cycles). The massacre at Coatepec took place during the "year-binding year," 2 Reed, according to some texts (e.g., *Crónica Mexicayotl*, Tezozomoc 1975:36; *Codex Aubin* 1963:11). This was the year that separated two adjacent 52-year cycles when the Mexica "bound the years" of the previous cycle into a bundle as part of the New Fire ceremony. The *Codex Aubin* further states that the year binding at Coatepec was the very first 52-year cycle the Mexica completed following their departure from the origin-place.

Several details, such as the occurrence during the year 2 Reed and the sacrifice of a female, indicate that other repetitions of this violent event occurred elsewhere during the Mexica migration. These similar episodes concern women who were not mother goddesses and were not related to Huitzilopochtli, but their sacrificial deaths took place in the same space-time and had the same result. In this way, the stories of these latter women, who as daughters of the barbaric human Chichimecs were absolutely opposed in nature to the mother goddesses, further illuminate the patterning of the Aztec histories and the meaning of this sacrificial event in terms of Aztec cosmology and related conceptions of rulership.

Daughters of Chichimecs

According to their traditions, after the Mexica departed Tollan, they eventually arrived in the Valley of Mexico, where they settled at

Chapultepec, from which they were later forcibly expelled. Chapultepec ("Grasshopper Hill," from *chapulin* = grasshopper + *tepetl* = hill), an impressive promontory on the western lakeshore, was the site of a natural spring that later supplied drinking water to Tenochtitlan via an aqueduct. The military leader of the Mexica at this time was named Huitzilihuitl in the many prose and pictorial documents that relate this episode. He is frequently referred to as Huehue Huitzilihuitl (Huitzilihuitl the Elder) to distinguish him from the second Tenochtitlan king of the same name. The accounts state that when the Mexica were attacked at Chapultepec, Huitzilihuitl was taken prisoner and killed in sacrifice, usually by the Culhua, together with one or more women. These women are usually indicated as his daughters, but there is some variation concerning their names and their relationship to him.

Huehue Huitzilihuitl's parentage is also of interest here, and it is given in detail in Chimalpahin's *Memorial Breve* (1958:56–57). His mother was a princess of Tzompanco, daughter of the king. His father was a Mexica whose name is not given. Huitzilihuitl became a leader of the Mexica by succeeding the former chief, Toxcuecuex, and as this text emphasizes, he became chief because his mother was of royal blood. Thus Huitzilihuitl played a role similar to that of Acamapichtli, the first *tlatoani* of the Mexica in Tenochtitlan. Like Acamapichtli, Huitzilihuitl had a Mexica father, but his mother was a princess, and she thereby endowed him with royalty. However, this first infusion of nobility into a Mexica "ruling family" was very short-lived, which is why Acamapichtli had to restart the process of lineage ennoblement later.

The different versions of the death of Huitzilihuitl that indicate he was sacrificed with other named family members are presented here as brief synopses, their details summarized in Table 3.1. To continue the story from the *Memorial Breve*, the Mexica under Huitzilihuitl were attacked at Chapultepec by ten of the valley cities led by the Tepanec city of Azcapotzalco. This event, like the massacre at Coatepec, occurred during the year-binding year, 2 Reed, one indication of a linkage between the two episodes as part of Mesoamerican conceptions of cyclical time. The Mexica could not defend themselves against such an attack, and Huitzilihuitl and his second daughter, ♀Chimalaxochitl (*chimalli* = shield + *atl* = water + *xochitl* = flower), were taken prisoner by the Culhua.

The account gives the added detail that when the two prisoners were brought before the king of Culhuacan, Coxcoxtli, they were

Table 3.1
Summary of the Episodes of Huehue Huitzilihuitl's Daughters

Source	Persons associated with Huitzilihuitl	Gender (m or f)	Relationship to Huitzilihuitl
Memorial Breve	♀Chimalaxochitl*	f	daughter
of Chimalpahin	♀Toxpanxochitl	f	daughter
	♀Coaxochitl	f	daughter
	Acolnahuacatl	m	son
Second Relación	♀Chimalxochitl*	f	niece/daughter
of Chimalpahin	♀Toxpanxochitl	f	niece/daughter
	♀Coaxochitl	f	niece/daughter
	Acolnahuacatl	m	son
Seventh Relación	♀Chimalaxochitl*	f	sister/daughter
of Chimalpahin			
Crónica Mexicayotl	♀Chimalaxochitl	f	sister
	Toxpanxochitl	m	brother
Third Relación	Acacitli	m	son
of Chimalpahin	Azcatlxochitl	m	son
Fifth Relación	♀Azcatlxochitl*	f	(none given)
of Chimalpahin			
Codex Aubin	♀Toxpanxochitl	f	daughter
	♀Azcatlxochitl*	f	daughter
Fragment de l'Histoire	♀Azcatlxochitl*	f	daughter
des Anciens Mexicains	Acacitli	m	son
	♀Toxpanxochitl	f	(none given)
Historia de los Mexicanos	♀Toxpanxochitl*	f	daughter
por sus Pinturas	♀Chimalaxochitl*	f	daughter
Anales de Tlatelolco			(or none given)
Codex Azcatitlan			
Codex Ríos			
Origen de los Mexicanos			
Anales de Cuauhtitlan	♀Chimalaxochitl*	f	daughter (or
Codex Boturini			none given)
Tira de Tepechpan	♀Toxpanxochitl*	f	(none given)
Eighth Relación	all his unnamed children		children
of Chimalpahin	were killed with him		

*sacrificed with Huitzilihuitl

totally naked, having been deprived of their clothing. ♀Chimalaxo-
chitl begged the king to allow them the decency of having their
bodies covered, but he refused to give them clothing. Huitzilihuitl
and his daughter were then sacrificed, the usual fate of war captives. His other two daughters, ♀Toxpanxochitl (banner-flower is her
glyph) and ♀Coaxochitl ("Serpent-Flower"), were also killed, the first

in Xochimilco and the second in Xaltocan. Huitzilihuitl's one son, Acolnahuacatl, escaped with some of the Mexica to Azcapotzalco, and they were not heard from again. (Acolnahuacatl is the name of one aspect of the Underworld deity [Nicholson 1971b:Table 3].)

The same story is told in the *Second Relación* of Chimalpahin (1965:58–59) except that while ♀Chimalaxochitl, ♀Toxpanxochitl, and ♀Coaxochitl are again said to be sisters, the text states that ♀Chimalaxochitl was sacrificed with her *uncle*, Huitzilihuitl the Elder. This implies that the three women were his nieces rather than his daughters. But later in the same account the author wrote that the deaths of these women destroyed the royal line begun by Huitzilihuitl because his *daughters* had died and his son Acolnahuacatl had fled to Azcapotzalco (1965:61). In this context, ♀Chimalaxochitl was now his daughter, not (just) his niece.

The same thought—that with the death of these women a royal lineage was terminated—is found as well in Chimalpahin's *Seventh Relación*. As in the *Second Relación*, a different relationship is given for ♀Chimalaxochitl, for she is first referred to as Huitzilihuitl's elder *sister* when the two are to be sacrificed in Culhuacan (1965:273). But when the author stated that Huitzilihuitl's bloodline was terminated, it was due to the death of his two *daughters* (1965:274). There is no mention of his son in this version. Therefore, in the second and seventh relations, ♀Chimalaxochitl is named as Huitzilihuitl's niece, and as his sister when the two are put to death. But later reference is to the death of a number of women (sisters) who were his daughters (they were clearly the same as this niece and sister) when it was the author's intent to explain that the first attempt at a royal dynasty infused with noble blood was a failure.

In these various texts, all written by Chimalpahin, there is no consistency as to the relationship of the women to Huitzilihuitl, or even as to how many there were, except at the point of referring to the end of a possible Mexica dynasty, when they must be his daughters regardless of any earlier statements. These texts are notable as well in their mention of a son of Huitzilihuitl who for some unstated reason could not carry on his father's royal line even though he survived the attack at Chapultepec. Again, the implication is that only females are legitimate carriers of the right to rule, with which they endow their husbands and sons.

The *Crónica Mexicayotl* (authored in part by Chimalpahin) has ♀Chimalaxochitl as Huitzilihuitl's elder sister (not daughter) and

Toxpanxochitl as his sibling as well, with the difference that here
Toxpanxochitl is male rather than female and is the younger brother
of Huitzilihuitl (Tezozomoc 1975:37). Neither of his siblings is mentioned as being sacrificed with Huitzilihuitl in Culhuacan. This gender change, putting a man in the position of a person usually indicated as female, with a feminine name, occurs also in some other
versions, including the third and fifth relations of Chimalpahin.

In the *Third Relación* (Chimalpahin 1965:70) no daughters are
explicitly given for Huitzilihuitl (he is sacrificed with a nameless
woman), but he does have two sons (1965:95). The elder son is Acacitli ("Reed-Hare") and the younger is named Azcatlxochitl ("Ant-
Flower," a feminine name), who was killed during the war. In the
Fifth Relación (1965:147–48), Acacitli does not appear, but this time
a female ♀Azcatlxochitl does, and she is the woman who was sacrificed with Huitzilihuitl. This account includes the fact that the two
prisoners, Huitzilihuitl and ♀Azcatlxochitl, were brought naked before Coxcoxtli of Culhuacan, but it does not state that ♀Azcatlxochitl
was Huitzilihuitl's daughter. Other accounts, however, do indicate
that ♀Azcatlxochitl was indeed his daughter.

One of these other accounts is the *Codex Aubin* (1963:36), which
states that ♀Toxpanxochitl was the elder daughter of Huitzilihuitl
and that ♀Azcatlxochitl was his younger daughter. Only ♀Azcatlxo-
chitl was taken captive with Huitzilihuitl to Culhuacan. In a reversal
of the roles found in the *Memorial Breve* account, described above,
here it is Huitzilihuitl who was upset that his daughter (but not he)
was naked and begged the king of Culhuacan, Coxcoxtli, to give her
something to wear, which Coxcoxtli refused to do. What happened
to them in Culhuacan is not told in this text. The accompanying
illustration (Fig. 3.4) shows Huitzilihuitl and his daughter facing the
king of Culhuacan, Coxcoxtli, who is the only individual with a
name glyph. The woman is not totally nude, for she wears a skirt,
but her upper body is unclothed, and she is shown covering her chest
with her arms.

A document that in some aspects parallels the *Codex Aubin*, the
Fragment de l'Histoire des Anciens Mexicains (1981:fol. 4r), is also
similar to Chimalpahin's *Fifth Relación* with regard to the story of
Huitzilihuitl. In this account ♀Azcatlxochitl is again given in the
text as the daughter sacrificed with Huitzilihuitl, and Acacitli is his
son who survived the slaughter at Chapultepec. A woman named
♀Toxpanxochitl is also mentioned, but no relationship to Huitzili-

Figure 3.4. Huitzilihuitl and his half-naked daughter, ♀Azcatlxochitl, face Coxcoxtli of Culhuacan in the year-binding year, 2 Reed, following the battle at Chapultepec (*Codex Aubin* 1963:36).

Figure 3.5. Huitzilihuitl and his daughter, ♀Azcatlxochitl, appear bound and totally naked in the year 2 Reed after the battle at Chapultepec (*Fragment de l'Histoire des Anciens Mexicains* 1981:fol. 4r).

huitl is indicated for her. A picture accompanying the text (Fig. 3.5) shows Huitzilihuitl and ♀Azcatlxochitl tied together by a rope that binds their wrists, and both are completely naked. According to the written text, they were brought before Coxcoxtli of Culhuacan, at which time Huitzilihuitl lamented that his daughter had nothing to wear and asked the Culhua king to give her some clothing, a request that was refused. Their fate is not told in this part of the account but is revealed later when Acacitli, speaking to the assembled Mexica, makes reference to the death of his father and his younger sister, ♀Azcatlxochitl, at Chapultepec (1981:fol. 6r).

Acacitli's speech in the *Fragment de l'Histoire* is very similar to the words given to him by Chimalpahin (1965:95) in his *Third Relación* above, except that in the latter version Acacitli refers to his younger brother, not his younger sister, named Azcatlxochitl. In this same *Third Relación*, however, a female ♀Azcatlxochitl does appear (1965:82). She is said to be the daughter of "Huitzillatl," a Mexica, and the mother of Coxcoxtli, king of Culhuacan (see Fig. 2.8). Thus she was the mother of the Culhuacan king who in other versions ordered the death of a woman of the same name. Ixtlilxochitl's history (1975:298) also has an ♀Azcatlxochitl as a princess of Culhuacan. She was the daughter of Pochotl and ♀Toxochipantzin (♀Toxpanxochitl, elsewhere the sister of ♀Azcatlxochitl). In Ixtlilxochitl's account, ♀Azcatlxochitl was the sister of Achitometl, another king of Culhuacan (see Fig. 2.2).

In all these versions there is thus the same ambiguity of gender affecting the sacrificed Chichimec woman that characterizes the multiple stories of ♀Ilancueitl and the mother-earth goddess ♀Toci. They are also linked by the repetition between the names of the daughters of Huehue Huitzilihuitl and Culhua noblewomen important in the founding of the Tenochtitlan dynasty. These similarities reveal an equivalence between the daughters of the Mexica chief and these Culhua princesses in their "nobility," especially with regard to the establishment of a Mexica royal family, and in the multiple kinship roles they are assigned with reference to the major male personages in these histories.

The remaining versions of the story of Huitzilihuitl have either ♀Toxpanxochitl or ♀Chimalaxochitl, or both, as the women sacrificed with Huitzilihuitl, and either they are explicitly given as his daughters or else no relationship is indicated. Both women are named in the *Historia de los Mexicanos por sus Pinturas* (1941:224), in which they were taken to Culhuacan to face King Achitometl (rather than Coxcoxtli); the *Origen de los Mexicanos* (1941:265); the *Anales de Tlatelolco* (1948:36); the *Codex Azcatitlan*, in which they are shown half naked (Fig. 3.6); and the *Codex Ríos*, where the two women and Huitzilihuitl are completely nude (Fig. 3.7). Only ♀Chimalaxochitl is mentioned in the *Anales de Cuauhtitlan* (1975:18), which is the only version in which she is saved from sacrifice by marrying the king of Cuauhtitlan, and in the *Codex Boturini*, a pictographic source that differs from the other illustrations in showing her completely clothed (Fig. 3.8). ♀Toxpanxochitl is the only woman

Figure 3.6. Huitzilihuitl and his half-naked daughters, ♀Chimalaxochitl and ♀Tox-panxochitl, are taken prisoner after the battle at Chapultepec (*Codex Azcatitlan* 1949)

Figure 3.7. Huitzilihuitl, ♀Chimalaxochitl (left), and ♀Toxpanxochitl (right) stand naked before the ruler of Culhuacan in the year 2 Reed (*Codex Ríos* 1831:Pl. 101; not shown are two male prisoners depicted below Huitzilihuitl).

accompanying Huitzilihuitl in the *Tira de Tepechpan*, a pictographic year-count document in which she is shown partially undressed and Huitzilihuitl is apparently naked as they appear before Coxcoxtli of Culhuacan (Fig. 3.9). The short *Eighth Relación* of Chimalpahin (1983:125) gives the most abbreviated account of the loss of Hui-tzilihuitl's family, indicating only that he and all his children were killed.

Figure 3.8. Huitzilihuitl and ♀Chimalaxochitl come before Coxcoxtli of Culhuacan in the year 2 Reed following the battle at Chapultepec (*Codex Boturini* 1975).

Figure 3.9. Huitzilihuitl and ♀Toxpanxochitl, shown half-naked, are prepared for sacrifice in the year 2 Reed. They are seated above Coxcoxtli of Culhuacan. To the left is the battle of Chapultepec (*Tira de Tepechpan* n.d.).

The Crónica X sources are notable in their failure to mention any daughter or other woman sacrificed with Huitzilihuitl. Instead, he is named as the leader of the Mexica who was killed in the battle at Chapultepec by the Culhua. These same accounts fail to give the story of ♀Coatlicue's miraculous conception at Coatepec. On the other hand, they do tell the story of ♀Toci in greatest detail, and she is structurally equivalent to both ♀Coatlicue and the daughters of Huitzilihuitl. One aspect of this equivalence is the naked condition of the daughters of Huitzilihuitl in many accounts. This detail, often graphically illustrated, seems an odd thing to be emphasized so strongly. It does stress the miserable state of the prisoners and of the Mexica themselves, who had nowhere to live and were preyed upon by the stronger powers in the valley. It may also indicate their barbaric status, for nudity was associated with the Huaxtecs of the Gulf Coast, a people whom the Aztecs considered inferior, whereas fine clothing was a mark of superior status.

Beyond these considerations, however, the nudity of the daughters of Huitzilihuitl is the same fate suffered by ♀Toci—the removal of her outer covering. The equivalence is confirmed by the fact that the Nahuatl root *xip-*, meaning to flay, skin, or peel something, appears in the word *xipetzoa*, to take off one's clothing (Karttunen 1983:325). This similarity further expresses an identity between the Culhua-Toltec princess, whose sacrifice resulted in her becoming the mother of the gods, and the Mexica-Chichimec "princess," whose sacrifice ended the line of nobility she would have begun. The results of their "uncovering" were opposed in each case: the nudity of ♀Chimalaxo-chitl/♀Toxpanxochitl/♀Azcatlxochitl revealed her exterior feminine characteristics, while for ♀Toci her femininity was obscured by the man inside her skin.

What these episodes have in common is the sacrifice of a woman together with Huitzilihuitl, which culminated in the flight of the Mexica from Chapultepec, a hill associated with water. Consequently, although the Culhua were the ones who sacrificed the Mexica leader and his daughter or daughters, they allowed the remaining Mexica to inhabit a part of their territory known as Tizaapan. As noted, in some versions this event occurred in the year 2 Reed or the preceding year, 1 Rabbit (e.g., *Anales de Tlatelolco, Codex Aubin, Codex Ríos, Crónica Mexicayotl,* and *Tira de Tepechpan*), at the boundary between two adjacent temporal cycles. This fact further links the Mexica women to the mother-earth goddesses who were sacrificed in Coatepec, as well as to the later princesses who renewed the nobility of the Tenochtitlan kings at the juncture of the genealogical cycles. But unlike the subsequent royal women of Tenochtitlan, Huitzilihuitl's daughters were put to death, preventing them from carrying on the nobility of the royal lineage, which would have to be recreated.

Again, the nobility factor reveals that the role of these women was very similar to that already outlined for ♀Toci and ♀Ilancueitl, and for ♀Coatlicue and ♀Coyolxauhqui. Like ♀Ilancueitl, the daughters of Huitzilihuitl had the inherent power to ennoble the future kings, a power that was lost with their deaths despite the survival of a son, their brother. Thus, the names ♀Azcatlxochitl and ♀Toxpanxochitl occur in other versions for important Culhua queens or princesses with ties to the founding of the Tenochtitlan dynasty (see Chapter 5 on the even more important role of an equivalent woman with the *chimal-* root in her name). Like ♀Toci, the Mexica women were sacrificed, but here the ethnic groups are reversed: instead of the Mexica sacrificing a Culhua princess, ♀Toci, the Culhua killed a Mexica princess, in both cases removing their outer covering. And like ♀Coyolxauhqui and ♀Toci, the result of their violent deaths was to sever the social and spatial relationships of the Mexica, to wrench them from their homes and propel them onward in their migration, an act symbolized in the cutting up of their bodies in the sacrifice.

History, Cosmology, and Royal Genealogy

Placing these events in chronological order according to when in Mexica history they occurred puts the death of ♀Coyolxauhqui first. This act forced the Mexica away from Coatepec and toward Tollan. The death of Huitzilihuitl's daughter or daughters came next, moving them out of Chapultepec to Tizaapan-Culhuacan. Finally there was the sacrifice of ♀Toci, which led to the Mexica movement out of Tizaapan to their ultimate capital, Tenochtitlan. These sites of Mexica settlement—Coatepec, Chapultepec, and Tizaapan—were similar to one another and to the eventual Mexica capital, Tenochtitlan, in a way that links them to one of the traditional homelands of the Aztecs, the island paradise known as Aztlan (equivalent in this sense, though not in form, to Chicomoztoc).

Their similarity lies in their association with water. In the center of Aztlan was a mountain with a spring that formed a river like that of Chapultepec (*Historia de los Mexicanos por sus Pinturas* 1941: 218), or as it is drawn in the Aubin and Boturini codices, Aztlan was an island in a lake adjacent to the place known as (old) Culhuacan. When the Mexica settled at Coatepec, the river was dammed to form a lake with the "Serpent Hill" as an island in it. The springs of Chapultepec were a major source of water for Tenochtitlan, and Tizaapan is described in one document (*Relación de la Genealogía* 1941:249) as having a water source as large as that of Chapultepec.

It is significant to note, therefore, that the death of the noble genetrix–mother goddess is associated with the movement of the Mexica away from certain cities on the route of their migration from Aztlan to Tenochtitlan, cities that have characteristics like the Mexica's beginning and ending settlements. However, the Mexica stopped at many other places along the way very uneventfully, a fact that begs the question as to why the episode of female sacrificial death appears with regard to some settlements and not others.

There was one other time when a woman was sacrificed, and it gives a clue to the importance of these episodes. In the *Leyenda de los Soles* (1975:126–127) and more briefly in the *Anales de Tlatelolco* (1948:34), there is the story of the sacrifice of ♀Quetzalxochitl ("Quetzal Feather-Flower"; the quetzal is a tropical bird with green plumage), daughter of the Mexica leader Toxcuecuex, who preceded Huitzilihuitl. According to the *Leyenda de los Soles*, the collapse of the Toltec civilization was marked by a drought sent by the rain gods to punish the last Toltec ruler, Huemac, who ruled from the capital, Tollan. After four years of famine, the rain gods appeared at Chapultepec and demanded the sacrifice of the daughter of Toxcuecuex. The Toltecs knew that when this was done, their age would come to an end and Mexica ascendancy would begin. The Mexica were living in Xicococ at that time, but the girl was taken to Pantitlan by her father, where she was sacrificed. Then the gods placed her heart on the head of her grieving father, along with all the different kinds of food that the Mexica would eat, foods of which the gods had deprived the Toltecs.

With this sacrifice the drought was over, the rains came, and the plants grew once more. (In this context one should note that Sahagún referred to Toxcuecuex as a rain deity [1950–82:Bk. 2:225.]) This is the reverse of the outcome of the sacrifice of ♀Coyolxauhqui at Coatepec, in which the water dried up and the plants died. Furthermore, like the episode of the expulsion of the Mexica from Coatepec and Chapultepec, this event occurred in the year-binding year of the Mexica, 2 Reed.

In several ways, the daughter of Toxcuecuex is equivalent to the females previously analyzed. She has the name (though the two parts are reversed) of one of the mother-earth goddess aspects, ♀Xochiquetzal. She is the daughter of a Mexica leader, in this case Toxcuecuex, the immediate predecessor of Huitzilihuitl. Like ♀Coyolxauhqui and Huitzilihuitl's daughter, she was sacrificed at the point in time between adjacent calendrical cycles. More important, she provides a most emphatic clue concerning the consequences of the sacrifices of all these women, in that her death brought to an end the era of Toltec dominion. That is, her sacrifice occurred at the boundary between two world ages, the time of the Toltecs and the time of the Aztecs. It is the relationship between these oppositions—civilized Toltec (Culhua) and barbarian Chichimec (Mexica)—that becomes a salient factor linking the fate of these women. Their deaths result in either a conjunction or a disjunction between the Mexica and the Toltec-Culhua, in terms or codes that are geographical (spatiotemporal), political, and familial.

Adding this episode in chronological order to those already analyzed completes the sequence that began with the dismemberment and heart sacrifice of the goddess ♀Coyolxauhqui at Coatepec. This "supernatural" event led to the departure of the Mexica from Coatepec toward Tollan, a geographic conjunction of Toltecs and Mexica-Chichimecs (although Coatepec and Tollan are somewhat synonymous in other sources). Then followed the sacrificial death of ♀Quetzalxochitl, daughter of the Mexica leader Toxcuecuex, a sacrifice to the gods but of a mortal woman, which led to the downfall of the Toltecs at Tollan (a temporal and political disjunction). After this event the Toltecs abandoned Tollan and the Mexica, now under the leadership of Huitzilihuitl, went to Chapultepec. Huitzilihuitl, born of a noble woman and a Mexica man, would have begun the first royal house of the Mexica, but his line was doomed, for the time of Mexica royalty would not begin until they were in their promised city. He and his daughter or daughters were sacrificed in Culhuacan following the battle at Chapultepec, which resulted in the Mexica departure from that site and their settlement at Tizaapan in Culhuacan territory. The death of the Culhua princess, ♀Toci, then caused their final movement from Tizaapan to establish Tenochtitlan.

It is after this point in the story that ♀Ilancueitl and ♀Atotoztli appear. They were not sacrificial victims, for the Mexica were no longer to move, but their fate was equivalent in the sense that they united oppositions via kinship ties, and sacrifice is equally a unifying event, relating the victim to the person in whose behalf the sacrifice was performed (see Chapter 7). Instead of being put to death, these Culhua princesses provided the ultimate conjunction of the two opposed forces—Toltec and Chichimec—in the marital/maternal union of female Culhua and male Mexica, thereby providing the

generative power that legitimated and established the most important ruling house of the Aztec peoples.

The pertinent relationships and events in the four episodes concerning the sacrifice of women, plus those of ♀Ilancueitl and ♀Ato-
toztli, are summarized in Table 3.2 arranged in chronological order
according to when they occur in the Mexica migration. This ordering reveals an "evolutionary" progression in time, space, and relationships for all these events. Such a progression is in keeping with
Mesoamerican conceptions of history, in which past actions have a
direct effect on, and continuity with, future events, and it is also a
consequence of the narrative form of the accounts, since the migration story has a definite beginning and end. There is a temporal sequence beginning with the cosmogonical actions of gods and leading
to events that relate the Mexica to the Toltecs, people of the distant
past, and finally to events that relate the Mexica to the Culhua of
the more immediate past and the present. As part of this progression
in time, there is a movement of the Mexica in literal and figurative
space from the realm of the creator gods at Coatepec to the realm
of the Toltecs at Tollan and to the ethnically diverse realm of the
Aztecs within the Valley of Mexico.

The episodes in Table 3.2 in columns 1 (for ♀Coyolxauhqui) and
2 (for ♀Quetzalxochitl) are closely related to one another, both referring to actions by divine beings distant in time and outside the Valley
of Mexico. Columns 3 (for ♀Chimalaxochitl) and 4 (for ♀Toci) form
another set of linked episodes, since they occur later within the valley itself and refer to sacrificial actions by mortal men. Nevertheless,
other aspects link these two sets of stories together, revealing their
essential unity. The two inner columns (2 and 3) and the two outer
columns (1 and 4) also form paired sets of stories. ♀Quetzalxochitl
is like ♀Chimalaxochitl, both being mortal, sacrificed daughters of
Mexica leaders. ♀Toci, like ♀Coatlicue/♀Coyolxauhqui an aspect of
the mother-earth goddess, suffers the same fate, being sacrificed by
her brother/son Huitzilopochtli. Column 5 is different from the first
four episodes because, as noted, the combined woman, ♀Ilancueitl/
♀Atotoztli, was not put to death. Nevertheless, her affinity with
♀Toci is quite obvious, since they are both daughters of the same
Culhuacan king given in marriage to a Mexica leader (divine in the
case of ♀Toci, mortal in the case of ♀Ilancueitl), with implications of
royal incest.

Table 3.2

Relationships Revealed in Episodes Involving the Key Women

	1 ♀Coatlicue/ ♀Coyolxauhqui	2 ♀Quetzalxochitl	3 ♀Chimalaxochitl/ ♀Toxpanxochitl/ ♀Azcatlxochitl	4 ♀Toci	5 ♀Ilancueitl/ ♀Atotoztli
Nature	goddess	mortal with goddess's name	mortal	mortal turned goddess	mortal with goddess's name
Relationship	mother/sister of Huitzilopochtli, Mexica patron god	daughter of Toxcuecuex, Mexica chief	daughter/sister/niece of Huehue Huitzilihuitl, Mexica chief	wife/mother/grandmother/sister of Huitzilopochtli, Mexica patron god	wife/mother/grandmother/aunt of Acamapichtli, Mexica king
			{ mortal }		
			{ daughter of Culhua king }		
Fate	sacrificed by god; heart removed and eaten; dismembered	sacrificed by gods; heart removed and placed on father's head	sacrificed by Culhua; nudity	sacrificed by Mexica; skin flayed	married
Result	Mexica leave Coatepec for Tollan	Toltecs leave Tollan; Mexica go from Xicococ (near Tollan) to Chapultepec	Mexica leave Chapultepec for Tizaapan-Culhuacan	Mexica leave Tizaapan for Tenochtitlan	founding of Culhua-Mexica dynasty at Tenochtitlan
Mexica-Toltec spatial relationship	conjunction	disjunction	conjunction	disjunction	conjunction
Year-binding, 2 Reed	yes	yes	yes		

It has already been noted that the Culhua-Toltecs, as civilized, town-dwelling agriculturalists indigenous to the Valley of Mexico, function in the Mexica histories in opposition to the Mexica-Chichimecs, who are barbaric, nomadic hunters from the outside. On the other hand, both the Chichimecs and the Toltecs are alike in their opposition as mortal beings on earth to the supernatural deities. In this respect, however, there is actually a tripartite relationship. The opposition is not simply between the gods and mankind, because the Toltecs played an important role in Aztec thought as mediators between the two. They were mortals considered more godlike than the Aztecs in their level of cultural achievement and their position in time (in the distant past) and in space (outside the valley) in Aztec history.

In the totality of the Aztec past, a past that represented a regression in some respects, the gods appeared first and set the world in order. The era of creation was followed by the age of the Toltecs (some of whose kings were also apotheosized). As Fr. Sahagún (1950–82:Bk. 10:168–169) observed, the Toltecs began the worship of the gods, including the practice of sacrificial offerings. They also instituted agriculture and all the arts and crafts of civilized peoples. The Toltecs exemplified the most divine accomplishments mortals could hope to attain. Sahagún credited all of the ancient ruins of civilization in Mexico to this single people, who lived in a golden age of postcosmogonic unity and peace.

The end of the Toltec civilization coincided with the rise of the Chichimecs, a diversity of squabbling ethnic groups who only gradually attained the characteristics of civilization, primarily by imitating the remnant survivors of the Toltec culture. The Toltec mediating position between gods and Chichimecs was subsumed by their descendants, the Culhua, as seen in the instance of a Culhuacan king who in one account gives his daughter (♀Toci) to be mother-wife of a powerful deity, and in another account gives his daughter (♀Ilancueitl/♀Atotoztli) to be mother-wife of, and thereby to ennoble, a Chichimec king.

Exploring these episodes further from a structuralist orientation reveals basic themes, which become salient as alternations between opposed elements in the different stories (see Heusch 1982 for an analysis of similar themes in Bantu myths of kingship). For instance, in terms of familial relationships, the stories of ♀Coatlicue/♀Coyolxauhqui, ♀Toci, and ♀Ilancueitl/♀Atotoztli emphasize the mother-son tie between the mother-earth deity and the Tenochtitlan tutelary god and king, while on the other hand, the episodes with ♀Quetzalxochitl and ♀Chimalaxochitl deal with the father-daughter tie. The two fathers in these stories are Chichimecs and hence are on a lower cultural plane than either of the other two males, Huitzilopochtli, a god, and Acamapichtli, who embodied a mixture of Culhua and Mexica blood, or of their goddess/ennobling daughters.

The sacrificial deaths of the first four women are also linked by an alternation between the internal and external. The first two females had their hearts removed and then treated in opposing ways. The heart of ♀Coyolxauhqui was consumed by Huitzilopochtli, her innermost organ internalized by him as his food, and thus was begun the practice of feeding the gods with human hearts. The heart of ♀Quetzalxochitl was also removed, this time by the rain gods (the antithesis of the solar aspect of Huitzilopochtli), but it was not eaten. Instead, it was placed on her father's head (becoming external to him) together with the food of men so that her sacrifice would feed humans rather than gods.

The next two women suffered a sacrificial death dealt by men, not gods, and are similar in having their external covering, rather than their internal organs, removed. Again, the fate of the human female was less extreme than that of her divine counterpart, and the human father participated in the death of his daughter. The only detail provided for the sacrifice of Huitzilihuitl's daughters is the loss of clothing, not body parts, since the form of their deaths is not stated. ♀Toci's loss was more severe since not only her clothes but her entire skin was removed.

The mutilation of ♀Toci's body, ordered by Huitzilopochtli but carried out by the Mexica, is similar to the cutting up of ♀Coyolxauhqui, both women suffering a change from continuity (whole body) to discontinuity (separated body parts). After their deaths, however, ♀Toci's skin was removed intact from the rest of her body, unlike the scattering of ♀Coyolxauhqui's parts. Furthermore, ♀Toci's body was put back together but in the wrong fashion, a man's inner being substituted for her female inner being. Thus ♀Toci's fate was to become a female outer covering over a male internal being, while in ♀Coyolxauhqui's case, a female inner organ lay within a male external being. In both cases there was a conjunction of the two previously distinct genders as a result of the disjunction of their body parts.

In this way, these two women are aligned with the last female, who also has some divine qualities as an aspect of the mother-earth goddess. The fate of the wife/mother of the first Tenochtitlan king was a conjunction in the context of kinship between the oppositions male-female and Chichimec-Toltec, represented first by her marriage to the Mexica king but strengthened by the detail that he was also her son, linked to her further by ties of descent. The incestuous sexual union of the king and queen, a relationship considered "too close" in the kinship code, is a further manifestation of the union of ♀Coyolxauhqui and her brother/son Huitzilopochtli, their relationship becoming "too close" in the alimentary code (see, e.g., Lévi-Strauss 1966:105–106 and Leach 1964:42 on the transformation from sexual to alimentary codes in New World mythology).

A further alternation in these episodes deals with spatial and political relationships between Culhua-Toltec and Mexica-Chichimec, an alternation expressed as conjunction and disjunction in a cyclical fashion. This is revealed in the geographical movements of the Mexica into and out of cities inhabited by the Toltecs and Culhua (even though all these places are metaphorical representations of the "promised land," Tenochtitlan). Coatepec, Tollan, Chapultepec, and Tizaapan were occupied by Toltecs or Culhua, and the Mexica tried to settle in these places. At the death of one of the women, they left all these cities (at ♀Quetzalxochitl's death it was the Toltecs who were forced to leave Tollan, but this cleared the way for the Mexica, at nearby Xicococ, to go to Chapultepec; see below). Thus, a true union of the Toltec-Chichimec opposition, attempted on both a divine and a human level, was not achieved by the Mexica after leaving Aztlan/Chicomoztoc, the origin-place, until they reached the fifth and final manifestation of the promised city, Tenochtitlan itself. At this point the Mexica completed their labyrinthine journey. Tenochtitlan was not a previously Toltec-occupied place but a city to be built by the Mexica themselves from scratch.

Instead of a spatial conjunction of Toltec and Chichimec, here union was finally achieved by a kinship relationship in a dynasty that mingled the blood lines of both of these groups. The city of the barbarian Mexica Chichimecs, on the edge of more powerful domains of other groups, grew to become the most civilized center of an empire and to rule them all. In Tenochtitlan—the fifth and final try at Toltec-Chichimec conjunction—the Mexica lived under the guidance of Huitzilopochtli. There they constructed a cosmic center as well, with its principal temple pyramid, the Templo Mayor, dedicated to Huitzilopochtli and to the ancient rain god, Tlaloc. As the Tenochca they lived out the age of the fifth and final "sun," or world era, the sun of the center of the world. This sun sustained them until its demise, when the Aztecs were defeated by the Spanish.

The fact that the fifth sun or era, like the sun in the sky overhead, was identified in some way with the deity Huitzilopochtli requires an investigation of the cosmogonical aspects of the episodes concerning the sacrificed women. For a number of years Mesoamerican scholars have recognized that the story of Huitzilopochtli's birth, as Sahagún related it, can be construed as an astronomical allegory (León-Portilla 1978:24–25). Huitzilopochtli is the sun; ♀Coatlicue, his mother, is the earth; his sister, ♀Coyolxauhqui, is the moon; and the Four Hundred (innumerable) Huitznahua, his brothers, are the stars. In astral terms, therefore, the story refers to the daily emergence of the sun out of the earth at dawn, dispersing the moon and the stars from sight by its rays of light (the *xiuhcoatl*, fire-serpent, held by Huitzilopochtli).

Beyond this fairly simple symbolism, further implications of the cosmological relationship between the earth and the sun are revealed by examining, in turn, the different episodes of the women who share affinities with the mother-earth goddess. The first event was the birth of Huitzilopochtli from ♀Coatlicue, which Sahagún placed in his *General History* in the book dealing with the origin of Aztec gods rather than Mexica history. All the individuals involved are identified as deities. The action occurs at Coatepec, a totally sacred locality in this story. A detail provided in another account shows that Coatepec is actually at the boundary between the supernatural and natural domains. In the *Crónica Mexicana* (Tezozomoc 1980: 226) Coatepec is located at the *edge* of Tonalan, the place of the sun, and thus is at the threshold between the realm of the gods and the realm of mankind, at the point where the sun moves from the earth to the sky.

Similarly, the "historical" Coatepec functioned as a doorway for people to have access to the gods (León-Portilla 1978:6). For example, in a story told by Durán (1967:II:216–222), Motecuhzoma I sent ambassadors to find Aztlan, also known as Chicomoztoc. The messengers traveled in the conventional manner as far as the "real" Coatepec, described as lying in the province of Tollan, but from there they were magically whisked to Culhuacan, a mountain surrounded by water in Aztlan. Here they visited with ♀Coatlicue, the mother of Huitzilopochtli. Because Coatepec served as the threshold between the sacred and mundane worlds, it is therefore located near, and becomes synonymous with, Tollan, capital of the Toltecs, who mediated between gods and men. Postconquest Maya documents explicitly indicate that Tollan was the passageway used by the sun to enter and exit the Underworld (e.g., *Annals of the Cakchiquels* 1979: 45; *Title of the Lords of Totonicapan* 1979:169).

Coatepec is a doorway not only in its figurative geographical location but also in its form as a mountain, for in Aztec thought horizontal distance was equated with vertical distance, and both were equated with distance in time. The *coatepetl*, serpent hill, was an Aztec Tower of Babel with its base on earth and its summit connecting the earth to the sky. It linked people on the surface of the earth with the gods in the Upperworld beyond them. In this sense, too, Coatepec represents a point of continuity between the terrestrial and celestial spheres. Finally, the fact that it was a "serpent" hill shows its mediating qualities, for serpents were viewed as connectors of the vertical layers of the cosmos throughout Mesoamerica. The same association is seen in the name of ♀Coatlicue, the "serpent skirt" under which Huitzilopochtli was born and thus the pathway by which the sun emerged from under the earth.

In the story of Huitzilopochtli's birth, ♀Coatlicue, the earth itself, stood in the temple on top of Coatepec, at the closest point to the sky. She became impregnated by feathers floating down from the sky, indicating the joining of these two spheres. Since the unborn sun was still within the womb of the earth, only the nocturnal bodies were present, the moon and the stars. Night reigned uninterruptedly, for there was no separation yet between day and night. The disjunction between the two occurred when the sun, Huitzilopochtli, was born and left the earth at dawn. He dispersed the moon and stars, providing for a discontinuity between earth and sky in the diurnal alternation of day and night. In this context the earth is on the side of the night as opposed to the sun and day sky, and thus there is an identity between ♀Coatlicue (earth) and ♀Coyolxauhqui (moon) already revealed in the different versions in which both women are given as the mother of Huitzilopochtli. The addition of lunar characteristics to the mother-earth deity is established as well by other data (Nicholson 1971b:421).

Although a daily cycle was established by this act, there was as yet no seasonal alternation. The alternation of the seasons, rainy and dry, is referred to in the other version of the story of Huitzilopochtli at Coatepec as part of the Mexica migration narrative. In this tradition, Huitzilopochtli had already been born long before the Mexica arrived at Coatepec, so there is no mention of a miraculous conception and birth; that is, the diurnal alternation was in place. The Mexica sojourn at Coatepec in these accounts began with Huitzilopochtli creating a lush paradise by damming a river or creating a source of water. Thus Huitzilopochtli, a deity with solar aspects, is shown here to be a master of terrestrial waters and is thereby opposed to Tlaloc, with whom he shared the summit of the Templo Mayor of Tenochtitlan. Tlaloc was the master of celestial waters (rain) but his name refers to the earth (*tlalli*), and he was said to live under the earth, a further opposition between the sun of the daytime sky and him.

When Huitzilopochtli decided to punish those among the Mexica who wished to stay at Coatepec rather than continue their journey, he killed the traitors in the middle of the night, opened their chests, and ate their hearts. He cut off ♀Coyolxauhqui's head and threw it into the center of the ballcourt, at the place known as the *itzompan*, the place of the skull. Then he broke the dam, letting all the water run out to create a desert devoid of plant and animal life. In these accounts Huitzilopochtli is not the day sun dispersing the stars with his rays but instead is associated with the night. The massacre takes place at midnight while the sun is at nadir on its journey in the bowels of the earth, as it travels to the east to emerge as the day sun.

Sahagún's version of the story emphasizes the beginning of the daily cycle of the sun rising out of the earth, initiating the alternation of day and night, and thus the head of ♀Coyolxauhqui remained on top of the mountain close to the sky, where the moon should be as an astral body of the night sky. In the latter accounts, on the contrary, the head of ♀Coyolxauhqui was placed in the ballcourt, which is an entrance to the Underworld (Gillespie 1985), the counterpart of the *coatepetl* as the entrance to the realm of the day sky. More precisely, her head was placed in a hole containing water in the ballcourt (Tezozomoc 1980:229), and ♀Coyolxauhqui as the moon is associated with water (Hunt 1977:139). The result here was a permanent conjunction of earth and sky (represented by the moon), such that normal seasonal alternation was impossible, and thus there is a permanent dry season (drought). Huitzilopochtli, who ate the heart of the moon and thus conjoined himself with it as well, is further associated with the dry season, which he brought about in this version, because he was armed with the *xiuhcoatl,* a symbol of the dry season (Caso 1953:100). Also, he is the "Hummingbird on the Left," to the left of the sun's east-west axis, namely, the south, which is where the sun is during the annual dry season (see Hunt 1977). This drought was to continue until the instigation of the alternation of rainy and dry seasons.

The sacrifice of the next woman, ♀Quetzalxochitl, provided the motive for the beginning of the seasonal cycle. In the *Leyenda de los Soles* version, her death was ordered by the rain gods, the *tlaloque,* who live underground, specifically to relieve the drought that in this text they themselves had created by their withdrawal of celestial (rather than terrestrial) water. In opposition to the fate of ♀Coyolxauhqui, whose heart was eaten by her brother/son, the heart of this girl was placed on her father's head with cultivated foods, indicating the return of rain and the earth's fertility as well as the beginning of Mexica reliance on cultivated instead of wild foods. This event is appropriate for the ♀Xochiquetzal manifestation of the mother-earth goddess, for she was the youthful pregnant or childbearing (fertile) aspect of this deity (Nicholson 1971b:421).

The change of seasons that began with the sacrifice of ♀Quetzalxochitl occurred simultaneously with the political changeover from the era of the Toltecs to that of the Aztecs, for the rain gods meant the sacrifice to signal the end of Toltec hegemony. This act established a political discontinuity, marking the beginning of the cyclical rise and fall of various powers (Toltec, Culhua, Tepanec, Tenochca). The place where the gods first requested this sacrifice was the hill of Chapultepec, then occupied by Toltecs. Chapultepec in this sense functions as the doorway into the Valley of Mexico, since it is within the valley (the Tenochca domain) but was inhabited by Toltecs, and in this text it was the first place the Mexica settled once they entered the valley.

At that time the Mexica were said to be living in Xicococ, a name that refers to navel (*xictli*), that is, in the navel or womb of the earth. Since Tollan—the capital of the Toltecs, the mediators between humans and supernaturals—was adjacent to Coatepec, which joined the earth to the sky, it is no surprise to discover that Tollan was also adjacent to Xicococ, the entrance to the Underworld (see Davies 1977:40). In fact, Sahagún (1950–82:Bk. 10:165) referred to

"Xicocotitlan, now called Tollan," identifying the two places as one. Xicococ also appears in a drawing of events at Tollan during the Toltec era in the *Leyenda de los Soles* (Fig. 5.3). The location at Xicococ (the opening in the earth's surface leading into the Under-world) is equivalent, and yet opposed in its spatial relationships, to the earlier actions at Coatepec (the threshold between the earth's surface and the sky).

These cosmogonical oppositions are summarized in Table 3.3. The dynamic spatiotemporal relationship between the earth and the sun, expressed as diurnal and seasonal alternation, takes place in the first two episodes of the women, those dealing with the Mexica migration from Coatepec to Tollan and to Chapultepec. Both epi-sodes involve sacrifice performed by gods in contexts that are more supernatural than mundane, and both refer to a movement from the otherworld of the gods, at its threshold with the world of mortals, toward the world of living humans in the Valley of Mexico.

♀Coyolxauhqui and her brothers were the leaders of a group of Mexica who wanted to stay in Coatepec, a relationship "too close" in geographical terms to the realm of the gods. They were therefore disjoined from that place by the Mexica patron deity, who insisted that they move on to a more distant place, away from the gods and away from the past. This act created the essential separation between mankind and the supernaturals, mirrored in the daily discontinuity between sky and earth as the cycle of the sun's emergence out of and disappearance into the earth.

Next, ♀Quetzalxochitl was put to death by the rain gods to bring about the end of the Toltec era, to force them to leave Tollan and dis-perse to the four corners of the world. This act created seasonal dis-continuity simultaneous with a political disjunction of major spatio-temporal proportions. It allowed the Mexica to adopt agriculture and ultimately to inherit the legacy of the Toltec civilization, with which they traveled to Chapultepec. The Toltec era was past now, as was the golden age of semidivine unity under their leadership.

After the death of ♀Quetzalxochitl, the Mexica entered the eth-nically diverse Valley of Mexico, where they began a series of alter-nating relationships with the Culhua, at that time the leading repre-sentatives of the Toltecs. First they went to the hill of Chapultepec, located on land belonging to other ethnic groups. Although they were attacked by armies from many cities, the sacrifice of Huehue Huitzilihuitl and his daughters was carried out by the Culhua, who

Table 3.3
Introduction of Diurnal, Seasonal, and Political Cycles in Mexica History
Initiated by the Sacrifice of the Mother-Earth Goddesses

Sacrificial episode	1 ♀Coyolxauhqui (birth of Huitzilopochtli)	2 ♀Coyolxauhqui (heart sacrifice)	3 ♀Quetzalxochitl	4 Huitzilihuitl's daughters
Sacrificer	Huitzilopochtli (as day sun)	Huitzilopochtli (as night sun)	Underworld rain gods	King of Culhuacan
Effect on victim's body	head is above and outside on coatepetl, where earth meets sky	head is below and inside the earth; heart is internalized	heart is above and outside, externalized	external covering is removed, hidden external body parts revealed
Result	provides celestial fire	withdraws terrestrial water	provides celestial water	withdraws terrestrial fire (nudity = raw)
Effect on cosmological/political relationships	earth/moon–sun disjunction, diurnal alternation	earth–sky conjunction, lack of seasonal alternation	seasonal alternation, political (Toltec-Mexica) alternation	Culhua/Toltec–Mexica spatial conjunction, marital conjunction

thereby terminated the line of royalty that the Mexica had hoped to establish. As for the Mexica, they were not ready for this preeminent position because their own island city was still off in the future, and at Chapultepec they were only at the threshold between the Valley of Mexico and the outside world.

By this point in the histories, the cosmogony had been completed, and the cycle of political hegemonies had been put in motion by the ouster of the Toltecs and the rise of ethnic diversity. While Huitzilopochtli and the mother-earth goddess are still important in the narrative, the spatial conjunctions/disjunctions of the Mexica with regard to the Culhua-Toltecs now refer less to cosmological alternations than to the political alternations of the different groups on the mundane level of historical events. Sacrifices are now performed by the two opposing peoples against one another, rather than by gods.

First there was the sacrifice of the daughters of Huitzilihuitl by the Culhua king. The fact that there are often three daughters given for Huitzilihuitl, when in the related previous episodes only one woman was sacrificed, may indicate an identity between these women and the three hearthstones of the domestic fire, which were frequently thought of as female (Hunt 1977:126, 158). They would therefore represent terrestrial fire, the final element in Table 3.3, and their deaths would result in the withdrawal of terrestrial fire, that is, the Mexica loss of domestic fire for cooking (and hence culture itself, which would be gained when the Mexica intermarried with the civilized Culhua). The inability to cook foods, thereby leaving them raw, is associated with the loss of clothing these women suffered, an example of the transformation in New World mythology from the category "raw" to the category "naked" (Lévi-Strauss 1981:362). The extinguishing of domestic fires was also a part of the New Fire ceremony, and the ouster from Chapultepec (like the episodes of the sacrifice of ♀Coyolxauhqui and ♀Quetzalxochitl) took place in the year-binding year, when the New Fire was lit. The consequence of this event, however, was that the Mexica went to Tizaapan-Culhuacan, where they intermarried with the Culhua, in particular with Culhua women, and thus began the conjunction in the marital as well as the spatial codes between Mexica and Toltec-Culhua.

The final sacrifice was when the Mexica ritually killed the Culhua princess who would become the wife/mother/grandmother/sister of their god. In this fashion they achieved the ultimate formula for the conjunction between sun and earth, in the marriage

on the divine plane between Huitzilopochtli and ♀Toci. The Tenochca then repeated this conjunction on the mortal level with
the marriage between their first king, as representative of Huitzilopochtli, and his mother, another Culhua princess who is also an
aspect of the mother-earth goddess. In many of the accounts, as
noted in Chapter 2, the royal couple came to Tenochtitlan from
Coatlichan ("Serpent-Dwelling"), where ♀Ilancueitl had taken Acamapichtli during the night, and they were under the protection of
Acolmiztli, one of the aspects of the Underworld deity. Coatlichan
is thus equivalent in its threshold aspects to Coatepec. It is located
on the eastern side of the valley, the direction from which the sun
emerges from the Underworld on its daily cycle. Hence Acamapichtli was equated with the rising sun (like Huitzilopochtli), and his
wife/mother was the earth who bore him on his night journey. The
Tenochtitlan dynasty they initiated thus represented another alternation of sun and earth, but in this case the alternation was in the
context of the genealogy. The Tenochca queen cycled throughout the
dynasty, reappearing at patterned intervals with respect to the reigns
of the kings (representing the sun), in the immortal self-regenerating
form of the earth goddess.

The role and function of all these women, the sacrificed goddesses
and princesses and the "queens" of Tenochtitlan, may be parsimoniously summarized by stating that they bound various series of events
that were cognized as alternating cycles. They actually caused the
next cycle to begin, providing the dynamism necessary to keep the
cyclical succession going at the end of one cycle and the beginning
of the next, in the alternation of days and seasons, of political hegemonies, and of kings. This is another aspect of their merging of
kinship roles, since they must continually reappear in each cyclical
episode, as well as in the genealogy, as grandmother, mother, sister, wife, and daughter of the major male personages, who are also
equivalent to one another. All of these characteristics mesh with
their identification with the mother-earth deity, who is described as
"our beginning" and "our end" (*Codex Telleriano-Remensis* 1899:
160). She is at the beginning and the end because her many manifestations correspond to the four stages of life—youth, fecundity,
middle age, and old age to death (Sullivan 1982:30)—as a metaphor
for the cyclical nature, and hence immortality, of the cosmos.

This female deity is represented in Aztec history and in the genealogy as women of different ages in both ascending and descending

generations. She is immortal, not because she does not die, but because she does age and die but is then reborn. She is the earth and the
maize (Brundage 1979:242) that grows from it to sustain mankind
in its seasonal permutations of conception, growth, maturity, and
death—that is, planting, nurturing, harvesting, and eating. Maize is
"killed" and eaten by the people to give them life; thus the fate of
many of these women was violent death in the context of sacrifice
and sometimes of being eaten.

The reality faced in Aztec cosmology was that death was essential for the completion of a cycle (Klein 1975:83), thereby paving
the way for the birth of a new cycle and the continuance of life.
The deaths of the women propelled the Mexica onward in a cyclical
fashion, for although they ostensibly traveled to different cities prior
to finally founding Tenochtitlan, they were actually returning each
time to the metaphorical promised land—Aztlan, Coatepec, Chapultepec, Tizaapan, Tenochtitlan—which was both the beginning and
the end of the cycle. Only the movement from the actual beginning
place of the journey (Aztlan) to the actual endpoint (Tenochtitlan)
was not marked by sacrificial deaths of the mother deity, for such
deaths occurred only at the *completion* of the cycle. The start of
the migration from Aztlan was the beginning of the first cycle, so
there was no sacrifice. For this reason, ♀Coatlicue was considered
to be still living at Aztlan/Culhuacan in Durán's account of how
Motecuhzoma I sent messengers to find the Aztecs' original homeland. Similarly, after the people settled Tenochtitlan—the last of the
promised-land manifestations—they were not to leave, and the cycle
was not to end until their world ended (which it did with the arrival
of the Spanish).

This long digression into the stories of Mexica female sacrifices
has served to show how ♀Ilancueitl/♀Atotoztli was part of a larger
scheme, as genetrix and mother-earth goddess. She was the quint-
essential female, who continually reappeared in the genealogy by
playing all the major kin roles with respect to the kings. The Tenochtitlan queen was the only woman of all these who was not sacrificed,
for rather than severing relationships, her marriage finally bound
the Mexica with the ancient and original ruling lineage. Following
the model more explicitly laid out by ♀Toci, she was grandmother,
mother, and wife of the first Tenochca king, Acamapichtli (and if
Huehue Acamapichtli of Culhuacan is a duplicate of Acamapichtli
of Tenochtitlan, his aunt/sister as well).

To complete the abstract model of royal incestuous marriage within the dynasty, she must also be the king's daughter. Thus far, the other women considered here have assumed all the primary kin roles, but within the Tenochtitlan genealogy, ♀Ilancueitl/♀Atotoztli has appeared primarily in Acamapichtli's generation and in his first and second ascending generations, not in a descending generation. As the following chapter reveals, however, this woman did reappear as daughter, not in the next generation, but as a great-granddaughter of the genetrix of the dynasty, following a cycle of four kings. The role she played was just as crucial as that of her ancestress, for she ennobled the dynasty once again, starting a new cycle just as her great-grandmother had done.

Chapter 4

Motecuhzoma's Daughters

To complete the abstract model of the merging of the primary female kinship roles (to conform to Fig. 2.15) requires a woman in a descending position, a daughter. This woman does exist in the genealogical histories for Tenochtitlan, and her characteristics make manifest her structural equivalence to the first queen. However, she appears in the dynasty not as the daughter of the first king but as the daughter of the fifth king, Motecuhzoma I. Her positioning in the genealogy at this point confirms the dynastic cycle outlined in Chapter 1 and further isolates Motecuhzoma I from the second, third, and fourth kings, a separation that has already been discussed based on the generational placement in the succession of the kings.

The relationship of this second woman to the founding female is revealed most obviously in her name, for she too was named ♀Ato-toztli. Like her ancestress of the same name, she was the genetrix of half of the Tenochtitlan dynasty. Furthermore, in many of the historical traditions she provided the later kings with the right to rule. This quality is revealed in the different accounts concerning the succession to the throne following Motecuhzoma I's death. There is more inconsistency in the documents concerning who would follow Motecuhzoma I, and on what basis, than for any other Tenochtitlan king. It is at this ambiguous point that ♀Atotoztli appeared to rejuvenate the royal bloodline. According to some texts, she even ruled as queen in her own right, as did ♀Ilancueitl before her.

This key female—who is both daughter (to end one cycle of the dynasty) and mother (to begin the next cycle)—reappeared one more time in the genealogy, at the end of the line of Tenochtitlan kings, as the daughter of Motecuhzoma II. Her native name was ♀Tecuichpo, but she is more commonly referred to by the name she was given by the Spaniards, Isabel. ♀Tecuichpo is the only one among all these women who can be said to have a historical reality, since she survived the conquest and lived well into the colonial period. Because she played the final female role to end the second dynastic cycle of Tenochtitlan, she was paired with Cuauhtemoc, Motecuhzoma II's successor, the last of Tenochtitlan's leaders chosen by the Mexica people. Cuauhtemoc literally, and ♀Tecuichpo figuratively, attempted but failed to continue the era of Tenochtitlan hegemony, signaling the end of the Aztec "sun."

Because ♀Tecuichpo and her contemporaries, Motecuhzoma II and Cuauhtemoc, were known to the Spaniards and played out their roles at the critical point of contact between Europeans and Aztecs, the historical events of their lives became a focus for both sides in the creation and manipulation of historical traditions. This is revealed, for example, in conscious attempts to rewrite the Tenochtitlan genealogy so that both daughters of the two Motecuhzomas would marry a kinsman of exactly the same biological relationship, as detailed in this chapter, and in the emergence of traditions concerning Motecuhzoma I that would parallel events in the life of Motecuhzoma II, discussed in the next chapter. While these actions are part of the process of rewriting Aztec history to conform to their ideas of cyclical space-time, it is equally important to note the heavy Spanish contribution. In particular, the accounts dealing with the key females, who reappeared at cyclical intervals in the Tenochtitlan dynasty and who were an aspect of the mother-earth deity, cannot be understood without some reference to a European counterpart brought by the Spanish, namely, the Virgin Mary. Her similarities to the Tenochtitlan "queens" are discussed at the end of this chapter.

♀Atotoztli: Daughter of Motecuhzoma I

Although there is little mention in the historical traditions of the royal females in the Tenochtitlan dynasty, one woman in particular stands out because she appears right after the death of Motecuhzoma I. For no other point in the dynastic history of Tenochtitlan was there such variation within the documentary sources as to how the kingship was transmitted to the next *tlatoani*. These variations take four major forms: (1) the line of rulership passed through Motecuhzoma's daughter, ♀Atotoztli, to her son, Axayacatl, meaning ♀Atotoztli had an inherent quality that ennobled her children; (2) the line of rulership passed through Tezozomoc, son of Itzcoatl, the fourth *tlatoani* of Tenochtitlan, who happened to have been married to ♀Atotoztli, which allows for some ambiguity as to the part played by ♀Atotoztli in ennobling her children; (3) ♀Atotoztli and Tezozomoc are mentioned as husband and wife, parents of the later kings, but there is no indication as to which one passed the right of rulership on to their children; and (4) ♀Atotoztli is not mentioned, and the line passed directly through a male, either Motecuhzoma or Tezozomoc. Thus, some sources stress the female as the transit through which rulership passed, some stress the male, and others do not state how the line continued.

Most of this information is presented in the narrative texts, but ♀Atotoztli and Tezozomoc are depicted in at least two of the pictorial family trees. The *Genealogía de los Príncipes Mexicanos* illustrates the marriage between ♀Atotoztli and Tezozomoc (Fig. 4.1). They are shown below their respective fathers, Motecuhzoma I (right) and Itzcoatl (left), and a dotted line connects them, indicating that they were husband and wife. Below them sit their three sons who ruled as kings: from left to right, Tizoc, Axayacatl, and Ahuitzotl. This document was presumably drawn up by the heirs of Tizoc, since only his descendants are shown. From Tizoc's standpoint, and from the standpoint of his heirs, his mother and father were each one generation removed from him, his grandfathers two ascending generations away, and so they are shown in this family tree.

The author of this document presented genealogical information only so far back in the past as was necessary to prove the relationship of Tizoc's heirs to Itzcoatl and Motecuhzoma I, who according to tradition distributed much of the inheritable property and titles

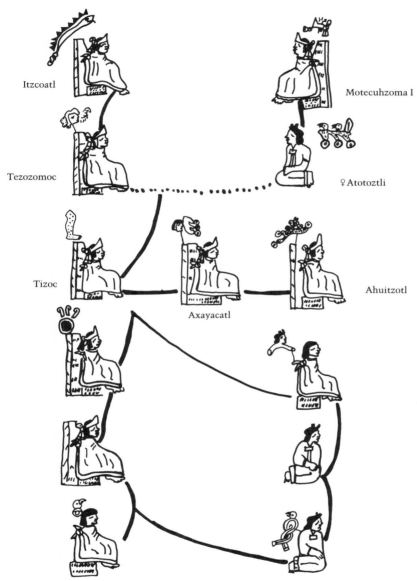

Figure 4.1. Latter half of the Tenochtitlan family tree as shown in the *Genealogía de los Príncipes Mexicanos* (1958:Pl. 1; text deleted).

(a)

Figure 4.2. The Tenochtitlan family tree in the *Codex Mexicanus* (1952:Pl. 16–17; minor personages deleted): (a) the first part, showing the ancestors of some of the females who married into the dynasty; Chimalpopoca is at bottom center; (b) the second part, starting with Acamapichtli at left, in front of the Tenochtitlan place glyph (in this part, generations are separated by curved lines).

at the fall of Azcapotzalco and the creation of the Triple Alliance headed by Tenochtitlan. But when the entire genealogy is shown, as outlined in Chapter 1, it is clear that Motecuhzoma I and Itzcoatl were not of the same generation, since Itzcoatl was one generation above Motecuhzoma.

In the Tenochtitlan family tree in the *Codex Mexicanus* (Fig. 4.2b), this difference in generation is quite explicit because the artist drew in thin curved lines to separate people of different generations. Interestingly, the crucial role played by ♀Atotoztli is revealed in the unique treatment given to her in this family tree. At the same time, a certain ambiguity is maintained as to exactly which kinship position she held with respect to Tezozomoc. As the daughter of Motecuhzoma I, she is connected to her father by a black line and depicted one generation separated from him. Like everyone else in the drawing, she faces to the right of the page, toward the future generations. But above her picture are footprints that lead up the page toward a second depiction of her, connected to her first image by a line. In her second appearance she faces to the left of the page, toward the

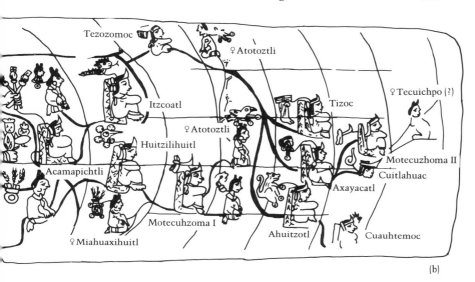

(b)

past generations, directly opposite Tezozomoc, son of Itzcoatl (whose name glyph is a stone, for the sound of "*tetl*"). No lines connect her to Tezozomoc or to their children; nevertheless, the implication is clear that she was his wife, because his children are two generations away from him and only one from ♀Atotoztli, who is already one generation removed from Tezozomoc.

What is depicted pictorially in the *Codex Mexicanus* is spelled out in narrative form in Ixtlilxochitl's *Historia Chichimeca* (1977:230–259) but not in his other histories. ♀Atotoztli was Motecuhzoma's only legitimate child in this version, so his line would have died out with her. She married Tezozomoc, son of Itzcoatl, her father's father's brother's son (FFBS), and their children included the next three kings, Axayacatl, Tizoc, and Ahuitzotl.

Some of the Franciscan-authored histories do not indicate the name of Motecuhzoma's daughter, but they attach increased importance to her. These texts explicitly state that not only did the line of rulership pass through her but she herself inherited the throne and ruled as queen (see also P. Carrasco 1984:44 for other postconquest documents supporting this claim). This role is given to her in the *Origen de los Mexicanos* (1941:274–275) and the *Relación de la Genealogía* (1941:253–254). Here Acamapichtli is given as the father of the three succeeding kings: Huitzilihuitl, Chimalpopoca, and Itzcoatl. The rule of succession, according to these two very similar accounts, was that brothers would succeed one another in birth order, and then the son of the eldest brother would inherit the throne. Thus, after Itzcoatl's death, Motecuhzoma I, as the son of the eldest brother, Huitzilihuitl, became *tlatoani*. In these versions Motecuhzoma lacked legitimate brothers to succeed him and had only one legitimate child, a daughter (unnamed). She inherited his throne and ruled as a female *tlatoani*, or ruled jointly with her husband, Tezozomoc.

In these two accounts Acamapichtli was not crowned *tlatoani* but was only a chief or important lord, and thus his son, Huitzilihuitl, is named as the first Tenochca *tlatoani*. This shift in the numbering of the kings makes the daughter of Motecuhzoma I, rather than he himself, the fifth *tlatoani* and keeps the number of pre-Hispanic Tenochtitlan rulers at nine. The Franciscan author or authors of these histories explain the absence of her reign as *tlatoani* in the year-count books as the result of prejudice on the part of the record keepers against a female ruler! In addition, these documents have Motecuhzoma's daughter marrying Tezozomoc, son of Itzcoatl, the last of the three earlier brothers to rule. Tezozomoc fathered her children, the next set of three kings to rule in birth order—Axayacatl, Tizoc, and Ahuitzotl—but it is clear that they inherited the throne directly from their *tlatoani* mother, not from their father.

These accounts fit most closely with the pattern discussed by Zantwijk (1978) in which kings number two through four and six through eight are brothers adhering firmly to a rule of fraternal succession (Chapter 1). The problem encountered at the end of Motecuhzoma I's reign, as explained in these documents, was that he lacked brothers, indicating that he did indeed stand alone in his generation in terms of succession considerations, and thus his heir had to come from a descending generation. The texts further state the fact that no legitimate male heir was available as a reason for the succession of a daughter. Interestingly, Tezozomoc was of the same generation as Motecuhzoma, as his classificatory brother. Furthermore, Tezozomoc was the son of a great *tlatoani*, Itzcoatl, whom he conceivably could have succeeded. Nevertheless, Tezozomoc was somehow excluded from the succession. He did not rule in his own right but served as consort of a female *tlatoani* and father of the next three kings.

These prose sources add yet another important detail concerning Motecuhzoma's daughter, namely, that she married Tezozomoc to insure that the right to rule would not leave the family line established by Acamapichtli (*Origen de los Mexicanos* 1941:274; *Relación de la Genealogía* 1941:253). This statement indicates that because of the lack of a legitimate son or brother of Motecuhzoma, the line went to his daughter and through her would have passed to her sons of whichever lineage she married into. To prevent the throne from being taken over by another family, she married a man who was a member of the Tenochtitlan lineage. In other words, *she* carried the right of rulership, not Tezozomoc, even though he was the son of Itzcoatl.

Two other Franciscan authors, Frs. Motolinía (1903:8) and Mendieta (1945:165), also wrote of ♀Atotoztli without mentioning her by name, but they emphasized even more that the line of rulership went through her. They noted that she inherited the kingship, but more important, these chroniclers failed to mention that her husband was the son of another ruler. Thus, there is no ambiguity in these texts that Axayacatl inherited the throne from his mother.

In contrast to these strong indications of ♀Atotoztli's ennobling qualities, other accounts downplay her role or fail to indicate any participation she may have had in the ennobling of the later Tenochtitlan kings. Chimalpahin's *Eighth Relación* (1983:129) says only that Axayacatl, Tizoc, and Ahuitzotl were Motecuhzoma's grandsons, implying that they ruled because of their inheritance from him but not giving any information as to whom their parent was who was the child of Motecuhzoma. Other texts are unclear as to whether rulership passed through a child of Motecuhzoma or a child of Itzcoatl. For example, the marriage between ♀Atotoztli and Tezozomoc is only implied in the *Seventh Relación* of Chimalpahin (1965:197, 206) and the *Leyenda de los Soles* (1975:128), and no indication is given as to whom the line of succession passed through. In Chimalpahin's history, Motecuhzoma's successors—Tizoc, Ahuitzotl, and Axayacatl—born in that order (and thus they did not rule in birth order in this text), are referred to as the sons of Tezozomoc and the grandsons of both Itzcoatl and Motecuhzoma. This ambiguity leaves one to assume the marriage of Tezozomoc to a daughter of Motecuhzoma, an assumption strengthened, of course, by the other accounts that state this explicitly. The *Leyenda de los Soles* version is even briefer, naming no children for Motecuhzoma or Itzcoatl but indicating that Axayacatl was the grandson of both rulers.

There are also versions that indicate rulership was handed down by Itzcoatl through his son Tezozomoc to Axayacatl, emphasizing the male line of succession and negating not only the feminine contribution but the entire lineage founded by Motecuhzoma's father, Huitzilihuitl. The *Crónica Mexicayotl* (Tezozomoc 1975:109, 111–112, 114), which was so detailed in its description of the roles of the mother and wife of the first king, says nothing about Tezozomoc's wife, mother of future kings, while the *Third Relación* of Chimalpahin (1965:97, 103) has her as a commoner, so there is no link between Tezozomoc and Motecuhzoma's daughter. Both these texts also name several children of Motecuhzoma I as possible heirs to his title, including a legitimate son, Iquehuac. Thus the problem of a lack of male issue to continue the rulership through Motecuhzoma's line never arises in these accounts. In fact, in the *Third Relación* Iquehuac is said to have ruled briefly after the death of his father before Axayacatl took over the throne.

The Spanish commentary appended to the pictures in the *Codex Mendoza* (1964:20–28), which gives two sons for Motecuhzoma I, nevertheless has the line of rulership running directly from Itzcoatl through Tezozomoc to Axayacatl and then to Axayacatl's sons, Tizoc, Ahuitzotl, and Motecuhzoma II (a rare and not unambiguous instance of Motecuhzoma II being a brother of the previous ruler). In this partial genealogy, as with the two accounts mentioned above, no relationship is given to link these latter kings to Motecuhzoma I. Motecuhzoma's line therefore appears to die out, and all the later rulers are from the line of Itzcoatl.

Finally, there is a further solution that avoids the problem of whether Axayacatl's right to succession came through Motecuhzoma I's daughter or through Itzcoatl's son: in some accounts Motecuhzoma is given as the father, rather than the grandfather, of Axayacatl. Removing the extra generation means that Axayacatl clearly inherited the throne directly from his father. This version is found in the Crónica X tradition (*Codex Ramirez* 1980:67; *Crónica Mexicana*, Tezozomoc 1980:411; Durán 1967:II:250; Tovar 1972:58), one of Ixtlilxochitl's histories (1975:410, but not his *Historia Chichimeca*, as noted above), and the *Historia de los Mexicanos por sus Pinturas* (1941:231, 233), although the relationship of Axayacatl to Tizoc and Ahuitzotl varies among these documents.

In the *Historia de los Mexicanos por sus Pinturas*, several generations are collapsed in that Motecuhzoma I, son of Huitzilihuitl, is indicated as the father of Axayacatl, Tizoc, and Ahuitzotl, and also of Motecuhzoma II and Cuitlahuac, obfuscating the issue of generational distance between these later kings. The Introductory Letter in Motolinía's *Historia* (1951:78) presents the most simplified version of all. In this account, Motecuhzoma I was succeeded by his daughter, who married a close relative (as in Motolinía's other text above). She was succeeded by her *son*, Motecuhzoma II, completely skipping Axayacatl, Tizoc, and Ahuitzotl.

Taken together, all these sources demonstrate a great uncertainty concerning the passage of the right of succession following the reign of the middle king, Motecuhzoma I, even though they generally agree on Axayacatl as his successor. In some texts, Motecuhzoma I had no brothers or heirs to succeed him in the usual fashion, setting the stage for the problem of succession. In others accounts, however, he had a son, Iquehuac, who could have succeeded but for some reason was passed over in favor of Axayacatl (see Zantwijk 1978). There is also a question in some accounts as to the birth order of the three succeeding kings and whether they ruled in that order or if a younger brother was chosen over his elder. More basically, there is ambiguity as to whom the line of succession passed through, since the parents of Axayacatl were both children of earlier *tlatoque.*

In this interregnum, eventually to be filled by Axayacatl, a woman played a very important role, a minor role, or no role at all. The same situation occurred at the founding of the dynasty and concerned the origin of the right of rulership of the first Tenochtitlan king. The first queen, genetrix of the Tenochtitlan ruling family, is said to have ennobled her husband-son and also to have ruled as *tlatoani* in her own right, but in some accounts she is not mentioned at all. The second ♀Atotoztli, who followed the fifth king, is structurally equivalent to the ♀Atotoztli/♀Ilancueitl pair associated with the first king, meaning that the same woman appeared at both the beginning and end of the first half of the dynasty. She ended the line of kings begun by Acamapichtli by being the daughter of Motecuhzoma I, and as some sources indicate, the line may have died out with him. She renewed the line by marrying Tezozomoc, a prince who did not rule himself. This act regenerated the dynasty and kept it in the already-established Tenochtitlan ruling house, preventing the removal of the kingship to a different lineage (according to some texts). Within the diversity of the historical traditions, it is nevertheless clear from various indications that ♀Atotoztli, the daughter of Motecuhzoma, like ♀Ilancueitl, had the power to ennoble the future kings.

Information from Classical Nahuatl kinship terminology further reveals the equivalence of these two key women. ♀Ilancueitl and the second ♀Atotoztli were related to one another as great-grandmother and great-granddaughter, respectively. There is a parallel construction in Nahuatl for the names of these positions which utilizes the elder-younger distinction applied to siblings in ego's generation (Gardner 1981:101). This construction has been formulated as a kinship terminology rule—the "Greatgrandkin-Sibling Merging Rule": "Let any person's older sibling be regarded as structurally equivalent to that person's greatgrandparent; conversely, let any person's younger sibling be regarded as structurally equivalent to that person's greatgrandchild" (Offner 1983:193).

An equation of elder-younger sisters with great-grandmother and great-granddaughter is exactly what is being communicated in the dynastic histories. The pairing of ♀Ilancueitl as elder sister of ♀Atotoztli at the founding of the dynasty is structurally equivalent to the pairing of ♀Ilancueitl with the second ♀Atotoztli as her great-granddaughter. ♀Atotoztli's reappearance as the daughter of Motecuhzoma I thus completed the first dynastic cycle.

♀Tecuichpo: Daughter of Motecuhzoma II

Just as a daughter renewed the dynasty after the death of Motecuhzoma I, the middle king, there was a daughter of the last king, Motecuhzoma II, who was said to possess her father's right to rule. This woman, ♀Tecuichpo, more commonly known by her baptismal name, Isabel, survived the conquest and died in 1551 (López de Meneses 1948:495). A few sources equate her explicitly with the daughter of the first Motecuhzoma by having her marry and thereby legitimate her father's cousin and successor (see, in addition to the sources below, P. Carrasco 1984:44). Thus, although she appears in fewer accounts, efforts were made to place her in the same role as the other two "queens" to whom she was structurally equivalent.

♀Tecuichpo is not named in the two most important eyewitness accounts of the conquest. One of the conquistadores who wrote a history of the conquest toward the end of his life, Bernal Díaz del Castillo (1970:230), recorded only that Motecuhzoma II told Cortés that he had one son and two legitimate daughters, while Cortés (1971:138) in his letters mentioned a son and two daughters who apparently died during the Spanish retreat from Tenochtitlan. The later prose historiographical texts, especially those written by natives, are more detailed with regard to Motecuhzoma II's descendants. His children are named in the *Origen de los Mexicanos* (1941: 276; one daughter and one son), the *Relación de la Genealogía* (1941: 254; one daughter and one son), the *Seventh Relación* of Chimalpahin (1965:275; two daughters and a son), the *Anales de Tlatelolco* (1948:65; two sons), Ixtlilxochitl's *Historia Chichimeca* (1977:306; three daughters and seven sons), the *Crónica Mexicayotl* (Tezozomoc 1975:150–158; nineteen children!). The *Anales de Cuauhtitlan* (1975:61) gives only two, unnamed daughters.

In all these sources, the child given the most prominence was the daughter named Isabel. Her pre-Hispanic name, found in a few texts, is usually ♀Tecuichpo or ♀Tecuichpoch. For example, the *Crónica Mexicayotl* (Tezozomoc 1975:156) refers to her as Isabel Tecuichpo, indicating that the daughter with the Nahuatl name of ♀Tecuichpo was the one renamed Isabel. In the *Historia Chichimeca* of Ixtlilxochitl (1977:306), however, her original name is given as ♀Miahuaxochitl (see Chapter 5 for a discussion of ♀Miahuaxochitl as the mother of Motecuhzoma I and the wife of Motecuhzoma II). ♀Tecuichpoch has been translated as "Royal Cotton Ball" (from *tecuhtli* = noble + *ichcatl* = cotton; López de Meneses 1948:471). Another translation, however, is more revealing of her significance in the genealogy: "Lord's Daughter" (Zantwijk 1985:305), from *tecuhtli* = lord + *ichpochtli* = daughter, a name that may actually have been a title (Zantwijk 1978:93).

Her appellation as a lord's daughter is graphically depicted in the late-sixteenth-century *Codex Cozcatzin*, which shows her with her father and a brother (Fig. 4.3a). The brief text accompanying the drawing gives her name as Isabel de Motecuhzoma and states that she married a Spaniard, Alonso de Alvarado (which should read Alonso de Grado) (Robertson 1959:Fig. 80). What is interesting about this picture is how her name is rendered glyphically. She and her brother are connected by lines to their father, who is sitting on a throne in front of the Tenochtitlan place glyph. Isabel is drawn directly opposite Motecuhzoma, gesturing to her father, while her brother is behind her in a less important position. Motecuhzoma's name glyph, the diadem of a lord (*tecuhtli*), is on top of the prickly pear cactus that forms part of the Tenochtitlan glyph. His son is named with a glyph that phonetically spells out Tlacahuepan

(a)

(b)

Figure 4.3. Representations of ♀Tecuichpo-Isabel: (a) drawing of Motecuhzoma II, his daughter, Isabel, and son, Tlacahuepan, in the *Codex Cozcatzin* (after Robertson 1959:Fig. 80; text deleted), in which Isabel has the same name glyph as her father, the ruler's diadem (his name glyph rests atop the prickly pear cactus that forms the Tenochtitlan place glyph); (b) ♀Tecuichpo at the surrender of Cuauhtemoc to Cortés in the *Lienzo de Tlaxcala* (1964:Pl. 48) (she is the only individual with a name glyph).

("Human-Beam," a face on a beam of wood; this name is also given to an aspect of Huitzilopochtli [Nicholson 1971b: Table 3]). Renamed Pedro, Tlacahuepan also survived the conquest and lived until 1570 (Barlow 1946a: 427), although he failed to receive the recognition from the Spanish Crown accorded to his sister (Duverger 1983: 54).

His sister's name glyph, however, is the same ruler's diadem that names her father. Perhaps the artist used the same glyph because both father and daughter have the sound of *tecuhtli* in their name, but the effect of the picture is that she has the same name as the ruling *tlatoani*, Motecuhzoma, while her brother does not. She appears to be more directly linked to her father's position by this fact and by her placement ahead of her brother. Conceivably, the artist was indicating her right to rule as a lord and to inherit her father's throne, a right denied to her surviving brother, just as her predecessor, ♀Atotoztli, was considered the legitimate heir of Motecuhzoma I in spite of the existence of her brother, Iquehuac.

The fullest account of the life of Isabel is found in the works of modern historians who have analyzed the archival records of the early postconquest period. She is usually identified as one of the three daughters of Motecuhzoma II whom he entrusted to Cortés's care along with her sisters, Maria and Marina (López de Meneses 1948: 472). She was baptized Isabel, possibly after the reigning queen of Spain (1948: 473), which may be coincidental or may reflect some belief that she was a "queen," the heiress of Motecuhzoma II. She was given in marriage to a Spaniard, Alonso de Grado, but after his death she became Cortés's mistress and gave birth to his daughter, Leonor Cortés Motecuhzoma, also known as Marina. This daughter was born after she had married another Spaniard, Pedro Gallego. Widowed once again, she was married for a third time in 1531, to Juan Cano de Suavedra (1948: 475–480).

What is of interest here is how in the postconquest histories she played a role in the royal genealogy similar to that of the daughter of Motecuhzoma I. The similarities to ♀Atotoztli are found in her marriage to her FFBS (in Isabel's case, Cuauhtemoc, successor to Motecuhzoma II) and in her right to the throne of Tenochtitlan, a right alluded to in the *Codex Cozcatzin*. However, the accounts differ as to whether she married Cuauhtemoc, whether Cuauhtemoc was her FFBS, and whether Isabel had any extraordinary claim to the inheritance of a right to rule.

A major point of disagreement among the different documents

concerns her marriage to Cuauhtemoc. Cuauhtemoc is said in several colonial sources, such as two testaments written in 1647 (Barlow
1946a:425), to have married a daughter of Motecuhzoma II, but this
woman was María Motecuhzoma Cortés Xochitlmazatl ("Flower-
Deer"). This information also comes from another pictorial document, the early-eighteenth-century *Codex García Granados* (Barlow
1945a), although there is no explanation given for the "Cortés" part
of her name. Bernal Díaz del Castillo (1970:328) also claimed that
Cuauhtemoc married one of Motecuhzoma II's daughters but did not
identify her by name. In her will, although Isabel referred to herself
as the heiress of Motecuhzoma (López de Meneses 1948:493), she
never claimed to have been the wife of Cuauhtemoc.

On the other hand, a few accounts indicate that Cuauhtemoc did
indeed marry Isabel Tecuichpo (e.g., P. Carrasco 1984:62). One is a
late prose account, the eighteenth-century history written by Clavijero (1976:378). This relationship is also implied in the pictorial
Lienzo de Tlaxcala in the scene showing the surrender of Cuauhtemoc (Fig. 4.3b). According to an interpretation of this scene (*Lienzo
de Tlaxcala* 1964:78, Pl. 48), Cortés is on the left with his native
interpreter, Marina, behind him. Cuauhtemoc stands before him (it
is assumed that the individual is Cuauhtemoc, though he is not
named). Above them, four women are watching the surrender, and
only one of them has a name glyph. It consists of an old person's head
(*tecul*), a cotton flower (*ichcatl*), and smoke curls (*pochtli*), giving the
sounds of the syllables in ♀Tecuichpoch. The picture indicates an
association between Cuauhtemoc and ♀Tecuichpo, that they surrendered to Cortés at the same time. Because this source lacks a text to
accompany the drawings (with the exception of a few brief glosses),
it remains unclear whether the two were actually married to one
another, although this seems a likely inference.

The most strident claim that Isabel was married to Cuauhtemoc
and that she was Motecuhzoma's principal heir was made by Juan
Cano, her third husband. Cano attempted on several occasions to
press claims on his wife's behalf for certain grants. In a letter to
Charles V of Spain, he stated that Motecuhzoma II and his one
legitimate son were killed and that Cano's wife had been wrong-
fully dispossessed of her inheritance as the only legitimate heir of
the empire headed by Tenochtitlan (López de Meneses 1948:487).
Cano's statement that Isabel had been married to Cuauhtemoc came
in an interview he had in 1544 with Gonzalo Fernández de Oviedo

y Valdés (1945:134). In this interview Cano asserted that his wife, Isabel, and her brother, here named Axayacatl, were the sole legitimate heirs of Motecuhzoma II. The brother was killed by Cuauhtemoc, Motecuhzoma's nephew, who had become ruler after the brief leadership of Cuitlahuac, Motecuhzoma's brother. In order further to establish himself as the rightful *tlatoani*, Cano said, Cuauhtemoc married Isabel, but they had no children. Thus, here is a claim for the marriage and for the legitimating qualities of ♀Tecuichpo, but Cuauhtemoc is given as a nephew, not a cousin, of Motecuhzoma II (a relationship also given in Durán's history [1967:II:549]).

Another source that speaks of this marriage is one of the two texts written by anonymous Franciscans at the behest of Juan Cano and sometimes known therefore as the *Cano Relaciones*: the *Relación de la Genealogía* and the *Origen de los Mexicanos*, dating from c. 1532. The *Relación de la Genealogía* (1941:254–255) says of Isabel that she was the daughter of Motecuhzoma and that she married Juan Cano. Motecuhzoma's legitimate son, again called Axayacatl, should have succeeded him but was killed by the Aztecs themselves (see also the *Crónica Mexicayotl* [Tezozomoc 1975:144], which has Axayacatl as her only full brother). Cuitlahuac and Cuauhtemoc are not mentioned in this narrative.

The *Origen de los Mexicanos* (1941:276–277), the companion document, provides the detail that Cuauhtemoc married Isabel after he was elected to rule. He did so, the document says, in order to legitimize his claim to the throne, the same statement Cano made later to Fernández de Oviedo y Valdés. This source thus implies that Cuauhtemoc himself did not possess a valid claim to ascend the throne of Tenochtitlan, even though he was the son of a great *tlatoani*, Ahuitzotl (by some accounts), and in any event a close relative of his predecessor, Motecuhzoma. It further assumes that Cuauhtemoc's claim could be strengthened by marrying the daughter of the late king. This is the same situation that occurred with Isabel's great-grandmother, ♀Atotoztli, daughter of Motecuhzoma I. In fact, the author of the *Origen de los Mexicanos* referred precisely to this earlier woman to explain Cuauhtemoc's behavior, stating that in his marriage to Isabel, Cuauhtemoc was following the pattern established by the marriage of Tezozomoc to ♀Atotoztli.

The genealogy given in the *Origen de los Mexicanos* has both women marrying the same kind of relative, although the biological relationships differ slightly from other sources in a most illuminating way. Here Isabel married her FBS, not the more usual FFBS, since Cuauhtemoc's father is given as Abocaci, a brother of Motecuhzoma II; thus Cuauhtemoc was Motecuhzoma II's nephew, not his cousin. The author then stated, but *only* in this context, that this was in the same manner that Motecuhzoma I had married his daughter to his nephew, Tezozomoc, the son of his *brother*, Itzcoatl. Earlier, however, the author had made it clear that Itzcoatl was the uncle, not the brother, of Motecuhzoma I, meaning that the daughter of the first Motecuhzoma had really married her father's cousin (FFBS), a generation above her (Fig. 4.4 displays these two variations). Thus, when he came to the point in the text of discussing the marriage of Isabel—with Cuauhtemoc already being given as the nephew, not cousin, of Motecuhzoma II—the chronicler changed the genealogical position of the first Motecuhzoma so that the marriage pattern would be the same for the two daughters. Adhering to the pattern of the genealogy was therefore more important to the author than maintaining a consistency with his previous statements concerning the exact biological relationships among the earlier kings.

In most of the other accounts where Cuauhtemoc's kinship relations are detailed (e.g., Ixtlilxochitl 1975:410; Ixtlilxochitl 1977: 306; *Historia de los Mexicanos por sus Pinturas* 1941:233; *Crónica Mexicayotl*, Tezozomoc 1975:163; *Seventh Relación* of Chimalpahin 1965:236), he is stated to have been a cousin of Motecuhzoma II, son of his uncle, Ahuitzotl. This does put him in the same kinship relation to Motecuhzoma II as Tezozomoc was to Motecuhzoma I, since Tezozomoc is given as the cousin of Motecuhzoma I, son of his uncle, Itzcoatl.

The *Cano Relaciones* are said to have been written so that Juan Cano could claim properties on his wife's behalf (Gibson and Glass 1975:345). Nevertheless, aside from any desire Cano may have harbored to manipulate history to suit his own purposes, these texts include some of the clearest indications of the dynasty's structural patterning, which was based on native conceptions (and they are also among the earliest surviving histories of the postconquest period). Isabel's rights to an inheritance may have been considered valid simply on the basis of her position as Motecuhzoma's daughter. From the purely legal point of view, there seems to have been no need to project back to an earlier daughter who ruled as queen in order to strengthen Isabel's claim, nor to assert that she was married to Cuauhtemoc in order further to legitimate *his* position; yet both

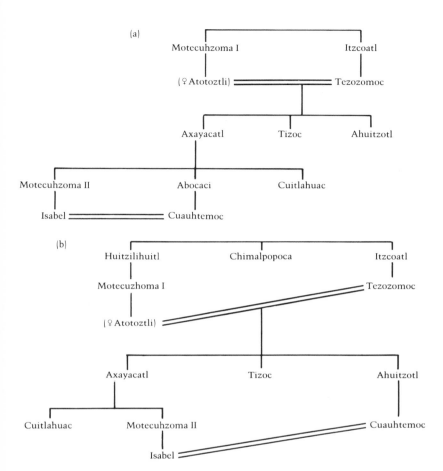

(a)

Motecuhzoma I — Itzcoatl

(♀Atotoztli) ══════════ Tezozomoc

Axayacatl — Tizoc — Ahuitzotl

Motecuhzoma II — Abocaci — Cuitlahuac

Isabel ══════════ Cuauhtemoc

(b)

Huitzilihuitl — Chimalpopoca — Itzcoatl

Motecuzhoma I ══════ Tezozomoc

(♀Atotoztli) ══════

Axayacatl — Tizoc — Ahuitzotl

Cuitlahuac — Motecuhzoma II ══════ Cuauhtemoc

Isabel ══════

Figure 4.4. Isabel assumes ♀Atotoztli's role in the *Origen de los Mexicanos*: (a) in the "revised" genealogy, both daughters of the two Motecuhzomas marry their father's brother's son (♀Atotoztli's name appears in parentheses because she is not named in this source); (b) in the usual version, Cuauhtemoc is the son of Ahuitzotl, and both women marry their father's father's brother's son (this is the complete model of the dynasty, showing the equivalent roles of the men and the women; compare to Fig. 1.5).

of these episodes are included in the *Cano Relaciones*. The Franciscan author or authors were aware of how history was used to explain current conditions; these chronicles thereby express aspects of the cyclical nature of the dynastic history, with Isabel reliving the part of an earlier queen, and Cuauhtemoc the part of an earlier prince, Tezozomoc.

A crucial distinction between Cuauhtemoc and his predecessor, Tezozomoc, is that Cuauhtemoc assumed the position of leader and Tezozomoc did not, although he has been called a "presumptive successor" (P. Carrasco 1984:61). However, in keeping with the pattern already presented with reference to the husbands of the key women, there is some dissension as to whether Cuauhtemoc was a true *tlatoani*. These are the same kinds of inconsistencies discussed previously for Acamapichtli and Tezozomoc (with the latter, the contradictions concerned whether the rulership passed through his wife or him).

Durán's history (1967:II:558), for example, has Cuauhtemoc crowned as king; Ixtlilxochitl (1975:410) called him the "last king." However, Fr. Acosta (1940:565), a later author in the Crónica X tradition, said that Cuauhtemoc was not a real king and that Motecuhzoma was the "last king." The illustrations of the kings in the Crónica X sources (Durán, Tovar's manuscript, *Codex Ramirez*), do not picture any of the *tlatoque* beyond Motecuhzoma II, glossed as "last" in Tovar's history. Nor are the kings after Motecuhzoma II pictured with their predecessors in the *Codex de Huichapan*, the *Anales de Tula*, the *Codex en Cruz*, the *Codex Mendoza*, or the *Codex Azcatitlan*. Chimalpahin (1958:12; 1965:61, 271) made several references to the *nine* kings of Tenochtitlan or to Motecuhzoma II being the last (1958:127; 1965:122). On the other hand, Cuauhtemoc and Cuitlahuac do appear as *tlatoque* in the *Codex Aubin*, *Codex Cozcatzin* (Barlow 1946b), *Codex Mexicanus*, *Tira de Tepechpan*, *Plano en Papel de Maguey*, and Sahagún's list of kings (see Fig. 1.3). This disagreement over the true political status of Cuauhtemoc is typical of the uncertain rulership position of the men who were married to ♀Ilancueitl (Acamapichtli) and ♀Atotoztli (Tezozomoc), and of the ambiguity that occurs at the juncture of the completion of one dynastic cycle and the beginning of the next.

Adding ♀Tecuichpo as the daughter of Motecuhzoma II and wife of Cuauhtemoc completes the cyclical pattern for the royal genealogy (see Fig. 1.5). The dynastic cycle was begun by ♀Ilancueitl/♀Atotoztli, a female split into two manifestations (usually two sisters) so that she may appear in several generations and take on two kinship roles as wife and mother of the founder of the Tenochtitlan dynasty, Acamapichtli. As genetrix and ennobler, she is equivalent to the mother-earth goddess. Thus the events that transpired at the founding of the royal family, including the merging of kinship roles held by a single person, occurred in other episodes of the cycle of Mexica history that deal with the mother goddess under a variety of her known guises. The cycle she began was completed in her second manifestation, again as an ♀Atotoztli, daughter of Motecuh-zoma I, her great-granddaughter (= younger sister), where she was in a descending position with respect to her husband but upon her marriage joined his generation. She appeared once again as great-granddaughter, daughter of Motecuhzoma II. Her ability to renew the dynasty one more time by marrying her FFBS, as her predecessor had done, survives in later documents as part of this cyclical concept.

Basic postulates of Aztec cosmology and rulership that underlay the re-creation of the Tenochtitlan dynasty in the historical tradi-tions (the form of the actual dynasty is not at issue here) are thus revealed. These include the mother-earth goddess as ultimate gene-trix, the generative power derived from the union of oppositions, the role merger and positional succession whereby males and females in the royal dynasty constantly replace one another to maintain the descent line and essence of kingship, and the cyclical nature of space-time. The oppositions that—once united—founded and ennobled the dynasty were not just male *vs.* female but the more fundamental sociocultural separation, Chichimec *vs.* Toltec (Culhua), in the same way that all things were created from the generative powers of the god of duality.

The origin of the dynasty is mirrored in the preceding origin of the tutelary deity, a celestial god, out of the earth, his mother (the original cosmic separation that also served as a metaphor for the diurnal and seasonal cycles). In this way, the creation of the geneal-ogy was grounded in the primordial space-time of the original cos-mogony, since the mother of the Tenochtitlan kings was also the mother of the gods and is the earth which gives birth to all life. It also occurs within the space-time at the threshold between the realm of the gods and the realm of men, since the mother of the Tenochtitlan kings was also the mother of all humanity at Chico-moztoc. It was in the space-time at the boundary between the golden age of the Toltecs and the new age of the Aztecs, since the mother of the Tenochtitlan kings was derived from the Toltec past but be-gan the Aztec present. Finally, it should have been recreated in the space-time juncture of the Aztec and European eras, since Isabel—who joined the Aztec world to the Spanish world most obviously in her liaison with Cortés, the ostensible ruler of this new political power—was the ultimate manifestation of this crucial female who functioned to continue the cycles of time and space by linking their male elements.

The Spanish Mother-Queen

At this point it is instructive to ask how much of this model may be postconquest in date (a result of the dialogue between Spaniard and native) and how much is preconquest (see also Chapter 6). It was noted in Chapter 2 that the ancient Egyptians had ideas identical to those of the Aztecs concerning the merging of primary kinship roles in the pharaonic line patterned to correspond with the actions of their gods. This may seem to be evidence for independent, parallel conceptions of genealogical modeling (see Chapter 7), but in fact the Spanish brought the Egyptian model to the New World, because biblical history incorporated the pharaonic positional succession model (Leach 1983). The merging of kinship roles occurs most explicitly and in greatest detail in the Holy Family, although like the Aztec texts, the "biblical versions baulk at the more extreme incestuous implications" (1983:54), and as with the Tenochtitlan queens and kings, avoid these implications by splitting the role of the essential female and male among several personages.

The Virgin Mary seems to have been the principal deity the Spaniards brought to New Spain. According to the letters of Cortés (1971) to the king of Spain and the history of the conquest written by Díaz del Castillo (1970), wherever the Spanish went, they erected wooden crosses and placed with them images of the Virgin. Compared to Mary, Jesus was a minor deity, appearing only in such weaker manifestations as a baby, a dying man on a cross (Kurtz 1982:206), and a dead man residing in the afterworld.

The high degree of Marianism among the early conquistadores (Lafaye 1976:224, 226; Vargas Ugarte 1947:28–29, 46), combined with the intense interest the Indians exhibited in the Virgin, contributed to the most powerful synthesis of Aztec and European mother goddesses, the Virgin of Guadalupe. Inspired in part by the Guadalupe Virgin of Extremadura, Spain, the home province of many of the conquerors, including Cortés (Lafaye 1976:217, 226; Uchmany 1980:33), she is still the most important religious manifestation in Mexico and is the singular image of native-Christian syncretism (see especially Kurtz 1982 and Lafaye 1976 on the creation of the Virgin as an outcome of dialectical processes between the two cultures).

According to the origin myth of Guadalupe (Kurtz 1982:194), the Virgin appeared to an Indian in 1531 at the hill of Tepeyacac, or Tepeyac, north of Tenochtitlan. Tepeyacac was a preconquest sanctuary and pilgrimage center (Gibson 1964:133) dedicated to ♀Tonan, "our mother," an important aspect of the mother-earth goddess (Sahagún 1956:Bk. 11:352). When the bishop of Mexico ordered that a shrine be built to the Virgin at the place where she appeared, he was actually allowing the Indians to continue a pre-Hispanic religious practice, something that did not escape the notice of clerics such as Sahagún and Durán (Uchmany 1980:33–34) who were knowledgeable about indigenous beliefs.

In addition to this synthesis of a new goddess, after the conquest many of the stories of the parthenogenic conceptions of Mexica gods and kings were influenced by the New Testament account of the birth of Christ (see especially in Chapter 5 the conception of Topiltzin in the *Codex Ríos*). It is even conceivable that if the principal deity of the conquerors was a woman whose son, the god-king, was conceived by a Holy Spirit, then the natives may have adopted that model for their own mother goddesses and their god-king offspring. This hypothesis becomes more intriguing in light of the fact that another woman and her royal son came to New Spain with Cortés along with the Virgin and her son, who would thereby have reinforced this model. This other woman was the queen of Spain; Spain at that time was ruled by Charles V and his mother, Queen Juana. The Aztecs were instructed by the Spaniards not only to worship the Virgin Mary and her son, Jesus Christ, but also to obey Queen Juana and her son, Charles V (Cortés 1971:xii). Less is known about the natives' knowledge of and reaction to Queen Juana, but she must have reaffirmed their view of the Spaniards as being ruled by queen mothers who were as powerful as their royal sons and who had divine counterparts in the Virgin Mary and Jesus.

More significantly, the Aztec mother-earth goddess and the Virgin Mary are key players in virtually identical royal genealogical models. The Virgin corresponds to the "woman of discord" in the dynastic model of the Tenochtitlan kings in her assumption of all the major kinship roles. In the Christian trinity, God is the father of us all, so God was the father of Mary. In the manifestation of the Holy Spirit, God the father impregnated Mary and thereby acted as spouse, as genitor of her son, Jesus, the third aspect of God as the son. Therefore, God was the father, husband, and son of Mary, just as she was daughter, wife (the Bride of Christ), and mother of God (Leach 1983).

Mary has a number of other manifestations as well, because her personality is split into the three Marys who witnessed Christ's resurrection (Leach 1983:46). These three women vary slightly in the four Gospels of the New Testament, and their merged identity is most apparent in the Apocrypha, especially the Gnostic texts. For instance, from the *Gospel of Philip* (Brown et al. 1978:246), a second-century collection of Gnostic meditations, comes this passage (59:6): "There were three who always walked with the Lord: Mary, his mother and her sister and Magdalene, the one who was called his companion. His [*sic*] sister and his mother and his companion were each a Mary." In the second sentence, which contradicts the first in a most meaningful way, Mary was Jesus' mother, sister, and companion (= wife). As mother, sister, wife, and daughter of Jesus/God, Mary reveals the same pattern of relationships for an Old World deity that has been shown to apply to Aztec deities and their mortal representatives, the Tenochtitlan kings.

While it is possible that the Aztecs borrowed a non-native virgin mother model, there is compelling evidence to support the idea of the independent creation of this kind of deity in both the Old and New Worlds in order to resolve similar philosophical dilemmas, especially because the Aztec mother-earth goddess differs in significant ways from the Virgin Mary. An obvious clue to the preconquest existence of the beliefs concerning the Aztec goddess is that the story of the sacrifice of ♀Toci was reenacted at the annual Ochpaniztli ceremony, and the birth of Huitzilopochtli at Coatepec at the annual Panquetzaliztli ceremony (Chapter 7). These pre-Hispanic practices reveal a coincidence of Spanish and Indian conceptions. In addition, the Aztec goddess was considered to have both female and male attributes, an androgynous quality found in deities of many cultures as an "expression of totality" (Eliade 1969:111). The Franciscans were well aware of the dual sexual nature of ♀Tonan, "our mother," who had been converted into the Virgin of Guadalupe, and they feared that the Virgin would be worshiped as a god rather than as a female saint (Lafaye 1976:239).

Furthermore, while the Virgin Mary in her multiple relationships with the Christian God is like ♀Toci in her relationships with Huitzilopochtli, there is a fundamental dissimilarity in the two ideologies which is part of their contrasting conceptions of time. The Virgin's relationships with God the Trinity took place in her lifetime, and her body was lifted up to heaven after her death (the Assumption). Mary was considered not to have aged, always appearing in the iconic imagery as a young woman (Leach 1983), whereas Jesus, her son, went through the stages of life from birth to death to rebirth. In contemporary Mesoamerican folklore, Jesus is identified with the sun going through its daily and annual cycles (e.g., Gossen 1972; Ichon 1973). Thus Christ may be considered equivalent to the Aztec Huitzilopochtli in having a solar aspect and in being born from the mother goddess.

In contrast, however, in Aztec tradition ♀Toci did not become wife, sister, mother, and grandmother of the Aztec god until after her death, which was accompanied by the mutilation of her body. It was the mother goddess, not her son, who represented the stages of life from youth to old age, while Huitzilopochtli was similar to the Virgin in his constant appearance as a young adult; in fact, he emerged from the womb fully grown.

The incorporation of the Virgin into postconquest Aztec culture, as seen most prominently in the Virgin of Guadalupe transformation, was thereby facilitated by parallels between the mother goddesses of both groups. But there were differences as well, which indicate that the multiple role merging of the genetrix in Tenochtitlan dynastic history and her reappearance at the juncture of the dynastic cycles were not necessarily postconquest, Franciscan creations, as some have thought (e.g., Duverger 1983:53; Stenzel 1980: 23). The repeating deaths of the mother-earth deity on the cyclical Mexica migration, like the repeating appearance of the Tenochtitlan "queen," were necessary for the emergence of the next cycle, and this is at variance with Christian tradition concerning Mary.

This coincidence—the development of positional succession and royal incest in the modeling of the divine families of the Old and New World cultures that clashed in 1519—is of great significance and is discussed further in Chapter 7. First, however, other aspects of how the royal genealogy was manipulated in order to deal with social reality must be examined. The Tenochtitlan dynastic model encompasses more than the reappearance of queens as genetrix and the positional succession of kings. Like all representations of time, the genealogy had a cyclical form, going through periods of generation, death, and regeneration. It died in one sense with Motecuhzoma I but was renewed through his daughter. It died again with Motecuhzoma II, when the Spanish put an end to the dominion of the Aztecs.

Also, as a cycle the genealogy is tied to other temporal periods in

Aztec history, some of which have been discussed. When the final dynastic cycle ended with the unanswered claims of Isabel's supporters, thus also ended the age of the Aztecs, and the age of the Europeans began. But for the age of the Aztecs to have begun, the antecedent Toltec cycle had had to end, at which point the mother-earth goddess also appeared (♀Quetzalxochitl in the *Leyenda de los Soles*). As with all cycles, the genealogy and these ages, Toltec and Aztec, were most clearly marked at their close, for only at its completion can a cycle be said to have existed. Although some versions of Aztec dynastic history pay little attention to the women who began the genealogical cycles, they do refer to the endpoints of those cycles in ways that further reveal the cyclical quality of the genealogy and its relationship, as a cycle, to earlier, pre-Aztec periods of history.

These endpoints, at the boundaries of the Tenochtitlan dynastic cycle, are the two kings named Motecuhzoma, the subject of the next chapter. Discovery of the organizing principles that resulted in the merging of their identities, already alluded to by their sharing of a single name, illuminates the processes by which the royal genealogy, as history, was a medium for understanding the present by incorporating actual—and hence, by default, nonactual—events in the transformation of the past.

Part 2

The Recycled King

Chapter 5

Motecuhzoma and Quetzalcoatl: On the Boundary

The royal dynasty of Tenochtitlan was conceived as a repeating cycle, according to the cyclical paradigm that structured other aspects of Mexica history. Up to this point, the women who personified the generation and binding of the two halves of the dynasty have been discussed in detail and related to the mother-earth goddess and cosmogonical events. The discussion now turns to the key males in the dynasty and how they further reveal organizing principles in Aztec thought. This chapter is concerned with the men who appeared at the ends of the generational cycles: the two kings named Motecuhzoma. The dynastic model shows that these two kings merge into one, as is indicated by their sharing a single name. The implications of the positioning of the Motecuhzomas at the ends of the dynastic cycles and the reasons why only these two of the nine kings have the same name remain to be explained.

The meaning assigned to the placement of these kings within the Tenochtitlan dynasty is most clearly delineated when another king, from another place and another era, is considered. This other king is Ce Acatl Topiltzin Quetzalcoatl, who headed the earlier Toltec civilization. The native historical traditions treat Topiltzin Quetzalcoatl and Motecuhzoma in very similar ways, so much so that they become equivalent personages, one belonging to the age of the Aztecs

124 THE RECYCLED KING

and one to the age of the Toltecs. Their equivalency results from the identical function they serve in the histories, the function of marking the beginning and ending—the boundaries—of cycles.

Examining the similarities that link Motecuhzoma I and II and also equate both Motecuhzomas to Topiltzin Quetzalcoatl and his alter egos invokes the related questions of why these similarities exist in the historical accounts and when they became incorporated into the Aztec past as viewed by both natives and Spaniards. A critical event for the shaping of these personages in the histories was the conquest itself, which placed Motecuhzoma II on the boundary between the Aztec and Spanish eras and hence presupposed both the ordering and nature of the earlier Motecuhzoma and his Toltec counterpart, the ruler named Topiltzin Quetzalcoatl.

It is in this aspect of Aztec history—the relationship between Motecuhzoma and Topiltzin Quetzalcoatl as recurrent markers of cyclical endpoints—that the re-creation of the past as shaped by the needs and events of the present is best revealed. And it is also here that the royal genealogy is more completely manifested as the model for history par excellence. It incorporates in the most essential and efficient form the basic concepts that underlay Aztec visions of the cosmos, state, and society. The rapidity with which dynastic history was modified after the conquest, as shown in this and the following chapter, further indicates its preeminence as the paramount historical narrative.

Motecuhzoma I and II

Of the nine *tlatoque* in the Tenochtitlan dynasty, two (the fifth and ninth) shared a single name, Motecuhzoma. Although there are a few other Motecuhzomas scattered through the historical traditions from central Mexico, this name repetition within the Tenochtitlan royal family cannot be considered coincidental or simply the result of a practice of retaining names within a lineage. Instead, it reflects the cyclical patterning of the dynasty as it was conceived by the Aztecs. As noted in Chapter 1, a similarity in details in the narrative histories links the structurally equivalent kings in the abstract model of the dynasty, most notably Tizoc and Chimalpopoca but also the two kings named Motecuhzoma.

In addition, only these two kings are equated in the pictures of the rulers, particularly the illustrations in the Spanish-authored Crónica X documents (Durán's history, Tovar's history, and the *Codex Ramirez* of Tovar). Of the nine Tenochtitlan kings pictured in these sources, only the two named Motecuhzoma are depicted in the act of being crowned with the *xiuhuitzolli,* the turquoise diadem that was both the symbol of rulership and the motif of their name glyph. The other *tlatoque* are shown already wearing the diadem of office.

Furthermore, only the two Motecuhzomas are depicted wearing a device on their left arms, the *quetzalmachoncatl* (named in Sahagún 1950–82:Bk. 8:28, pictured in Bk. 12:Fig. 53; see also Seler 1902–23:II:542, Figs. 48, 49). The *quetzalmachoncatl* consists of an armband with a sheaf of green (*quetzal*) feathers, worn at about the elbow. It appears in association with other kings' corpses (e.g., Ahuitzotl and Nezahualpilli in Durán's illustrations, 1967:II:Figs. 36, 49), but only the two kings named Motecuhzoma are shown wearing it (Fig. 5.1). Lest one think that this is a device worn only at the crowning of a *tlatoani,* which would explain why only the two Motecuhzomas wear it, Durán's history pictures Motecuhzoma I wearing it on the sculpted likeness of himself that he had carved at Chapultepec (Fig. 5.2a). The device may also appear in a very abbreviated form in the *Lienzo de Tlaxcala* as three feathers coming off the left hand of Motecuhzoma II (Fig. 5.2b). Despite these appearances in European-ized illustrations, the feather armband does not seem to occur in the pictographic documents of the native style, in which all the *tlatoque* are represented in nearly identical fashion, distinguished from one another only by their name glyphs.

These details link the two kings named Motecuhzoma and thereby separate them from the other *tlatoque* of Tenochtitlan. The similarities are a manifestation of the cyclical conception of dynastic history, which equated these kings because of their placement at the endpoints of their generational cycles, when the cycle is most marked. Because of their position on the edge of their respective cycles, the mytho-logic results in the attribution of certain characteristics to the two Motecuhzomas that identify their role as boundary markers.

By their nature, boundaries have certain characteristics cross-culturally and cross-phenomenally, a result of the process of their creation. Boundaries are constructed when people use symbols to classify the world around them, a world in which all phenomena are

(a)

(b)

Figure 5.1. In these drawings, Motecuhzoma I and II are shown to be equivalent in wearing the *quetzalmachoncatl* and in being depicted at their coronations (*Codex Ramirez* 1980:Figs. 12, 16): (a) Motecuhzoma I, with the Ilhuicamina name glyph, is being crowned by Nezahualcoyotl of Texcoco; (b) Motecuhzoma II (lacking a name glyph) is being crowned by Nezahualpilli of Texcoco, son of Nezahualcoyotl.

Figure 5.2. In these drawings, Motecuhzoma I and II wear the *quetzalmachoncatl* on occasions other than their coronation: (a) Motecuhzoma I has his figure sculpted at Chapultepec ("Grasshopper Hill"), and only his likeness wears the *quetzalmachoncatl* (Durán 1967:II:Fig. 19); (b) at the encounter between Motecuhzoma II and Cortés, Motecuhzoma is shown with feathers coming off his left hand, an abbreviation of the usual feather sheaf worn on the left arm (*Lienzo de Tlaxcala* 1964:Pl. 11). In drawing (b) he is named by the ruler's diadem glyph, but the style of the ruler's crown conforms to Tlaxcalan rather than Tenochca conventions, as a band with a feather ornament (he wears it, and it also appears in front of him as a name glyph). The glyphic elements above the building in which Cortés sits give the name of Motecuhzoma the Elder, whose palace housed Cortés and his men. It consists of an old man (*huehuetl*), a stone (*tetl*), a jar (*comitl*) with sand in it (*zoquitl*), and a hand (*maitl*), yielding huehue [mo]te-co-zo-ma (*Lienzo de Tlaxcala* 1964:30).

potentially continuous. When these continuua are divided into different classes of things, events, or relations, the separations thereby imposed between them are in that sense artificial. The boundaries that divide these culturally separated categories may thus be recognized by their contrast with the phenomena that they divide. "A boundary separates two zones of social space-time which are *normal, time-bound, clear-cut, central, secular,* but the spatial and temporal markers which actually serve as boundaries are themselves *abnormal, timeless, ambiguous, at the edge, sacred*" (Leach 1976:35; emphasis is in the original).

Belonging not to the normal, secular world, boundaries are therefore often embued with taboo or other supernatural (as opposed to natural) qualities (Leach 1983:15). Where the boundaries are personified, the individuals marking the boundary are necessarily ambiguous or anomalous beings such as incarnate gods and virgin mothers (Needham 1979:47; as in Chapters 3 and 4 above), twins, tricksters, bisexual beings, sibling pairs, or even messiahs (Lévi-Strauss 1963:226). Such individuals are very powerful, not only because they bridge opposed phenomena, but also because they transcend the categorization of phenomena itself and thus have the power to create order out of potential chaos. They are necessary for the orderly division of space-time into culturally understood categories and relationships.

As for Motecuhzoma I and II, it is already known that they appeared at the "edge," positioned at the endpoint of the dynastic cycles, rendering them timeless (recurrent or "recycled"). Furthermore, in the historical traditions their reigns are marked by ambiguity with regard to their succession. But other details portray Motecuhzoma I especially as an anomalous being in the most classic sense: his parthenogenic conception and his relationship with a "twin."

The *Crónica Mexicayotl* (Tezozomoc 1975:90–95) provides the story of the parthenogenic conception of Motecuhzoma I in an account that links the birth of Motecuhzoma to the miraculous conception of the deity Huitzilopochtli at Coatepec. According to this document, Motecuhzoma's father, Huitzilihuitl, second *tlatoani* of Tenochtitlan, was married to ♀Miahuaxochitl (*miahuatl* = corn tassel + *xochitl* = flower). He sought as a second wife the daughter of the king of Cuauhnahuac (modern Cuernavaca), a fertile agricultural land south of the Valley of Mexico. This woman was named

♀Miahuaxihuitl (*miahuatl* = corn tassel + *xihuitl* = a precious blue-green stone, turquoise). Her father, Ozomatzintecuhtli, who was a sorcerer, hid his daughter from her many prospective suitors in the palace, guarded by wild beasts, spiders, centipedes, serpents, bats, and scorpions. However, Huitzilihuitl was able to make contact with the princess by shooting an arrow ("*ce acatl*" in the Nahuatl text) over all the barriers. Inside the arrow he had placed a precious stone (a *chalchihuitl* = jade), which the princess found when she retrieved and broke open the arrow. She swallowed the stone and became pregnant by this act with her son, Motecuhzoma Ilhuicamina (here the meaning of Ilhuicamina as the "Archer of the Skies" was actually a part of his conception).

The chronicle continues that this action resulted in a forty-year war between Tenochtitlan and Cuauhnahuac, ending in the conquest of this southern province by Tenochtitlan. The princess of Cuauhnahuac, ♀Miahuaxihuitl, is thus like the other woman of discord (♀Toci) in being the cause of a war. Here the struggle resulted in a conjoining of the Mexica Tenochca by conquest and marriage to a southern agricultural land highly desired for its fruits and other plant products, just as the southern agricultural city-state of Culhuacan was eventually united with Tenochtitlan by marriage and conquest.

♀Miahuaxihuitl can also be compared to ♀Coatlicue, the mother of Huitzilopochtli, who conceived by "swallowing" another precious substance, feathers, although here there is an opposition between sky (feathers) and earth (stone) as the agents of the conception. On the other hand, the jewel (synonymous with the green stone in ♀Miahuaxihuitl's name) came from the sky, in the arrow, just as the feathers that conceived Huitzilopochtli came from the sky. The conception of ♀Miahuaxihuitl's son, the mortal ruler Motecuhzoma, was as unnatural as the conception of the deity Huitzilopochtli, but there is greater representation of sexual union in the begetting of Motecuhzoma. First, he does have an acknowledged father. Second, his father shot an arrow (= phallus) toward the woman, part of which she ate (a sexual metaphor). Thus, Huitzilihuitl did have a part to play, albeit not the usual one, in the conception of his son.

Note that because he was conceived by a jewel in such a manner, Motecuhzoma I was therefore not a product of the lineage founded by Acamapichtli, as his predecessors were. In other words, the dynasty actually breaks with him in a true sense. Furthermore, he received his life and his right to rule ultimately from his mother, a "Toltec-like" princess, another woman of discord. In this sense, he is akin to Acamapichtli and to Huehue Huitzilihuitl before him, both of whom founded new Mexica dynasties via their ennobling through their mothers.

♀Miahuaxihuitl is named as the mother of Motecuhzoma I—but without the supernatural implications—in the *Seventh Relación* of Chimalpahin (1965:183), the *Codex Mexicanus* (in the pictorial family tree; Fig. 4.2b), the *Historia de los Mexicanos por sus Pinturas* (1941:229), and the *Carta* to the king of Spain by Nazareo de Xaltocan (1940:122). According to this last source, ♀Miahuaxihuitl, the wife of Huitzilihuitl of Tenochtitlan, is given as the daughter of another ♀Miahuaxihuitl, who was the wife of the king of Cuauhnahuac, which would make ♀Miahuaxihuitl both the mother and grandmother of Motecuhzoma I. In this document and in the *Historia de los Mexicanos por sus Pinturas*, the Cuauhnahuac king's name was Itzcoatl rather than Ozomatecuhtli, the same name as that of the predecessor of Motecuhzoma I as the ruler of Tenochtitlan. Nazareo de Xaltocan (1940:121) also had Itzcoatl of Tenochtitlan married to a woman of a similar name, ♀Miahuaxochitl, mother of Tezozomoc who married ♀Atotoztli. As mentioned above, this is the same name as that of the first wife of Huitzilihuitl, brother of Itzcoatl, in the *Crónica Mexicayotl* account.

The similarity of the two names—♀Miahuaxihuitl and ♀Miahuaxochitl—becomes a merger of the two women when later documents are consulted. Torquemada (1975:148–149) and Clavijero (1976:77) named ♀Miahuaxochitl (not her counterpart, ♀Miahuaxihuitl) as the mother of Motecuhzoma. Furthermore, ♀Miahuaxochitl appeared again in the dynasty, as the wife of Motecuhzoma I in another late source (Veytia 1944:I:373) and as the wife of Motecuhzoma II in the *Crónica Mexicayotl* (Tezozomoc 1975:152) and in Clavijero's history (1976:363). A final role is given to a woman named ♀Miahuaxochitl in Ixtlilxochitl's *Historia Chichimeca* (1977:306), where she is the daughter of Motecuhzoma II who was renamed Isabel! Here is another instance of the role merging of an important female associated with the kings who stand alone in their generation in the dynastic model. ♀Miahuaxihuitl/♀Miahuaxochitl appears variously as grandmother, mother, and wife of Motecuhzoma I and as wife and daughter of Motecuhzoma II.

Another wife given for Motecuhzoma I (Nazareo de Xaltocan 1940:122) was ♀Chichimecacihuatl ("Chichimec-Woman") of

Cuauhnahuac, the hometown of his mother, and she was the mother of ♀Atotoztli. Her name embodies exactly the opposite qualities one would expect of a native of Cuauhnahuac, a city more akin to the civilization of the Toltecs, the antithesis of the barbaric Chichimecs. On the other hand, ♀Chichimecacihuatl appears as an early apotheosized queen along with ♀Coatlicue (mother of Huitzilopochtli), ♀Yaocihuatl (equivalent to ♀Toci; see Chapter 3), and ♀Miahuatl (whose name has the same root as the merged woman who was mother and wife of Motecuhzoma) (*Anales de Cuauhtitlan* 1975:6). In Chimalpahin's *Third Relación* (1965:103, 89), ♀Chichimecacihuatl was the daughter, not the wife, of Motecuhzoma I, and his sister was ♀Yaocihuatl, also in the list above. Thus Motecuzhoma I and II were additionally linked by multiple primary kinship ties to a manifestation of the mother-earth deity, as befits their position in the genealogical cycle in which this goddess continually reappears in association with the three marked kings.

Like Motecuhzoma I, Motecuhzoma II was the product of a miraculous conception, not his but his father's, in an episode found in the sixteenth-century history of Fernández de Oviedo y Valdés (1945:100). According to this account, a virgin was cleaning the idol of Huitzilopochtli in the temple in Tenochtitlan when a feather fell down from above. She put the feather in her bosom and later dreamed that Huitzilopochtli came and slept with her. She discovered she was pregnant and gave birth to a son named Guatezuma, whose name is a composite of Cuauhtemoc and Motecuhzoma (López Austin 1973: 14), just as this story is a composite of the birth of Huitzilopochtli at the beginning of Mexica history and of the rulers at the end of that history.

The story continues that the people of Tenochtitlan were angry at the temple virgin for obviously neglecting her responsibilities, and they forced her to leave the city. She told them, however, that her son would be their king, and later Guatezuma did prove himself a very great ruler. He died in a battle against Tlaxcala, but his son, Motecuhzoma, succeeded him to the throne of Tenochtitlan. In this account, Motecuhzoma II was thus directly descended from the Mexica patron god, Huitzilopochtli, and the mother goddess, and he is also merged with his counterpart and successor, Cuauhtemoc.

This is not the only occasion when Motecuhzoma appears in the histories with a double or merged personality. Both Motecuhzoma I and II, like other major figures in the historical traditions, have counterparts with whom they may be opposed, with whom they may be related by kinship or paired in an altruistic partnership, with whom they may appear one after the other, and with whom they may be combined. Examples of this same phenomenon have already been presented for ♀Ilancueitl and ♀Atotoztli. This kind of doubling is a notable feature of Aztec thought, as if two elements were needed to represent a single idea (Kubler 1972a:5). It allows for ambiguity and contradiction, which are necessary to express complex concepts.

The major counterpart for Motecuhzoma I was his "twin" brother, Tlacaelel. Tlacaelel's life is so intermingled with Motecuhzoma's in the different histories that they become in effect the same person. Tlacaelel appears most prominently in the Crónica X versions of Tenochtitlan history, where he is given a dominant role in the victory over the Tepanecs of Azcapotzalco and the formation of the Triple Alliance. He held the office of *cihuacoatl* (woman-serpent, one of the names of the mother goddess; see Chapter 3)—second only to the king—during the reigns of Itzcoatl, Motecuhzoma I, and Axayacatl, but he was most firmly identified with Motecuhzoma. For instance, Tlacaelel and Motecuhzoma had certain privileges and markers of status denied to everyone else (*Crónica Mexicana*, Tezozomoc 1980:353). In Chimalpahin's *Seventh Relación* (1965:205), Tlacaelel is even described as coruler with Motecuhzoma I, and some sources give him the credit for the accomplishments of Motecuhzoma's reign (e.g., Acosta 1940:555). Yet while he appears so prominently in some sources, Tlacaelel is given less importance or not mentioned at all in others.

Because of these inconsistencies among the various texts, the true nature of his influence has long been a subject of debate. As early as the seventeenth century, Fr. Torquemada (1975:236–237) even doubted that he ever existed, wondering how such an important figure could be missing from so many pictorial and prose writings, especially the many detailed writings from the Texcoco area. Modern scholars are not so quick to deny the historical existence of Tlacaelel, but his treatment at the hands of the early colonial period writers has somewhat fused him with Motecuhzoma I. For example, a comparison of the different versions of the Crónica X tradition reveals that in some accounts certain speeches were attributed to Tlacaelel, while in others the same words were put into Motecuhzoma's mouth (Gillmor 1964:xiv, 209).

This merging of the two men in the documents has been attributed to the "possible influence of twin legends" (Gillmor 1964:xiv, 210), referring to the pan-American mythology of creator twins who originally created world order by separating phenomena into spatial, temporal, and social categories, and thereby prepared the world for mankind (Métraux 1946). Perhaps the best-known Mesoamerican example of the creator twins are two brothers transformed into the sun and moon in a late highland Maya tradition, the *Popol Vuh* (1971). The twinlike treatment accorded to Motecuhzoma I and Tlacaelel, by which they became substitutable for one another, reflects their creator role—they created a new political and social order. More pertinent, however, is the fact that they were brothers, indeed twins of a sort.

Chimalpahin, in his *Seventh Relación* (1965:183–184), provided the details of the birth of these two brothers: Motecuhzoma Ilhuicamina Chalchiuhtlatonac (jade + sun), son of Huitzilihuitl and ♀Miahuaxihuitl of Cuauhnahuac, was born at sunrise (and thus is associated with the day sun, because the *tlatoani* is the mortal representative of Huitzilopochtli). On the same day, another wife of Huitzilihuitl also gave birth to a son, Tlacaelel, just before dawn (associating him with Venus, the Morning Star, which accompanies the sun; he was surely a companion to the *tlatoani*, just as Venus and the sun are often paired in Mesoamerican mythology). These two half brothers were born on the same day, with Tlacaelel just a few minutes older than Motecuhzoma; yet Motecuhzoma became ruler, with his elder brother assuming a secondary role as *cihuacoatl*.

Furthermore, the office of *cihuacoatl* held by Tlacaelel had its own inherent twinlike quality. One meaning of the word has already been explained in reference to the goddess ♀Cihuacoatl as "Woman-Serpent." This goddess was always the mother of twins (Brinton 1890b:51). But there is a second meaning of the word: *coatl* also means twin, giving a translation as "female twin" or "female counterpart" (see also Zantwijk 1963, 1976, 1985). The two offices of *tlatoani* and *cihuacoatl* thereby conjoined the (male) ruler and his "female" counterpart, a duality that represents on the political level the supernatural union of Huitzilopochtli, the male patron deity of the Chichimec Mexica, and ♀Cihuacoatl (= ♀Toci, ♀Xochiquetzal, etc.), the female patron deity of the Toltec Culhua (P. Carrasco 1976:214), as well as the androgynous god of duality, Ometeotl, the generative power at the head of the pantheon, the source of all life (León-Portilla 1963:111). Thus Motecuhzoma I, who bounded the end of the first dynastic cycle, clearly had a twin or double in Tlacaelel. This is just one more aspect of his anomalous nature, a nature that marks him as a boundary figure. It also helps to link him to the most famous twin in Aztec historical traditions, the "precious twin," Quetzalcoatl.

Topiltzin Quetzalcoatl

The kings of Tenochtitlan were said to be the successors of the rulers of the old Toltec empire through their intermarriage with the Culhuacan dynasty, so the death of Motecuhzoma II at the hands of the Spaniards was seen as the termination of the indigenous kingship begun by the Toltecs. This notion is found in Chimalpahin's *Third Relación*, a text that ends at the year 1519 with the *entrada* of Cortés but has this final paragraph, which at first appears to be out of place in the chronology:

> After the death of Totepeuh and Topiltzin, no one reigned in Culhuacan for 100 years. For 52 years [the ritual cycle] Topiltzin had held in his care and charge the royal government, and 700 years later this government was terminated with the death of Motecuhzoma the Younger, Lord of Tenochtitlan. (Chimalpahin 1965:122)

Here the entry of the Spanish, and hence the end of Aztec hegemony under Motecuhzoma II, was related in the author's mind to the death of an earlier king, associated with the Toltecs, whose full name was Ce Acatl Topiltzin Quetzalcoatl (Ce Acatl = 1 Reed, a day name; Topiltzin = "Our Prince," a title; Quetzalcoatl = *quetzal* feather + serpent, or "Feathered Serpent"). Chimalpahin's linking of these two particular kings, the Aztec Motecuhzoma and the Toltec Topiltzin Quetzalcoatl, at the end of Motecuhzoma's reign has to do with their equivalent roles and positioning in the histories with regard to their respective kingdoms.

Ce Acatl Topiltzin Quetzalcoatl, like Motecuhzoma, functioned in the Aztec past as a boundary figure. As we have seen, for the age of the Aztecs, Motecuhzoma I and II were positioned at the endpoints of the two dynastic cycles in the Tenochtitlan royal genealogy. In the preceding Toltec era, Topiltzin Quetzalcoatl was also a boundary marker. He appears in different texts as the first or last ruler, or both, of the Toltecs. That is, some accounts speak of Topiltzin Quetzalcoatl as the first king of Tollan, as founder of the Toltec civilization, or as one of the early kings of the Toltecs, with Huemac as the last Toltec king. In other sources, however, Topiltzin and Huemac were contemporaries at the time of the collapse of Tollan, putting Topiltzin Quetzalcoatl at the end of the age of the Toltecs.

Topiltzin Quetzalcoatl's positioning as both "alpha and omega" (to use Davies's phrase [1982:106]) has generally perplexed scholars attempting to reconstruct the actual chronology of the Toltec period. Two contrasting schools of thought developed concerning the placement of Topiltzin Quetzalcoatl in Toltec history, each unable to reconcile its position with the other because of the many contradictions among the documents. Two distinguished Mesoamerican ethnohistorians took opposing sides in this controversy (Kirchhoff 1955; see a summary of their positions in Davies 1977:153–156, App. A). Wigberto Jiménez Moreno (1941, 1956) opted for Topiltzin Quetzalcoatl as the first ruler of Tollan, based on information in the *Anales de Cuauhtitlan* and the *Relación de la Genealogía*. To account for the other documents that put Topiltzin toward the end of the dynasty, he stated that Sahagún had erred in making Topiltzin and Huemac contemporaries (Jiménez Moreno 1956:34). Paul Kirchhoff (1955) preferred the other interpretation, with Topiltzin as the last ruler, relying on the accuracy of the *Memorial Breve* of Chimalpahin and Sahagún's lengthy account of the fall of Tollan but thereby having to denigrate the reliability of the sources Jiménez Moreno was using.

Nigel Davies (1977) attempted to reconcile these two positions by hypothesizing that there were at least two individuals named Topiltzin Quetzalcoatl who ruled Tollan, one at the beginning and one at the end of Toltec history. He accounted for the name repetition by noting that Quetzalcoatl was the name of a major deity worshiped by the Toltecs, and thus many of the Toltec priests and priest-rulers would have adopted his name. This proposal to account for the contradiction in the documents does not explain why only the first and last rulers of Tollan were named Topiltzin Quetzalcoatl, and none of those in the middle of the dynasty. More recently, Davies (1982: 107; 1984:209) has labeled the entire question as to whether Topiltzin Quetzalcoatl was the first or last ruler of Tollan as "irrelevant" and "sterile," recognizing that the prevalence of cyclical concepts in Mesoamerican thought would require that "if a Topiltzin reigned at the beginning of [Tollan], he had also to reign at the end, and vice versa" (Davies 1982:107; but see also López Austin 1973, and Nicholson 1957 and 1979 for discussions of Topiltzin Quetzalcoatl).

This recognition of the role of cyclical time in the purposeful rewriting of history is a more productive starting point for comprehending what the various sources on Toltec history are communicating. The dynamics of the cyclical concept require that the ending of one cycle coincide with the beginning of the next. Since this next cycle is structurally identical to the previous one, its ending must also share an identity with its beginning. If Topiltzin Quetzalcoatl is associated with the fall of Tollan, he must simultaneously be linked to its rise; he is the boundary marker of the Tollan "cycle." As such, he is characterized in the traditions by a number of attributes he shares with his Aztec equivalent, Motecuhzoma, for two reasons. First, Topiltzin Quetzalcoatl and Motecuhzoma were on the boundaries of adjacent cycles, so they share affinities because they belong to the same cycle series. Second, they are alike because both of them exhibit attributes that are typical of boundary personages in a more general sense. The qualities that mark Topiltzin Quetzalcoatl as a boundary figure and thus link him to Motecuhzoma include his birth from deities or by parthenogenic conception and a relationship with a counterpart in a "twinning" effect, as well as his positioning in the historical traditions as both the first and last kings of Tollan.

The stories about Topiltzin Quetzalcoatl are also similar to the accounts of Huitzilopochtli (recall that the births of Motecuhzoma I and II are also linked to that of Huitzilopochtli) in that both of these personages exist in the documents as both mortal men and gods. They are thus included in the category known as "man-god" or "hombre-díos" (López Austin 1973). Quetzalcoatl and Huitzilopochtli appear in the cosmogonic passages (e.g., in the *Historia de los Mexicanos por sus Pinturas*) as creator deities, but they also can be found in the historical episodes as human leaders of their respective groups, the Toltecs and the Mexica Aztecs. Thus, just as with Huitzilopochtli (Chapter 3), some accounts of Topiltzin Quetzalcoatl place him in the realm of the gods, some at the boundary of that realm and the realm of mortals, and some within totally mundane contexts, treating him as an ordinary man.

As a man-god, Topiltzin Quetzalcoatl was born from similar beings, having both divine and mortal attributes. His father is often given as the warrior deity Mixcoatl or Iztacmixcoatl (the husband of

the genetrix ♀Ilancueitl in Chapter 3), who was also known as Camaxtli. Mixcoatl ("Cloud-Serpent") is also associated with Tlahuizcalpantecuhtli ("Dawn-Lord," the Morning Star), the Venus aspect of
the deity Quetzalcoatl (Davies 1979:20). Other accounts name his
father as Totepeuh, a brother of Mixcoatl in the *Leyenda de los Soles*
and considered to be the same person as Mixcoatl (Davies 1977:429,
460). In addition to their deity manifestations, both Mixcoatl and
Totepeuh are treated as mortal rulers in the histories (e.g., Davies
1977, 1979). Ixtlilxochitl (1975:272, 398, 530; 1977:29) of the Aculhua tradition gives the father of Topiltzin as King Tecpancaltzin or
Iztaccaltzin, a mortal with apparently no divine associations. On
the other hand, his mother is virtually always given as one of the
mother-earth goddess manifestations. She is usually named ♀Chi-
malman ("Shield-Resting"), but ♀Coatlicue and ♀Xochiquetzal also
appeared in this role (Davies 1979:22; also, see below).

In addition to having divine parents, Topiltzin Quetzalcoatl was
conceived in an unnatural, miraculous way within the womb of
his mother, ♀Chimalman. According to the *Codex Ríos* commentary (1831:175–176), during the age of the fourth "sun" (the immediately preceding era), a messenger was sent from the supreme
deity to ♀Chimalman in Tollan to say that she would conceive a
son without connection to a man. ♀Chimalman was living with her
two sisters, ♀Xochitlicue ("Flower-Her Skirt") and ♀Coatlicue (elsewhere the mother of Huitzilopochtli). Although her two sisters died
of fright at the apparition, ♀Chimalman survived and did conceive
Quetzalcoatl, also known as Topiltzin, in this manner.

Other versions of Topiltzin's parthenogenic conception, in Fr.
Mendieta's history and the *Anales de Cuauhtitlan*, are remarkably
similar to the story of the conception of Motecuhzoma I in the
Crónica Mexicayotl. In the *Anales de Cuauhtitlan* (1975:7), where
his complete name is given, Ce Acatl Topiltzin Quetzalcoatl was
conceived when his mother, ♀Chimalman, swallowed a *chalchihuitl*, a precious jewel. His father, Totepeuh, had been dead for several years before this event, so he had no part in siring his son. In
the version relayed by Mendieta (1945:89), ♀Chimalman found the
chalchihuitl while sweeping, a detail that links this account to the
stories of the conception of Huitzilopochtli and of Guatezuma by
a virgin (♀Coatlicue, another mother goddess aspect) sweeping the
temple.

The *chalchihuitl* is the same object that impregnated ♀Miahuaxi-

huitl of Cuauhnahuac, indicating a relationship between Motecuhzoma I and Topiltzin Quetzalcoatl. The episodes of ♀Chimalman in
the *Anales de Cuauhtitlan* and of ♀Miahuaxihuitl in the *Crónica
Mexicayotl* are further merged and inverted in the *Leyenda de los
Soles* (1975:124). Here the story also takes place during the time of
the fourth sun, prior to the final creation. In this account Mixcoatl, a
hunter and warrior, went to conquer Huitznahuac, where he encountered ♀Chimalman. Huitznahuac refers to the south, a detail that
again relates ♀Chimalman to ♀Coatlicue, mother of the four hundred
Huitznahua, and to ♀Miahuaxihuitl and the Culhuacan princesses,
women of the agricultural south.

According to the story, ♀Chimalman, totally naked, approached
the advancing Mixcoatl. She had a shield and arrows but laid them
on the ground, leaving her completely unprotected. Mixcoatl shot
four arrows at her, but they went around her, so she was not harmed.
He then went away and began molesting the women of Huitznahuac. These women complained of their treatment to ♀Chimalman,
who had hidden in a cave (an appropriate place for an earth goddess). She went back to Mixcoatl, and the same thing happened—he
shot four arrows at her, and as before, one went over her head, one
next to her side, one she caught in her hand, and one went between
her legs. Having spent his arrows, however, this time Mixcoatl approached the woman, took her and slept with her, and from this
union Ce Acatl was born. ♀Chimalman died in childbirth, so her
son was nursed by ♀Quilaztli (another aspect of the mother-earth
goddess, elsewhere the sister of the god Mixcoatl [Davies 1977:433]).

Although the *Leyenda de los Soles* is a prose document, there is
one crude drawing on its pages referring to the story of Ce Acatl and
giving his other name, Topiltzin, plus additional details not mentioned in the prose account of his life (Fig. 5.3). In the top center
of the drawing is a place glyph (a hill) with the word *xicococ* above
it (Xicococ is the earth navel and the place near Tollan where the
Mexica were hiding when ♀Quetzalxochitl's sacrifice was demanded;
Chapter 3). Under the hill is a supine child with the words *ceacatl*
above it and *topiltzin* beside it. This little figure is connected by
chainlike lines to his parents, ♀Chimalman on the left and Mixcoatl
on the right. Below them is another upright figure of Topiltzin (now
an adult), the place glyph of Tollan (reeds) with the word *tollan* written next to it, and the four houses (rectangles) associated in other
texts with Topiltzin's rule of Tollan, related to the symbolism of the

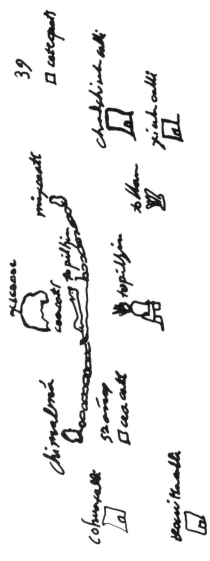

Figure 5.3. Ce Acatl Topiltzin is shown as a baby and as an adult in Tollan (*Leyenda de los Soles* 1975:fol. iv). His father, Mixcoatl, is to the right, and his mother, ♀Chimalman, is to the left. The place glyph for Tollan (reeds) is to the right of Topiltzin. On the edges of the drawing are his four houses. The hill glyph above him is labeled Xicococ.

four cardinal directions: *cohuacalli* (snake house, upper left), *chalchiuhcalli* (jade house, upper right), *teocuitlacalli* (gold house, lower left), and *xiuhcalli* (turquoise house, lower right). Two squares represent date glyphs of the years *ce acatl* (1 Reed), the year of Ce Acatl's birth as well as the year he left Tollan fifty-two years later (middle left), and *ce tecpatl* (1 Flintknife), the year of Mixcoatl's birth (upper right).

In prose and pictographs, the *Leyenda de los Soles* presents the union of Mixcoatl, the Chichimec-like warrior, and ♀Chimalman, woman of the south, as parents of Ce Acatl Topiltzin. In this text the encounter between these two is an inversion of the union of Huitzilihuitl of Tenochtitlan and ♀Miahuaxihuitl of Cuauhnahuac, although the "ethnic" identity of the major characters is essentially the same in both stories. ♀Chimalman was totally naked, seemingly defenseless, while ♀Miahuaxihuitl was enclosed in an impenetrable fortress surrounded by barriers. Yet ♀Chimalman was unharmed by the four arrows shot at her by Mixcoatl; she was defended by an inherent quality that is actually part of her name, *chimalli*, meaning shield, and further translated as "means of defense" and "armor" (Zantwijk 1957:84).

Thus ♀Chimalman was miraculously protected from the four arrows, all of which failed to hit their mark by going above, below, and to either side of her, but she was finally penetrated in the normal coital manner by Mixcoatl's "fifth arrow" piercing her in the center of her body (entry from below; union in the sexual code). In contrast, Huitzilihuitl's single (phallic) arrow found its target over all the visible barriers surrounding ♀Miahuaxihuitl, who was actually unprotected, and thus she became pregnant in a very unnatural way by swallowing the jewel within the arrow (entry from above; union in the alimentary code). In these details and the relationships they exhibit, the two stories reveal a unity that equates the products of the two conceptions, Ce Acatl Topiltzin Quetzalcoatl and Motecuhzoma Ilhuicamina.

As mentioned above, Ixtlilxochitl's history of the Toltecs, given in several of his accounts and representing Aculhua traditions, is much more mundane and lacks overt supernatural elements. Nevertheless, his version of the birth of Topiltzin is actually related to these others. The father of Topiltzin is given in several of Ixtlilxochitl's histories as Tecpancaltzin (*tecpan* = chief's house + *calli* = house), penultimate ruler of Tollan. In his *Sumaria Relación de Todas las*

Cosas (Ixtlilxochitl 1975:274–276), Tecpancaltzin was visited by a man named Papantzin, who with his wife and daughter, ♀Xochitl ("Flower"), had brought him a gift of *pulque* (maguey wine), which they had just invented. Tecpancaltzin seduced ♀Xochitl and hid her in a well-guarded fortress outside the city. There she gave birth to his bastard son, Maeconetzin ("Son of Maguey") in the year 1 Reed (*ce acatl*). His other name was Topiltzin, and he succeeded his father as the ninth and last king of Tollan (just as Motecuhzoma II was the ninth and last king of Tenochtitlan).

In a briefer rendition of the story in Ixtlilxochitl's *Sumaria Relación de la Historia General* (1975:531), the woman seduced by Tecpancaltzin was not the daughter of Papantzin but his wife (again, the principal female kin roles are interchangeable). More significantly, her name here is more completely given as ♀Quetzalxochitl. This is the same name as that of the young daughter of the Mexica leader, Toxcuecuex, who was sacrificed to bring about the end of Toltec hegemony in the *Leyenda de los Soles* (Chapter 3). She caused the same result in Ixtlilxochitl's history, playing a role as an agent in the downfall of the Toltecs. Her son, Topiltzin, succeeded his father to the throne of Tollan, but because he was the product of an adulterous union, his accession angered many people, and the empire was destroyed during his reign.

Unlike the Mexica woman of the same name, however, this ♀Quetzalxochitl had a sexual rather than a sacrificial role, as consort to Tecpancaltzin, just as the key women in the Mexica migration histories served both sexual and sacrificial functions in the conjunction and disjunction of Mexica and Toltecs. ♀Quetzalxochitl is again recognizable as ♀Xochiquetzal (e.g., Hunt 1977:84), the youthful aspect of the mother-earth goddess associated with carnal love and pregnancy (Nicholson 1971b:421). Her identity as a manifestation of this goddess further ties her to ♀Chimalman, the mother of Topiltzin in the other accounts.

The episode with ♀Quetzalxochitl, who was secluded away in a fortress by a man who had already abducted and impregnated her, is another inversion of the story of Huitzilihuitl and ♀Miahuaxihuitl, who was hidden in a fortress to prevent a man from touching her and by an immaculate impregnation was finally set free. Thus the stories of the conceptions of Motecuhzoma I and Topiltzin Quetzalcoatl are linked in a number of ways, as summarized in Table 5.1. The four episodes diagrammed in this figure are interesting not only in the

Table 5.1

Summary of the Relationship Between Motecuhzoma I and Topiltzin Quetzalcoatl
as Expressed in the Parallel Elements of Their Conception Stories

	1		2		3		4
	Crónica Mexicayotl		*Leyenda de los Soles*		*Anales de Cuauhtitlan*		Ixtlilxochitl
	Motecuhzoma I		Topiltzin Quetzalcoatl				
mother:	♀Miahuaxihuitl	≈	♀Chimalman (mother-earth goddess)	≈	Totepeuh	≈	♀Quetzalxochitl (mother-earth goddess)
father:	Huitzilihuitl		Mixcoatl				Tecpancaltzin
	mother guarded by beasts within the palace (visibly protected)	≈[a]	mother naked and defenseless (visibly unprotected)			≈	mother imprisoned in fortress outside city, after conception
	single arrow finds her (invisibly unprotected)	≈	unhit by 4 arrows (invisibly protected)				
	swallows jewel in arrow (unnatural conception, entry from above)	≈	impregnated in usual way (natural conception, entry from below)	≈	swallows jewel (unnatural conception, entry from above)	≈	impregnated in usual way (natural conception, entry from below)
	impregnated before marriage	≈	impregnated without marriage	≈	impregnated after marriage had ended	≈	impregnated without marriage
	father "too distant"	≈	father promiscuous	≈	father "too distant"	≈	father adulterous

[a] This symbol indicates a structural equivalency relating the motifs to one another.

identities posited for the mothers but also in the similarities of the four fathers.

All of the fathers have unusual sexual relationships with the mothers. In the case of Huitzilihuitl and Totepeuh, their contacts with the women are "too distant." Huitzilihuitl's part in the conception of Motecuhzoma Ilhuicamina was accomplished by the arrow he shot over the barriers to reach ♀Miahuaxihuitl. As for Totepeuh, he played no active sexual role, having been dead for several years prior to the conception of Topiltzin. On the other hand, the *Leyenda de los Soles* and Ixtlilxochitl's histories deal with men who force themselves on women outside of marriage. Tecpancaltzin had an adulterous relationship with another man's wife, while Mixcoatl promiscuously abused many of the women of Huitznahuac, including ♀Chimalman. Thus, even for the father's part, these episodes emphasize the abnormal conceptions of Topiltzin Quetzalcoatl and Motecuhzoma Ilhuicamina.

Quetzalcoatl was also an ambiguous figure because he appears in different episodes as both a mortal, the king of Tollan, and a deity, the "Feathered Serpent," associated with fertility, wind, and Venus. To distinguish these different qualities, the additional name of Topiltzin is often used to refer to the human being (Topiltzin Quetzalcoatl), and Ehecatl (the wind god aspect) to refer to the deity (Ehecatl Quetzalcoatl) (Nicholson 1979). This distinction cannot always be maintained, however, for the two roles were often combined (1979:41). Topiltzin Quetzalcoatl, the ruler of Tollan, was born of two deities and cannot therefore be considered fully mortal. Furthermore, in some of the illustrated texts, such as the *Codex Ríos* (Fig. 5.4a) and Sahagún's *Florentine Codex* (Fig. 5.4b), the king of Tollan is pictured wearing the deity attributes of Ehecatl, particularly the pointed cap (in 5.4a) and conch shell emblem (in 5.4b), but not the more characteristic buccal mask of the wind god.

Topiltzin Quetzalcoatl was also involved in a number of antagonist/twinning relationships that further mark him as an anomalous being. In keeping with his nature as a man-god, Quetzalcoatl was paired with counterparts on both of these conceptual planes, as part of the dualism in Aztec thought. Quetzalcoatl's dualistic qualities are especially prominent since his very name states that he was a "twin." As noted above, while *coatl* is most often translated as "serpent," and indeed the image of the feathered serpent has great antiquity in the New World, this Nahuatl word also means "twin."

Figure 5.4. Topiltzin Quetzalcoatl of Tollan wearing the deity attributes of the wind god, Ehecatl: (a) he enters the "Red Sea" (Tlapallan) wearing a cloak with crosses on it (*Codex Ríos* 1831:Pl. 15); (b) he is in a drunken sleep, the result of one of his "sins" (Sahagún 1950–82:Bk. 3:Fig. 14).

Quetzalcoatl was a twin par excellence, for the *quetzal* part of his name can mean "precious" as well as "feather" (León-Portilla 1983: 17–18).

As a deity, a mortal, and a combination of the two, Quetzalcoatl was opposed to the deity Tezcatlipoca and the mortal Huemac, two individuals who are also equated with one another as a combination man-god in their opposition to Quetzalcoatl. His struggles against these two figures occurred toward the end of his life, in association with the fall of Tollan (discussed below). However, an earlier battle, fought prior to his becoming a ruler, links him to the Tenochtitlan king Acamapichtli and the Mexica tutelary deity, Huitzilopochtli. This episode is found in the *Leyenda de los Soles*, the *Histoyre du Mechique*, and the parallel *Relación de la Genealogía* and *Origen de los Mexicanos*.

In the *Leyenda de los Soles* (1975:125), Mixcoatl, father of Ce Acatl Topiltzin by his union with ♀Chimalman (see above), was killed by his brothers, the four hundred Mixcoa ("Cloud-Serpents"), Ce Acatl's uncles. The four hundred Mixcoa are equivalent in this sense to the four hundred Huitznahua, uncles or brothers of Huitzilo-pochtli, who threatened him with death. Three Mixcoa in particular actually killed Mixcoatl: Apanecatl, Zolton, and Cuitlan. Ce Acatl Topiltzin avenged his father's death by killing these three uncles on top of the temple, the Mixcoatepetl, in which he had reburied his father's bones. Mixcoatepetl means "Hill of the Cloud-Serpent," further linking this episode with Huitzilopochtli's battle with the four hundred Huitznahua, which took place on the Coatepetl, the "Hill of the Serpent."

The *Histoyre du Mechique* (1905:34–35) has Topiltzin Quetzal-coatl's antagonists as his brothers rather than his uncles, the same substitution of collateral kinsmen previously seen in the various accounts of the birth of Huitzilopochtli. Unlike the Huitzilopoch-tli story, again it is Topiltzin Quetzalcoatl's father who is killed, rather than his mother. His father here was Camaxtli (another name for the god Mixcoatl), and his mother was the goddess ♀Chimal-man, who, despite her supernatural quality, died at the birth of her son. Camaxtli had other sons, but he antagonized them by favoring his youngest, Topiltzin Quetzalcoatl. In revenge, they killed their father, after which Topiltzin slew his brothers by shooting them with arrows (as befits the son of a hunting deity).

A similar account is found in the *Relación de la Genealogía* (1941: 242–243) and the *Origen de los Mexicanos* (1941:261–262). There are important differences as well: (1) Totepeuh, rather than Mixcoatl/Camaxtli, is named as the father of Topiltzin Quetzalcoatl, although, as mentioned above, Totepeuh has the same deity qualities as Mixcoatl; (2) Topiltzin has only one adversary rather than "innumerable" (four hundred) enemies; (3) his opponent is an affinal kinsman rather than a consanguineal one; and (4) the action takes place in Culhuacan or Teoculhuacan ("Divine Culhuacan," referring to one of the names of the origin-place of the Aztecs coincident with Chicomoztoc and Aztlan). Here, Totepeuh, ruler of Culhuacan, was killed by his brother-in-law, who then took over his kingdom. The usurper's name is Atepanecatl in the *Relación de la Genealogía* and Apanecatl in the *Origen de los Mexicanos* (which thereby links these two similar names; see below).

As in the other accounts, Topiltzin searched for his father's bones and reburied them in a temple he had built. Then he went after his adversary, his uncle, who was trying to kill him because he was the true heir. They met on top of the temple of Totepeuh, where Topiltzin killed Atepanecatl/Apanecatl by pushing him off the summit. Topiltzin then became the ruler of Culhuacan. The struggle with his uncle—the murderer of his father, who was the king of Culhuacan—was repeated later in the story of Acamapichtli the Elder, murdered by the usurper Achitometl, who also sought the death of his son, Acamapichtli the Younger, a story given prominence in the same two documents (see Chapter 2).

These deadly encounters with his father's murderers occurred early in the life of Ce Acatl Topiltzin, prior to his taking the throne, and appear as a struggle for the succession to his father's inheritance. They beg the question of who should succeed—a man's brothers, his eldest sons over his youngest, his brother-in-law—but in each case it was the youngest son, Topiltzin Quetzalcoatl, who, following his successful search to reclaim his father's body, was victorious and became king. Notwithstanding this early victory, in the various accounts a second struggle after he became ruler always resulted in his fall from power. His adversary this time was the *divine* counterpart of Quetzalcoatl, namely, Tezcatlipoca, in contexts that were either totally supernatural or a combination of mundane and supernatural.

The pairing of the two deities, Tezcatlipoca and Quetzalcoatl, was a recurring theme in Aztec cosmogony. Quetzalcoatl as a god was one of the quadripartite Tezcatlipocas born of the supreme male-female deity, according to the *Historia de los Mexicanos por sus Pinturas* (1941:209). These four sons, in birth order, were the Red Tezcatlipoca (who is also Mixcoatl-Camaxtli or Xipe Totec), the Black Tezcatlipoca (often referred to as *the* Tezcatlipoca, the most powerful of the four in many ways), the White Tezcatlipoca (Quetzalcoatl), and the Blue Tezcatlipoca (Huitzilopochtli) (Nicholson 1971b:398). Their order of birth is somewhat reflected in the stories of Topiltzin Quetzalcoatl in which Mixcoatl/Camaxtli, the oldest of the four, appears as a parent to Quetzalcoatl, the Black Tezcatlipoca is his contemporary and antagonist, and the final brother, Huitzilopochtli, belongs to a succeeding era, the era of the Aztecs.

As children of the supreme deity who created the universe, these brothers worked together, in pairs, to construct an order within the cosmos; this is a manifestation of the already-mentioned creator twin legends. Most frequently, one of the other three Tezcatlipocas was paired with Quetzalcoatl in one of his aspects, sometimes as companions and sometimes as opposites. For instance, this duo teamed up to create the earth and separate it from the sky (*Histoyre du Mechique* 1905:25; *Historia de los Mexicanos por sus Pinturas* 1941:210–211). However, they also struggled with one another to control the different "suns," and this adversarial relationship is more characteristic of their pairing (Davies 1979:19). In the *Historia de los Mexicanos por sus Pinturas* (1941:213), Tezcatlipoca and Quetzalcoatl each wanted to be the sun, and they alternated in their hegemony over the different world ages.

The opposition of these two deities in the cosmogony appears as well in the stories of Topiltzin Quetzalcoatl, the human Toltec ruler. For example, the *Codex Ríos* (1831:180, Pl. 14) account of Topiltzin's reign in Tollan shows him in a harmonious, paired relationship with one of the Tezcatlipocas, Xipe Totec, the Red Tezcatlipoca, working together in leading the people of Tollan. More frequently, however, when Tezcatlipoca appears in the story of the mortal Quetzalcoatl, he is the victorious adversary who forced Topiltzin Quetzalcoatl to leave his position as ruler and abandon his city and his people.

The exact cause of the exile of Topiltzin Quetzalcoatl from Tollan differs in the various accounts. In the *Histoyre du Mechique* (1905: 36–37), he had to leave Tollan because Tezcatlipoca stole the mirror that the Toltecs believed he used to control the rain (something expected of a fertility deity, which the *god* Quetzalcoatl was). According to the *Anales de Cuauhtitlan* (1975:10–11), Tezcatlipoca got Topiltzin drunk on *pulque* (which was also associated with agricultural fertility), and this resulted in such shame and guilt that Topiltzin felt he had to leave his city. In one of Ixtlilxochitl's histories (1975:277), Topiltzin committed grave sins, urged on by Tezcatlipoca, which offended other gods and brought disasters and political ruin to Tollan. The *Relación de la Genealogía* (1941:243) and the *Origen de los Mexicanos* (1941:262) state that Topiltzin left Tollan because he refused to perform human sacrifices as demanded by the gods Tezcatlipoca and Huitzilopochtli (see above; Huitzilopochtli is the Blue Tezcatlipoca). Huitzilopochtli and two of his deity manifestations, Titlacauan and Tlacahuepan (elsewhere the son of Motecuhzoma II; see Chapter 4), also beset Topiltzin Quetzalcoatl in Sahagún's *Florentine Codex* (1950–82) in Book 3, "The Origin of the Gods," a story given in a supernatural rather than a historical context. Durán (1967:I:9–15) also put the episode of Topiltzin and Tezcatlipoca's struggle in his section on the gods and ceremonies, not in the historical chronicle.

The fate of Topiltzin Quetzalcoatl following his departure from Tollan also varies among the sources. In some texts he was transformed into Venus, one of the deity aspects of Quetzalcoatl (*Anales de Cuauhtitlan* 1975:11; *Histoyre du Mechique* 1905:38; Mendieta 1945:88). In other versions he went to the seacoast (Durán 1967:I: 12) and to the place known as Tlillan Tlapallan ("Place of Black, Place of Red"; *Anales de Cuauhtitlan* 1975:11; Mendieta 1945:88; *Origen de los Mexicanos* 1941:262; *Relación de la Genealogía* 1941: 243; Sahagún 1950–82:Bk. 3:38). Ixtlilxochitl (1975:282) states that Topiltzin hid in a cave at Xicco (= Xicococ or Xicocotitlan, the entry into the earth) near Tollan prior to fleeing to Tlapallan.

The *Historia de Tlaxcala* of Diego Muñoz Camargo (1978:40), while not a principal source for this analysis, gives a number of interesting variations of the story of Topiltzin Quetzalcoatl. In this account, Quetzalcoatl was born of Mixcoatl Camaxtli and his wife, ♀Coatlicue, elsewhere the mother of Huitzilopochtli and like ♀Chimalman an aspect of the mother-earth goddess (see below, where the *Anales de Cuauhtitlan* also gives ♀Coatlicue as the mother of Topiltzin Quetzalcoatl). Here ♀Coatlicue is given as the ruler of Culhuacan, a variation of female rulership already seen in the multiple manifestations of ♀Ilancueitl, who is sometimes portrayed as a ruler. Quetzalcoatl appears as the ruler of cities in the Tlaxcalan area (as might be expected in a tradition from Tlaxcala). He was persecuted by Tezcatlipoca, but Muñoz Camargo (1978:5) added the fascinating detail that Tezcatlipoca's second name was Huemac.

Huemac is the third counterpart to Topiltzin Quetzalcoatl. The *Historia de Tlaxcala* makes clear that Huemac's relationship with Topiltzin was the same as Tezcatlipoca's by equating Huemac with Tezcatlipoca. The name Huemac means "Great Hand" or "Powerful Hand," a name also given to Tezcatlipoca (Jiménez Moreno 1956: 34). Thus it is not surprising that Huemac, like Tezcatlipoca, was paired with Quetzalcoatl in relationships that are both antagonistic and cooperative. His relationship was as partner, adversary, predecessor, successor, and the same person as Topiltzin Quetzalcoatl (Davies 1977:372–373 summarizes the accounts concerning Huemac). Unlike most of the stories about Tezcatlipoca and Quetzalcoatl, the episodes dealing with Huemac are more mundane and less supernatural, since they are the secular or historical manifestations of Quetzalcoatl's interaction with the deity Tezcatlipoca.

Ixtlilxochitl placed Huemac many years before Topiltzin, as his distant predecessor. In his *Sumaria Relación de Todas las Cosas* (1975:263–270), Ixtlilxochitl asserted that the Toltecs appeared after the destruction of the first of the five suns and that their homeland was Huehue Tlapallan (elsewhere the final destination of Topiltzin Quetzalcoatl, making the place where Quetzalcoatl ended his life the original homeland of the Toltecs). Later, during the time of the third sun, a group of people left Huehue Tlapallan under the leadership of Huemac, a great diviner. He led his people to Tollan and foretold that their end would come under the rulership of a king marked at birth by certain omens. These omens appeared at the birth of Topiltzin, the ninth king, under whose reign Tollan fell. Thus, in this story not only does Huemac precede Topiltzin by several centuries, but he also takes Topiltzin's usual place as a religious practitioner and as the first leader of the Toltecs. He is also associated with Topiltzin by predicting the destruction of the Toltecs during his tenure as king.

Huemac also appears as Topiltzin's predecessor in Chimalpahin's *Memorial Breve* (1958:8–13). This is his most complete account of the Topiltzin Quetzalcoatl story, but it gives two contrasting relationships for these two men. First Chimalpahin stated that Huemac, not Topiltzin Quetzalcoatl, was the son of Totepeuh, the king of Culhuacan, and he refers to Huemac by the title Topiltzin ("Our Prince"). Huemac was installed on the throne of Tollan, and after his death, Topiltzin Acxitl (= foot) Quetzalcoatl became the Toltec king. After stating these facts, Chimalpahin gives another version of the story, which has Topiltzin Quetzalcoatl and Huemac as contemporaries and enemies. Topiltzin Quetzalcoatl went into exile in the year 1 Reed (ce acatl), Huemac chased after him, and the two struggled. Huemac then fled to the cave of Cincalco ("Place of the Maize Houses") in Chapultepec.

The second version preserved by Chimalpahin is like Fr. Sahagún's account (1950–82:Bk. 3) in that Topiltzin Quetzalcoatl and Huemac were contemporaries, rather than successor and predecessor, at the time of the fall of Toltec civilization. Sahagún accounted for their contemporaneity at Tollan by splitting their roles between the secular and the religious, such that the two were partners in leading the Toltecs. In Book 3, "The Origin of the Gods," Huemac was the king of Tollan and Quetzalcoatl was a sorcerer, a nahualli capable of transforming his shape. (However, in Book 1, Appendix, Book 6, Chapter 41, and the Prologue to Book 8 of the Florentine Codex, Sahagún said that Topiltzin Quetzalcoatl was the king of Tollan.)

A third alternative relationship between Quetzalcoatl and Huemac was to have Huemac as a successor to Topiltzin Quetzalcoatl. This relationship occurs in the Histoyre du Mechique (1905:19; his succession after Topiltzin is only implicit in this version); the Origen de los Mexicanos (1941:262); the Relación de la Genealogía (1941:243); the Anales de Cuauhtitlan (1975:10–15), in which three other kings ruled in between Topiltzin and Huemac; and the Leyenda de los Soles (1975:125). In some of these texts, Huemac had no real struggle with Topiltzin Quetzalcoatl because Quetzalcoatl had already left Tollan when Huemac became ruler. Nevertheless, these stories reveal a relationship with the accounts of Sahagún and Chimalpahin's Memorial Breve in which the two men were contemporaries, especially in the details concerning Huemac's fate.

In the two Cano Relaciones (the Origen de los Mexicanos and the Relación de la Genealogía) there was a long interregnum after the exile of Topiltzin Quetzalcoatl before Huemac, a member of Topiltzin's lineage, was chosen to rule. Huemac, like Topiltzin before him, also departed Tollan and went into exile. As in the Memorial Breve version above, Huemac went to Chapultepec, where in despair he hung himself or entered a cave, which he never again left. He was succeeded by Nauhyotl, who led the Toltec people to Culhuacan in the Valley of Mexico. Thus ended the Toltec empire, its only legacy being the noble quality of the Culhuacan dynasty.

A similar fate befell Huemac in the *Leyenda de los Soles* account. A successor to Topiltzin Quetzalcoatl, he played ball with the rain gods, the *tlaloques*, who wagered *chalchihuitls* (jade jewels) and *quetzal* feathers that they would win. By this they meant green maize ears and leaves, the food of the people. But when Huemac won the game, he demanded real jewels and precious feathers, which they gave him. His failure to take the maize that was offered led to a drought, which was not ended until the Mexica sacrificed ♀Quetzalxochitl (Chapter 3), such drought befitting an individual who was opposed to the god Quetzalcoatl, a fertility deity associated with the rainy season.

Thus it was again during Huemac's reign that the Toltec era came to an end, and the Mexica took their place as the leading group in central Mexico, going first to Chapultepec. While the rest of his people dispersed in all directions (the diaspora that would begin the modern era of ethnic diversity), Huemac fled to Cincalco, where he entered the earth through a cave. As the *Memorial Breve* account above indicates (see also below), Cincalco was part of Chapultepec, meaning that the place where Huemac ended Toltec rule was the place from which the Mexica were to begin their ascendancy. The *Leyenda de los Soles* version is also linked thereby to the *Cano Relaciones*, which stated that Huemac fled to Chapultepec. The *Third Relación* of Chimalpahin (1965:69) refers to Chapultepec as Chapultepec Hueymacco, the "Place of Huemac," when the Mexica are said to have settled there, again tying Huemac to this site.

The same fate is found in the *Anales de Cuauhtitlan* version, an account that has other important details linking Huemac and Topiltzin Quetzalcoatl. Huemac's wife is named ♀Coatlicue, whom Topiltzin Quetzalcoatl previously referred to in this text as "my mother" (see above; she is the mother of Topiltzin Quetzalcoatl in the *Historia de Tlaxcala* as well). That Huemac's wife has the same name as Topiltzin's mother indicates a linkage of these two men via their kinship ties to the mother-earth goddess, mother of Huitzilopochtli. (It also further ties Topiltzin Quetzalcoatl, apotheosized leader of the Toltecs, to Huitzilopochtli, apotheosized leader of the Mexica Aztecs, in the same manner as the similar episodes of their struggles against innumerable collateral kinsmen on "serpent hills.") Furthermore, Huemac, like Topiltzin Quetzalcoatl, was plagued by Tezcatli-poca, whose evil influence caused the Toltecs to abandon their city of Tollan. After their dispersal they changed their name to Culhua. Huemac went to Cincalco at Chapultepec, to a cave where he hanged himself.

A slightly different pairing of these two figures occurs in the *Historia Tolteca-Chichimeca* (1976:133–135), an illustrated prose document little utilized in this analysis since it deals primarily with the history of the Puebla region, east of the Valley of Mexico. However, the text begins with the fate of the Toltecs. Huemac was the ruler of Tollan, which was home to two different ethnic groups, the Nonoalca Chichimeca and the Tolteca Chichimeca. Huemac, one of the Tolteca Chichimeca, sought to drive out the Nonoalca in order to rid Tollan of its multiethnic composition. He was abetted in this scheme by Tezcatlipoca. When war broke out between the two groups, as Huemac had intended, the two sides realized that the source of their conflict was really Huemac, and they joined together to get rid of him. Huemac escaped, but his enemies caught up with him at the cave of Cincalco, where they killed him. Both groups afterward abandoned Tollan. Quetzalcoatl appears in this document only as a deity, so, as in the *Anales de Cuauhtitlan*, Huemac plays both the role of the ruler (equivalent to Topiltzin Quetzalcoatl) who is tricked by Tezcatlipoca into leaving Tollan, and his more usual role as the doomed Toltec king who destroyed his people and fled to the cave of Cincalco.

As all these versions demonstrate, there are accounts in which Huemac was the adversary of Topiltzin Quetzalcoatl, his partner, his predecessor, his successor, and finally his equivalent, as he was also equivalent to Tezcatlipoca (see also Brundage 1982:273; López Austin 1973:35). A more complete identity between Topiltzin Quetzalcoatl and Huemac is found in the writings of Ixtlilxochitl and Durán. In a separate context from his stories of Huemac the diviner and of Topiltzin Maeconetzin, the last ruler of Tollan, Ixtlilxochitl (1975:529–530; 1977:23–25) wrote of a saintly man who lived during the time of the third "sun" whose name was both Quetzalcoatl and Huemac. Durán (1967:I:9–15), in his treatise on Aztec religion, made a similar equation. Topiltzin, he wrote, was a devout, priestly man whose name meant "Our Lord." Actually, Topiltzin means "Our Prince"; "Our Lord" is Totec, and we have already seen a pairing of Topiltzin Quetzalcoatl with the deity Xipe Totec in the *Codex*

Ríos. (Xipe Totec is further paired with Huemac, as explained below.) Durán continued to say that another name for Topiltzin was Huemac. He elaborated on this identity in an initially very confusing account of the downfall of Topiltzin, except that in his version he is talking about the downfall of Huemac. The confusion disappears once the reader realizes the two personages are equivalent.

Durán stated that the priest-ruler of the city of Cholula (whose patron deity was the god Quetzalcoatl) was named Huemac. This is the third "Toltec" city in which a struggle involving Topiltzin Quetzalcoatl occurred, the other two being Tollan and Culhuacan. Huemac was forced to abandon his city when wizards named Tezcatlipoca and Quetzalcoatl played a cruel trick on him. Here Quetzalcoatl is placed in the adversarial role against Huemac and is allied with Tezcatlipoca, whereas in the *Historia de Tlaxcala* version above, Quetzalcoatl was pitted against Tezcatlipoca Huemac! These two wizards placed a harlot in Huemac's room and then spread rumors about the presence of the woman in the chambers of a supposedly celibate priest, a gender inversion of the story of the sinless parthenogenic conception of the temple virgin ♀Coatlicue. A detail altogether in keeping with the construction of these stories is that the harlot's name was ♀Xochiquetzal, the aspect of the mother-earth deity associated with youth, lust, and carnal love, and elsewhere Topiltzin's mother in Ixtlilxochitl's account and the sacrificed daughter of the Mexica leader Toxcuecuex.

At this crucial point in the story, Durán used the name Topiltzin instead of Huemac; that is, once the act had occurred that would result in his exile. Topiltzin, insulted and shamed, left his country for the seacoast, and many years later his sons, the Spaniards, returned to avenge this cruel deed. When news of the Europeans' arrival reached Motecuhzoma II, said Durán, the Tenochtitlan king examined the ancient writings and knew that the newcomers were the sons of Topiltzin. As the Spaniards reached port, the lookouts saw them and spread the word that the sons of Huemac had arrived (Durán returned to the use of the name Huemac at the return, reserving Topiltzin for the exile).

Quetzalcoatl, Topiltzin, Huemac, and Tezcatlipoca are names given to antagonist/protagonist pairs involved in a relationship that is played out sometimes on a supernatural plane, sometimes on a mundane level, and often on both or somewhere in between. The actual pairing is quite variable: Quetzalcoatl *vs.* Tezcatlipoca, Quetzalcoatl *vs.* Huemac, Quetzalcoatl *vs.* Tezcatlipoca Huemac, Topil-tzin Huemac *vs.* Tezcatlipoca Quetzalcoatl, and so forth. The actual personages, though important in Aztec thought, take no permanent sides in this struggle, for what is paramount in this context in the histories is the relationship itself (see also similar conclusions for Maya traditions in Bricker 1981).

This multiple personality, in which aspects of a single personage can be split into an opposed pair, makes the otherwise contradictory versions of the events of the Toltec past all say the same thing: the age of the Toltecs ended when its last ruler struggled with some-one to whom he was structurally equivalent yet opposed, just as other cyclic periods (e.g., the previous "suns") ended in battles be-tween Tezcatlipoca and Quetzalcoatl, the winner and loser of which alternated. In more general terms, the beginning of a new cycle is equivalent, but opposed, to the ending of its predecessor, and this opposition takes the form of the struggle that occurs when one cycle succeeds another, all the while recognizing that the beginning and end are simply two sides of the same coin.

The twinning effect or paired opposition with someone who is simultaneously the same but different, together with a miraculous conception, reveals Topiltzin/Huemac and his deity counterpart, Quetzalcoatl/Tezcatlipoca, as anomalous and powerful boundary fig-ures. Aztec culture included a number of paired oppositions with regard to the god Quetzalcoatl. He was the patron deity of the *calme-cac*, the school for noble youths, while Tezcatlipoca was the patron of the *telpochcalli*, the school for commoners (Acosta Saignes 1946: 186, 188–189). As part of the dualistic nature of hierarchies, there were two top priests in Tenochtitlan who served the principal Aztec deities of the Templo Mayor, Huitzilopochtli and Tlaloc, both priests having the title of Quetzalcoatl (Sahagún 1950–82:Bk. 3:69). The twinning or doubling aspect that Quetzalcoatl incorporated in his name is also seen in his manifestation as Venus, the Morning Star (Tlahuizcalpantecuhtli, "Dawn-Lord"), for Venus has its double as well, the Evening Star. The deity associated with the Evening Star, Xolotl, was another aspect of Quetzalcoatl. Xolotl, whose name is translated as "Twins" (Zantwijk 1985), was the god of double things.

As the paramount boundary figure and twin par excellence, Que-tzalcoatl participated in the cosmogony, creating the earth and man-kind to people it, and providing maize to feed mankind (*Leyenda de los Soles* 1975:120–121; *Histoyre du Mechique* 1905:25–29). In keeping with this function in Aztec thought, in his more historical appearances Quetzalcoatl was the leader of the Toltecs, the people who appear in Aztec histories between the time of the creation of order by the gods and the time of the most recent people, the Chichimec Aztecs themselves. Sometimes sparring with gods, sometimes with men, Topiltzin Quetzalcoatl marked the boundary between the supernatural era, which preceded the fifth and current "sun," and the more natural or historical period of that sun, the age of the Aztecs.

On another level, Topiltzin Quetzalcoatl marked the boundaries of the Toltec era itself by existing at both its beginning and its end. Topiltzin and Huemac are one personage split into two manifestations so that he can be both the first and last Toltec king, as he indeed appears in the histories, as part of the Mesoamerican cylical view of time. When history is considered in terms of repeating cycles, the end of the Toltec era is seen as necessary for the beginning of the Aztec era. Quetzalcoatl, the leader/deity of the Toltecs of an earlier time, was replaced chronologically by one of his alter egos, Huitzilopochtli, the leader/deity of the ascending Mexica. As the *Leyenda de los Soles* and Ixtlilxochitl's histories make explicit, the end of the Toltec empire coincided with the entrance of the ethnically diverse Chichimec intruders into central Mexico. Ixtlilxochitl gave particular prominence to the most famous Chichimec leader, who led his people into the area immediately after the fall of Tollan. This man was named Xolotl, and he appeared in the Aztec past just when Topiltzin Quetzalcoatl made his exit, as may be expected since, as noted above, the deity Xolotl, the Evening Star, was the twin of Quetzalcoatl, and the two stars alternate with one another in the heavens. The historical Chichimec Xolotl, true to the pattern that has been elaborated, obtained a Toltec princess as wife for his son, Nopal (Ixtlilxochitl 1975:298). She was ♀Azcatlxochitl, the name elsewhere given to the daughter of Huehue Huitzilihuitl and a Culhuacan princess, ennobler of dynasties (see Fig. 2.2).

Motecuhzoma and Quetzalcoatl

Huemac's pairing with Topiltzin Quetzalcoatl leads further into the analysis of the relationship between Motecuhzoma I and Topiltzin Quetzalcoatl to show that the equivalence of the Toltec and Aztec kings goes beyond the fact that both are anomalous boundary markers. Both Quetzalcoatl and Motecuhzoma I are portrayed in the native historical traditions with twinlike counterparts, and other details reveal that these individuals merge with one another in some sense. The twin brother of Motecuhzoma Ilhuicamina, the *cihuacoatl* Tlacaelel, was given the additional title of Atempanecatl (Chimalpahin's *Third Relación* 1965:91; *Crónica Mexicana*, Tezozomoc 1980:240) or Atecpanecatl (Chimalpahin's *Seventh Relación* 1965:190). The title Atecpanecatl was also given to Huemac in the *Anales de Cuauhtitlan* (1975:12), which signifies a relationship between Tlacaelel and Huemac that further strengthens the already elaborated relationship between Motecuhzoma I and Quetzalcoatl (but see Davies 1977: 43, 370). Furthermore, we have already seen that Atepanecatl/Apanecatl was the adversary of Topiltzin Quetzalcoatl in the *Relación de la Genealogía*, the *Origen de los Mexicanos*, and the *Leyenda de los Soles*. Thus, this is a title or appellation given to personages who were paired in the histories with Topiltzin Quetzalcoatl and with Motecuhzoma I, as well as with Motecuhzoma II (see below).

Although the words *Atempanecatl* and *Atecpanecatl* are not identical, they were used interchangeably in the different accounts, particularly in reference to Tlacaelel. *Atecpanecatl* means "Lord of the Water Palace" (from *atl* = water and *tecpan* = palace), while *Atempanecatl* means "Lord of the Edge of the Water" (Davies 1977:43), or "the one in charge of the edge of the water" (*Crónica Mexicana*, Tezozomoc 1980:270). *Atempanecatl* was an Aztec judicial title (*Codex Mendoza* 1964:220; Sahagún 1950–82:Bk. 8:77), and a person with this title was a principal ambassador of Motecuhzoma II, sent as his go-between to deal with Cortés (Ixtlilxochitl 1977:210).

In addition, Atempan is a place name, a ward (*calpolli*) in the city of Tenochtitlan, as well as in Aztlan, the Mexica origin-place (Davies 1973:83) and Coatepec (*Crónica Mexicayotl*, Tezozomoc 1975:32), two of the metaphorical representations of Tenochtitlan. The patron deity (*calpolteotl*) of Atempan was ♀Toci, the mother-earth goddess (López Austin 1973:67; Sahagún 1950–82:Bk. 2:122). Both this *calpolli*, Atempan, and Chalman, the larger *calpolli* of which Atempan was a satellite (Zantwijk 1985:68), were said to be the home of the *cihuacoatl* Tlacaelel, who was also the *atempanecatl* (*Anales Tepanecas* 1903:51). Similarly, Atempan was the home *calpolli* of ♀Cihuacoatl, the goddess (Zantwijk 1966:182), as basically the same deity as ♀Toci. The pairing of Tlacaelel and Motecuhzoma again is confirmed as a manifestation of the pairing of the mother-earth goddess (♀Toci or ♀Cihuacoatl) with the *tlatoani* both as mortal representative of Huitzilopochtli and as the current holder of an office originally founded by Quetzalcoatl (see, e.g., *Crónica Mexicana*, Tezozomoc 1980:439).

Apanecatl is a third word that was substituted for Atecpanecatl/ Atempanecatl, as noted above (see also Davies 1977:436). Apanecatl was the name of Topiltzin's enemy, the uncle who killed his father, in the *Origen de los Mexicanos* and the *Leyenda de los Soles*, whereas in the *Relación de la Genealogía*, Atepanecatl was his name. *Apan* means "on the water" (M. Smith 1973:41), and *apanecatl* refers in general to the inhabitants on the banks or shore (*Fragment de l'Histoire des Anciens Mexicains* 1981:160), just as Atempanecatl also refers to the edge of water.

Apanecatl appears elsewhere in the Aztec histories in association with Huitzilopochtli, ♀Chimalman (Topiltzin Quetzalcoatl's mother), and Motecuzhoma II. An individual with this name was one of the four Mexica god-bearers who carried the deity image of Huitzilopochtli on the journey from Aztlan to Tenochtitlan (e.g., Chimalpahin's *Third Relación* 1965:66; *Codex Aubin* 1963:20; and *Crónica Mexicayotl*, Tezozomoc 1975:19). Another of these god-bearers was ♀Chimalman, already introduced as the mother of Quetzalcoatl and as an aspect of the mother-earth goddess. The Apanecatl associated with Motechuhzoma II appears in the *Codex Aubin*. According to this text (1963:58), after Motecuhzoma II died, Apanecatl bore the slain king's body out of Tenochtitlan to its final resting place, just as a predecessor of the same name bore the image of Huitzilopochtli on the long migration to Tenochtitlan.

All of these related names or titles—Atecpanecatl, Atempanecatl, and Apanecatl—given to Tlacaelel, Huemac, Topiltzin Quetzalcoatl's adversary, and an official associated with Motecuhzoma II have to do with water, especially the edge of water. Topiltzin Quetzalcoatl was also associated with the edge of water since he ended his mortal life at the edge of the greatest water of all, the sea, the primordial water. Huemac's fate, too, was at the edge of water, but this water was more directly concerned with the Tenochca in geopolitical rather than cosmological terms. It was at the edge of the valley's lake system, at the source of their drinking water, Chapultepec, that Huemac died.

With Chapultepec, the correlation of Tenochtitlan's dynastic history with Toltec history is complete, for this place was associated with the other boundary figure, equivalent to the final Toltec king, namely, the final Tenochtitlan king, Motecuhzoma II. The second Motecuhzoma reveals an affinity with Huemac (just as Motecuhzoma I is more associated with Topiltzin Quetzalcoatl) in that he, too, tried to flee to Cincalco-Chapultepec, to end his days with Huemac. The story of Motecuhzoma II's unsuccessful attempt to escape from Tenochtitlan before the Spaniards arrived is told in the *Florentine Codex* of Sahagún (1950–82:Bk. 12:26), in Durán's history (1967:II:491–497), and in Tezozomoc's *Crónica Mexicana* (1980:670–679).

As Fr. Sahagún told the story in the Nahuatl text of the codex, Motecuhzoma was deeply disturbed by reports that strangers had appeared on the coast (the Spaniards) and were asking to visit his city and talk with him. In anguish he asked his closest advisors where he could go to hide, and they mentioned the four following places: Mictlan, Tonatiuhichan, Tlalocan, and Cincalco. Motecuhzoma decided to go to Cincalco, but in the end he was too weak and dispirited to go. These four places are actually mythical locations (Sahagún 1950–82:Bk. 12:26), at the four corners of the world, where the earth's surface meets the supernatural realm. Mictlan, the place of the dead, is identified with the north; Tonatiuhichan, the place of the sun, with the east; Tlalocan, the paradise of Tlaloc, the rain deity, with the south; and Cincalco, the house of maize, with the west. The corresponding Spanish text authored by Sahagún (1956: Bk. 12:35) provides the information that Cincalco was a cave near Chapultepec, west of Tenochtitlan (see also above, where these two places are correlated).

The other two narratives that include this episode, part of the Crónica X tradition, are more detailed. Unlike Sahagún's account, they stress that the trip was secret, that it was almost accomplished, and that Huemac had a part in it. Durán related in his history that after many omens appeared to the Aztecs indicating that their empire was doomed, Motecuzhoma decided to flee to Cincalco. Since Cincalco was ruled by Huemac, his permission was needed to go there. Motecuhzoma sent his messengers to Huemac with gifts of human skins (associated with annual sacrifices to the god Xipe Totec), asking that he be allowed to reside there. At the cave entrance of Cincalco, the messengers met Huemac's servant, Totec (= Xipe Totec), who took them to Huemac. Here is an association between Xipe Totec and Huemac (see also Broda 1970:255; Krickeberg 1966:210) that is similar to the partnership of Xipe Totec and Topiltzin Quetzalcoatl in the *Codex Ríos*, where Xipe was Topiltzin's assistant.

Huemac's message to Motecuhzoma was that he should stay in Tenochtitlan and accept his fate. Motecuhzoma persisted in his decision, however, and sent his messengers back to Cincalco to receive further instructions on how to prepare for his journey there. He was told that Huemac would meet him on the hill of Chapultepec and that when Motecuhzoma saw Huemac, he was to go by canoe to Tlachtonco, where Huemac would receive him. When the time came, Motecuhzoma went out and saw at Chapultepec a brightly lit cave. His servants rowed him across the lake to Tlachtonco (Fig. 5.5), and there he waited for Huemac. But that night a priest in the temple was told in a dream that Motecuhzoma was escaping and that he should go after him. This the priest did, and upon meeting up with Motecuhzoma, shamed him into returning to Tenochtitlan.

The *Crónica Mexicana* version is similar and adds the significant detail that the Lord of Cincalco, Huemac, was the same as the ruler who had come from Tollan and that he was still alive because he was immortal. This account also states that Tlachtonco was not a separate place but was on top of Chapultepec. However, this text also put Chapultepec in the middle of the lake, which contradicts geographic reality, since the hill of Chapultepec was on the edge of the lake system, not in the center (but see below).

Motecuhzoma II thus became identified with Huemac, the ruler at the end of the Toltec era, by fleeing to his place of refuge, Cincalco-Chapultepec, at the end of the Aztec era. This seemingly unexpected episode is understandable when one realizes that in the colonial period Hernán Cortés had become identified with Quetzalcoatl as a returning god-king who had come to take Motecuhzoma II's place (see Chapters 6 and 7). The pairing of Motecuhzoma II and Cortés as leaders of the two confrontational groups, Aztec and Spaniard, is yet another manifestation of the paired opposition of Huemac/Tezcatlipoca and Quetzalcoatl. Just as the destruction of the previous "suns" and the fall of Tollan resulted from a struggle between two individuals who were ultimately related (Quetzalcoatl/Tezcatlipoca or Quetzalcoatl/Huemac), so the fall of Tenochtitlan was conceived as the result of a struggle between two equally paired personages, the last Aztec leader and the first Spanish leader.

In contrast to the association between Motecuhzoma II and Huemac, Motecuhzoma I was paired with Topiltzin Quetzalcoatl, while

Figure 5.5. Motecuhzoma II flees across the lake to Cincalco to escape from Cortés (Durán 1967:II:Fig. 52).

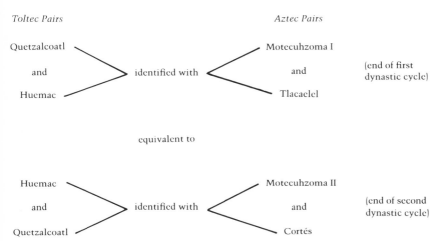

Figure 5.6. The paired oppositions expressed by the boundary figures of the Toltec era, Quetzalcoatl and Huemac, with Motecuhzoma I and II and their counterparts, Tlacaelel and Cortés, at the end of the two Tenochtitlan dynastic cycles.

his counterpart, Tlacaelel, was paired with Topiltzin's counterpart, Huemac. This series of paired relationships for the two Motecuhzomas at the endpoints of their dynastic cycles is summarized in Figure 5.6. Motecuhzoma I and Tlacaelel were "twins," working co-operatively as a "male-female" couple (*tlatoani* and *cihuacoatl*) to create a new order, known as the Triple Alliance, just as the twin brothers, Quetzalcoatl and Tezcatlipoca, created the cosmological order at the beginning of time. Motecuhzoma II and Cortés were opponents at the end of the Aztec era, just as Topiltzin Quetzalcoatl and Tezcatlipoca/Huemac were opposed at the end of the Toltec era. This battle marked the endpoint of the Toltec hegemony as it gave way to the Aztecs, and the opposition conceived between Cortés and Motecuhzoma II marked the changeover from Aztec to Spanish rule. But Quetzalcoatl also appears as the founder of his era, the age of the Toltecs, and thus Cortés became the "false" new Quetzalcoatl, starting a new era for the people of Mexico (Chapter 6).

On the Boundary

Having examined the accounts dealing with Topiltzin Quetzalcoatl and with the two Motecuhzomas, and their counterparts, it is now necessary to determine in more general terms why they are structurally identical. Their merged identity lies in the function they serve in the histories as boundary markers, which means that they should be abnormal, timeless, ambiguous, sacred, and at the edge (using Leach's attributions, noted at the beginning of the chapter). Quetzalcoatl and Motecuhzoma I and II were abnormal in their origins in parthenogenic conceptions and ambiguous in their "twinning" relationships, which were simultaneously opposed and united. They were timeless in that they appeared at both the beginning and end of cycles, and they were sacred in the supernatural quality of Quetzalcoatl as deity and the apotheosis of Motecuhzoma (discussed below).

The final and most obvious characteristic of a boundary figure is to be "at the edge." The anthropomorphized boundary markers here, belonging to both the earlier Toltec and the later Aztec eras, were on the edges of their temporal-political cycles, as discussed, but they were also on a spatial edge. They moved from the center, an island in the water (as both Tollan and Tenochtitlan are described) to the water's edge. In the case of Topiltzin Quetzalcoatl, this was the seacoast, to the east, where the earth's surface meets the sky, and thus he was transformed into a celestial object. For Motecuhzoma II, it was the edge of the more politically circumscribed Lake Texcoco system, to the west at Cincalco-Chapultepec, where the earth's surface intersects with the Underworld (the cave being an Underworld entrance), and thus Motecuhzoma has become apotheosized as an earth deity (see below). The significance of their ultimate fates on the edge of water is that bodies of water in myth often symbolize both death and regeneration (Eliade 1961:151).

These personages existed at the boundaries of many categories, and by their presence they united them. Both Topiltzin Quetzalcoatl and Motecuhzoma I were the offspring of a union of bipolar oppositions: their fathers were from the north, associated with hunters, barbarians, and Chichimecs, while their mothers were from the south, associated with farming, civilization, and Toltecs. Thus they ruled from a place in between these oppositions. Topiltzin Quetzalcoatl's palaces are described as lying between the plains and the spear house (hunting, Chichimec) to the north, and irrigated lands (agriculture, Toltec) to the south (Sahagún 1950–82:Bk. 10:166). The city of Tenochtitlan was founded at the boundary between the territories of the major political powers in the valley, the Tepanecs to the west and Aculhua to the east (1950–82:Bk. 10:196).

Here is another source of ambiguity—boundary figures are by definition on the edge, but because they exist in limbo between opposed categories, they are obviously at the center of the greater phenomenon that includes those categories. Thus, to be at the edge is simultaneously to be in the center. This seeming paradox was actually recognized in Aztec thought (Elzey 1976b). There are two terms in Nahuatl for "center." One of these is *tlalli ixco* or *in tlalxicco*, referring to the "navel of the earth" (from *xicotli*, navel, and *tlalli*, earth). This center is the " 'stable' place, the source of all creation, renewal, power, purity, and knowledge" (1976b:320). But another conception of center among the Aztecs was *nepantla*, "a marginal and ill-defined place or time, standing outside or between the normal and usual classes and categories" (1976b:325), an apt description of Victor Turner's (1972) "betwixt and between" state except that it refers to a center. As *nepantla*, the center is "a place of danger, uncertainty, ambiguity and anomaly. A place, state, figure or situation is *nepantla* when it is unstable and in transition from one status or position to another" (1976b:324).

In a stable, unchanging state, the center—the earth's navel—is the source of stability, truth, and the generative power of creation. The center lies at the boundary separating cosmic oppositions, the quadrants of horizontal space and the tripartite vertical space (Upperworld, surface, Underworld), and it allows access and communication between the natural and supernatural planes (Eliade 1961:40). From its position, the center unites these planes, thereby releasing the generative power that results from such unity. This most powerful place is the rightful locus of divine kings, such as the Tenochtitlan *tlatoani*, who was the product of a union of opposed forces and who served as a mediator between mortals and gods. However, when unity is disrupted due to change, to the transition from one state to another, which is what happens when cyclic periods end, then the center per se is lost, and what takes its place are the now-separated edges of the opposed phenomena. The center becomes the boundary, and it is uncertain and unstable.

This is what happened to the boundary figures Motecuhzoma and

Quetzalcoatl. They were born of mother goddesses from the navel of the earth and lived in centers that again represent this stable point, but since they marked the transition between periods, they also exhibited a number of anomalies, and their fates were associated with spatiotemporal edges. Their capital cities, the archetypal "sacred center" as pivot or balance point uniting the disparate planes of the cosmos, lay in the middle of water, so when these centers collapsed, the boundary figures went to the edge of water.

Although Quetzalcoatl and Huemac were more frequently associated with the fall of Tollan, in some texts both participated as well in its founding (see above; Huemac is an early Toltec leader in Ixtlilxochitl's histories, Topiltzin is the first king in the *Historia de los Mexicanos por sus Pinturas* [1941:217]; the *Leyenda de los Soles* [1975:125]; the *Histoyre du Mechique* [1905:35]; and the *Relación de la Genealogía* [1941:243]). As befits true boundary figures, they appear in the histories at both the beginning and the end of the Toltec cycle. However, thus far the two Motecuhzomas have appeared only at the middle and the end of the Tenochtitlan dynasty, at its cyclical endpoints. The fact that the founder of the Tenochtitlan dynasty was Acamapichtli, not Motecuhzoma, would seem to detract from the argument that Motecuhzoma was a boundary figure conforming to the same structural position in the histories for the Aztecs as Topiltzin Quetzalcoatl does for the Toltecs.

If Motecuhzoma and Quetzalcoatl were actually equated in the historical traditions by serving boundary functions, then there must have been an earlier Motecuhzoma, a first king of the Mexica people to correlate with Topiltzin Quetzalcoatl as the first Toltec king. Furthermore, for the argument to become more compelling, just as Cortés came to be perceived as a "false" Quetzalcoatl returning to oust the Aztecs, there should also be an end to the Spaniards' "cycle" heralded by the return of Motecuhzoma. In fact, several sources of information confirm both of these hypotheses. Not only was there a first king of the Mexica named Motecuhzoma, but native beliefs also included the notion that a new Indian "sun" would begin again with a king named Motecuhzoma.

In Chimalpahin's *Memorial Breve* (1958:16–17) and in the *Crónica Mexicayotl* (Tezozomoc 1975:15–16, written in part by Chimalpahin) there is a Motecuhzoma who was the very first king of the Mexica, while they were still living in Aztlan, the origin-place. This first Motecuhzoma had two sons. The older, who is unnamed, was made leader of the Huaxtecs, the people who lived on the Gulf Coast during the Aztec period. The younger son was Mexi Chalchiuhtlatonac, and his inheritance was to rule the Mexica, a people named for him. His older brother resented the fact that he was passed over for this inheritance and was bequeathed an inferior people, the Huaxtecs. (This is another instance of the recurrent theme of the usurpation of the elder's inheritance by a younger brother or nephew.)

Mexi Chalchiuhtlatonac led the Mexica out of Aztlan, starting them on their first cycle out of the origin-place. The second part of his name is significant because elsewhere in Chimalpahin's writings (e.g., 1965:97, 183), Chalchiuhtlatonac is one of the names of Motecuhzoma Ilhuicamina of Tenochtitlan, tying the story of the Motecuhzoma in Aztlan to the middle king in the Tenochtitlan dynasty of the same name. Furthermore, in Ixtlilxochitl's histories (1975: 530; 1977:10) Chalchiuhtlatonac is the name of the first Toltec king, again linking the boundary figures of the Toltecs and the Mexica Aztecs.

In another document, the *Histoyre du Mechique* (1905:17), the first king of the Mexica-Tenochca at Tenochtitlan, not Aztlan, is given as Motecuhzoma. According to this text, Motecuhzoma the Elder, usually considered the middle king, was the *first* king of Tenochtitlan. Thus, several versions of the traditional histories refer to Motecuhzoma as a first king, confirming his position as a boundary figure who marks the beginning and end of dynastic cycles.

As a boundary marker, Motecuhzoma should also have played a part in the generation of the next cycle of the Aztecs, the one that would follow after the eventual defeat of the Spanish (which may explain why Motecuhzoma II has a daughter named ♀Ilancueitl in the *Crónica Mexicayotl* [Tezozomoc 1975:153]). Interestingly, however, the role of Motecuhzoma as the harbinger of a new political era was strikingly manifested among the colonial period Maya. It was especially among this southern Mesoamerican people, who were difficult to subdue and who sought for several centuries to overthrow their European overlords, that the name Motecuhzoma again came to prominence, being adopted by the rebellious Indian leaders.

During the activity connected with the Virgin Cult in 1712— in which several towns in Chiapas, a highland Maya area, rebelled against their Spanish subjugators—the Virgin Mary supposedly appeared to the Indians and told them that Motecuhzoma would be resuscitated to help them defeat the Spaniards (Bricker 1981:60).

Similarly, the Quisteil rebellion in Yucatan in 1761 included the crowning of an Indian king who called himself King Jacinto Uc Canek, Little Motezuma (1981:73). In this same rebellion another man, Francisco Uex, was supposed to have had himself crowned king and changed his name to Montezuma (1981:74). Even a present-day legend from Yucatan alludes to the name Motecuhzoma as the key to the expulsion of the Europeans. In this legend, a dwarf tells the native people that he has a marvelous rope which, on the cry of "Moc-te-zumaa," would be strung across the Caribbean Sea and on which all the "conquerors" would cross out of Yucatan (1981:166). These are specific indications that the last Indian king, the one who was most clearly opposed to Cortés, leader of the Spanish conquest, must therefore be the messiahlike figure who would start a new cycle of Indian hegemony.

Furthermore, Motecuhzoma has been incorporated into the pantheon of a number of groups in Mesoamerica. In northwest Mexico, Motecuhzoma was worshiped by the Pames (Soustelle 1970:249). Modern Otomis, Tepehuas, and Nahua-speakers revere an earth spirit named Montezuma, who provides health, agricultural fertility, and other good things, and who will someday come again (Sandstrom and Sandstrom 1986:20, 251). Among the present-day Sierra Totonac of Veracruz and Puebla, Motecuhzoma is also the name of the earth god (Ichon 1973:146). In contemporary highland Maya ritual in Zinacantan, dancers known as White Heads, who wear the attributes of the rain god, are also called Montezumas (Bricker 1981: 138–139). A twentieth-century tale from Guerrero in West Mexico tells of King Moctezuma, who changed himself into an eagle to defeat a serpent who had been eating the people of a village, a role assumed elsewhere in similar myths by Quetzalcoatl (Weitlaner and Weitlaner 1943:174–175). This last myth indicates that a linkage between Quetzalcoatl and Motecuhzoma continues to the present day, a final merging of their identities as the superhuman ruler who is both first and last, and who will be first again in the new era.

An issue that requires further discussion is the role of the Spaniards themselves in the construction of these cycles and their personified boundaries. Since Motecuhzoma II would not have been the last king of Tenochtitlan had the Spanish not intervened, he became a boundary figure by default. He was henceforth marked as the end of a dynastic and ethnopolitical cycle, and his placement necessarily structured the modeling of his predecessors in the genealogy.

It has always been taken for granted that the accession of the second Motecuhzoma (Motecuhzoma the Younger) in 1502 automatically resulted in the renaming of the fifth *tlatoani* as Motecuhzoma
the Elder (Huehue Motecuhzoma). However, the dynastic model as
it has been constructed here points to a more radical name change
for the fifth *tlatoani* that occurred not at Motecuhzoma II's accession but at his defeat. The end of Aztec hegemony during the reign
of Motecuhzoma II, rendering him the last king, structured the dynastic cycle such that the middle king, and eventually the very first
king, were also to be named Motecuhzoma once the cyclical model
achieved its final form during the postconquest period. Thus, according to the present argument, Motecuhzoma the Elder was not necessarily originally named Motecuhzoma. Instead, he may have been
assigned this name based on his position in the patterned genealogy, a position equivalent to that of Motecuhzoma II at the end of a
dynastic cycle of four rulers.

This proposition—that a ruler's name was altered very soon after
the Spanish conquest—would require a profound and rapid changing
of "history" (see Introduction and Chapter 6). In fact, there is good
evidence that the fifth *tlatoani*'s name was *not* Motecuhzoma. He,
of all the rulers, is the only one with another name of significant
usage, as shown by the name glyphs in particular. This other name
is Ilhuicamina, which is represented by an arrow piercing the sky. As
a listing of his names from the different prose and pictorial sources
demonstrates (Table 5.2), the first Motecuhzoma is rarely referred to
by that name alone. He is most frequently called Huehue Motecuhzoma, or Motecuhzoma the Elder, in the prose accounts. In several
cases, Ilhuicamina is added as a second name in the written texts.

In contrast, many of the pictorial representations give only the
name Ilhuicamina, even if an added text refers to him as Motecuhzoma. The *Codex de Huichapan* and the *Genealogía de los Príncipes Mexicanos* do the opposite, calling him Ilhuicamina in the text
and giving him the Motecuhzoma glyph, the royal diadem of a lord
(*tecuhtli*). Even in the Spanish-authored illustrated chronicles, such
as the *General History* of Sahagún and the *Codex Ramirez* and *Historia* of Tovar, he is Ilhuicamina in the pictures but Motecuhzoma in
the text. Some of the pictorial codices use both name glyphs, such as
the *Codex Azcatitlan*, while in the *Codex Mexicanus* he is glyphically named Ilhuicamina at his birth and when he attains the throne,
but Motecuhzoma when he is shown at his death. In Durán's illus-

Table 5.2
Variation in Motecuhzoma Ilhuicamina's Name

A. Pictorial and Illustrated Documents

Document	Name in Text	Name Glyph
Codex Aubin 1576–96	ilhuicaminatzin veue moteuhcçoma; at death, Ilhuicamina	Ilhuicamina
Codex Azcatitlan 16th century		Ilhuicamina + Tecuhtli
Codex Cozcatzin 1572	Huehue Motecuhçuma Ilhuicaminatzin	Ilhuicamina + Tecuhtli
Codex García Granados 1700–43	Rey ylhuycaminqui	Ilhuicamina + Tecuhtli (arrow piercing shield?)
Codex en Cruz 1553–69		Tecuhtli
Codex de Huichapan 16th–17th century	Ilhuicamina	Tecuhtli
Tira de Tepechpan 1596		Tecuhtli
Anales de Tula 16th century	veve moteuhçomatzin	(not available)
Plano en Papel 1557–62		Ilhuicamina
Códices Matritenses 1559–75	motecuçoma ylhuicamina	Ilhuicamina
Florentine Codex 1575–80	veue motecuçoma	Ilhuicamina
Codex Mendoza 1541–42	huehuemotecçuma	Ilhuicamina
Codex Telleriano-Remensis 1562–63	huehuemoteuhcçoma	Tecuhtli
Codex Mexicanus 1571–90		Tecuhtli (family tree) Ilhuicamina (birth, accession) Tecuhtli (death)
Genealogía de los Príncipes Mexicanos 1554	Ilhuicamina	Tecuhtli
Durán's Historia 1579–81	Huehue Moteczoma, Motecuhzoma primero, Motecuhzoma El Viejo	combination: arrow (?) piercing diadem
Codex Ramirez 1583–87	Mutecuczuma	Ilhuicamina
Tovar's Historia 1583–87	Motecuçuma, primero de este nombre	Ilhuicamina

Table 5.2 Continued

B. Prose Documents

Document	Name in Text
Anales de Tlatelolco 1528	Ueuemotecuhzomatzin
Origen de los Mexicanos 1532	Mocrecisma, Motezuma
Relación de la Genealogía 1532	Moteczuma
Historia de los Mexicanos por sus Pinturas 1535	Iluicanminazi, changed to Mutizuma
Histoyre du Mechique 1543	Ueuemont Cumaci
Leyenda de los Soles 1558	Ilhuicaminatzin Motecucçomatzin el viejo
Carta of Pablo Nazareo 1566	Moteuczuma el viejo
Anales de Cuauhtitlan 1570	Moteucçomatzin el viejo, whose name was Ilhuicamina
Ixtlilxochitl's *Relaciones* 1600–1640	Moteczuma, Moteczuma primero de este nombre
Historia Chichimeca 1600–1640	Motecuhzomatzin Ilhuicaminatzin
Chimalpahin's *Eighth Relación* *Third and seventh relaciones* 17th century	Huehue Moteuhczoma Ilhuicaminatzin Huehue Moteuhczoma Ilhuicaminatzin Chalchiuhtlatonac
Crónica Mexicayotl early 17th century	Huehue Moteuczoma Ilhuicamina Chalchiuhtlatonac
Crónica Mexicana early 17th century	Moctezuma el viejo
Mendieta's *Historia* 1596	Huehue Moctezuma
Motolinía's *Historia* 1536–43	Huelme Moteuczoma
Motolinía's *Memoriales* 1536–43	Veve Motecçuma or Motezumacin el viejo
Anales Tepanecas (of Chimalpahin) c. 1615	Moteuhzoma Ilhuicamina

trations, the name glyph for both Motecuhzomas seems to be a shaft piercing the diadem, perhaps as a combination of both motifs (Figs. 5.2a and 5.5).

Other evidence that supports the hypothesis that the fifth *tlatoani*'s real name was Ilhuicamina and that Motecuhzoma was a later appellation comes from prose accounts that state quite explicitly that there was a name change, although they place this change within Motecuhzoma's own lifetime. The author of the *Anales de Cuauhtitlan* (1975:66) was emphatic that this *tlatoani*'s real name was Ilhuicamina. The earlier *Historia de los Mexicanos por sus Pinturas* (1941:229) provides the additional detail that his father, Huitzilihuitl, changed his son's name from Ilhuicamina to Motecuhzoma, which means "Angry Lord," because many people did not want Huitzilihuitl to be their ruler, and his anger at them resulted in the name change for his son. Despite this latter scenario, it is conceivable that his name change from Ilhuicamina to Motecuhzoma, which is probably a title (Rodriguez 1935:6), happened much later, after the conquest, in order to identify more firmly the position of the last (ninth) king with a middle (fifth) king in the genealogy.

The structural modeling of the dynasty that resulted in this name change developed gradually in the early colonial period, reaching its greatest expression in the writings of the Chalco native Chimalpahin in the early seventeenth century. Chimalpahin was the one who asserted the existence of the very first Motecuhzoma in Aztlan, corresponding to the last Motecuhzoma. In the *Third Relación* (1965: 122), he also equated the Spanish conquest with the downfall of Topiltzin and Tollan, showing that the surrender of Aztec hegemony to the Spanish was the same as the surrender of Toltec hegemony, and he similarly equated both of these events with the earlier Mexica defeat at Chapultepec, when the noble line established by Huitzilihuitl I and his daughters was ended (Chimalpahin 1958:127–128; 1965:61–62).

Chimalpahin further emphasized the sacredness of the number of Tenochtitlan kings—nine—in his accounting of Mexica history (1958:11, 127; 1965:61, 274). This point is elaborated even more in his *Seventh Relación* (1965:271–274), in which he stated that there were actually three sets (cycles) of nine Mexica kings. Up to the founding of the city of Tenochtitlan, he said, the Mexica were ruled by nine leaders. In order of rule, these were: (1) Huitzilton, a man later deified as Huitzilopochtli, who led the Mexica from Aztlan to

Coatepec (and who thus takes the place of Mexi Chalchiuhtlatonac, son of the first Motecuhzoma, in the *Memorial Breve* and *Crónica Mexicayotl*); (2) Cuauhtlequetzqui, who took over the leadership in Tollan (he elsewhere plays an important role in the establishment of Tenochtitlan); (3) Acacitli (see Chapter 3, in which he is described as a son of Huitzilihuitl the Elder; he is also frequently named as one of the founders of Tenochtitlan); (4) Citlallitzin; (5) Tzimpan; (6) Tlazotzin; (7) Toxcuecuex (see Chapter 3, in which he is described as the father of the sacrificed ♀Quetzalxochitl); (8) Huehue Huitzilihuitl, their first leader with royal blood, who was taken prisoner at Chapultepec and whose noble line died out with the sacrifice of his daughters in Culhuacan (Chapter 3); and (9) Tenoch, who took over the leadership of the Mexica while they were in Tizaapan and established Tenochtitlan, the city with his name, in 2 Reed, the year-binding year.

With this act—the founding of the capital city—the first cycle of nine leaders was completed. Then came the nine kings of Tenochtitlan, from Acamapichtli to Motecuhzoma II, prior to the arrival of the Spaniards. After the Spanish *entrada* (the essential act that created a boundary for Chimalpahin), there were nine more rulers of Tenochtitlan, beginning with Cuitlahuac and Cuauhtemoc, who surrendered to Cortés, up to the ninth, a grandson of Ahuitzotl, after which Tenochtitlan was deprived of having Spanish-controlled native governors. Chimalpahin's counterpart from Texcoco, Ixtlilxochitl (1975:276, 530; 1977:31), writing at the same time, stated that there were nine kings of Tollan, with Topiltzin as the last and Chalchiuhtlatonac as the first, again equating the Toltec era with the Aztec era in his use of this ritual number. The structure of the dynastic cycle and the sacredness of the number nine governed these aspects of colonial-period historiography.

These many manifestations in the various traditions of the boundary position assumed by the kings named Motecuhzoma are therefore considered to be postconquest developments, resulting from the dialectical processes involved in the construction of "history." They include the ascription of similar qualities and events of the two Motecuhzomas to a boundary figure of an earlier era, Topiltzin Quetzalcoatl/Huemac. Thus the next logical question to be addressed is whether the Quetzalcoatl/Huemac episodes were pre-Hispanic stories later applied to the creation of historical accounts dealing with Motecuhzoma I and II, or on the contrary, whether the stories of both Motecuhzoma and Quetzalcoatl developed in concert with one another during the postconquest period.

The following chapter presents the case for the latter hypothesis, showing how the defeat of the Aztecs at the hands of the Spaniards was projected into the past as the defeat of an earlier people and their king, Topiltzin Quetzalcoatl, who was modeled on a pre-Hispanic deity. An analysis of the stories of Topiltzin Quetzalcoatl of Tollan, detailed in Chapter 6, not only places the pre-Hispanic existence of this king in doubt but also provides an example of how quickly and profoundly the Spanish conquest influenced colonial-period Aztec conceptions of their past accomplishments, their present situation, and their hopes for the future.

Chapter 6

The Creation of Topiltzin
Quetzalcoatl

The cyclical patterning of the Tenochtitlan genealogy and the structural equivalence between the Tenochtitlan kings named Motecuhzoma and the Toltec king Topiltzin Quetzalcoatl have a strong postconquest component. The intervention of the Spaniards in 1519 was
the singular event that rendered Motecuzhoma the last pre-Hispanic
tlatoani, set the pattern for the cyclical reconstructions of dynastic
history in accordance with Aztec conceptions, and made Motecuhzoma the boundary figure identical with Topiltzin Quetzalcoatl of
the earlier period. The saga of Topiltzin Quetzalcoatl, the Toltec king
who was both first and last, accommodated the fundamental notion
of the cyclical recurrence of phenomena by grounding the events
of the conquest in a past era. With this story of an earlier empire
that had risen and fallen, the Aztecs created for themselves a more
specific destiny of conquest and destruction after that conquest had
already taken place.

Determining how and when the stories of Topiltzin Quetzalcoatl
and Motecuhzoma were created requires an examination of the contributions of both the Aztecs and the Spaniards to the dialogue in
which the historical traditions were reshaped. With the surviving
documents in the native historical tradition written by representatives of both cultures, one can hypothetically reconstruct the unfold-

ing conversation between the two sides by which they attempted to glean from the past some understanding of their present situation. In particular, the documents that relate the saga of Topilztin Quetzalcoatl and the Toltecs can be reviewed in chronological order to reveal how fragments from different contexts coalesced into a major synthesis, an epic of great meaning and satisfaction for both the Aztecs and their conquerors.

Such chronological analyses have been previously attempted (especially Stenzel 1980; see also Lafaye 1976 and Wagner 1944), although not with the hermeneutical perspective that has oriented the present study. There are, however, several obstacles to this undertaking. The documents are few in number, they often cannot be dated to a particular year or even decade, and their authors cannot automatically be assumed to represent the group from which they derive (native or Spaniard, or native of a particular city). Many voices and events are not represented at all in these traditions; for example, the Spanish authors are primarily drawn from the clergy, while most of the known native authors represent an elite stratum. Furthermore, because of the early, pervasive Spanish influence, by which is meant both the shock of the conquest itself and later Spanish acculturation, it is often difficult to determine which elements of the Topiltzin Quetzalcoatl saga reflect pre-Hispanic Aztec culture and which elements are already transformed.

Another factor to be considered is the presumption that Topiltzin Quetzalcoatl of Tollan was a genuine historical personage, the events of whose life have become mythicized (Nicholson 1979:39), which is the dominating paradigm in studies of Aztec history (see also D. Carrasco 1982:60 and López Austin 1973:10). Despite the fact that no undeniably pre-Hispanic (archaeological) evidence confirms the existence of a Toltec king named Topiltzin (Nicholson 1979:40), his historicity is usually maintained, at the very least, as a "working hypothesis" (1979:39). A number of lengthy studies (e.g., D. Carrasco 1982; Davies 1977; López Austin 1973; Nicholson 1957, 1979; Stenzel 1980) have been devoted to determining which aspects of Topiltzin Quetzalcoatl's life as presented in the colonial-period documents are "mythical" or refer to the deity Quetzalcoatl and which are "historical" and refer to the real priest or king of the Early Postclassic period Toltecs.

It has been suggested that the mythologizing of Topiltzin Quetzalcoatl began among the preconquest Aztecs in order to legitimize their own empire as having been modeled on that of the Toltecs (Davies 1977:344–345; see especially Davies 1987), or to justify their own rise to power by creating the story of Topiltzin's fall (Pasztory 1983:20). Other accretions to and elaborations of the story of the Toltecs are recognized as due to Spanish influence (López Austin 1973: 31). Not the least of these is the identification of Topiltzin Quetzalcoatl as a Christian saint, an idea that the Spaniards promulgated partly for their own purposes, to relieve them from the unsettling thought that God had unjustly left half the world's souls unproselytized (Lafaye 1976:186). This identification would also have appealed to the indigenous peoples as a historical link between their conquerors and themselves, and as an explanation for their conquest.

Thus, attempting to "disestablish the historicity of Topiltzin Quetzalcoatl" is acknowledged as a difficult undertaking (Bierhorst 1974:5). On the other hand, this study does not employ the ethnohistorical method. Instead, the emphasis is on how events construed as occurring in the past were manipulated according to basic principles in order to comprehend what was happening in early colonial New Spain, and the processes by which two cultures in prolonged contact became accommodated to the presence of the alien other. The following analysis further reveals the more profound meanings of the Topiltzin Quetzalcoatl saga, dealing with conceptions of the nature of rulership, which will explain why this story appears as well in the historical traditions of other cultures (Chapter 7).

The Aztec and Spanish Contributions to the Saga

What *is* known about preconquest Aztec beliefs is that Quetzalcoatl was a deity. His cult was not particularly strong in Tenochtitlan but was actually centered outside the Valley of Mexico in Cholula, a town in the modern state of Puebla (Cortés 1971:468). As a deity, Quetzalcoatl had several aspects, appearing primarily as Ehecatl, the wind (see especially Nicholson 1979). His manifestation as Ehecatl overlaps the stories of Topiltzin Quetzalcoatl of Tollan, since most of the few illustrations of Topiltzin Quetzalcoatl show him wearing the vestments and other attributes of Ehecatl (Fig. 5.4). As noted in Chapter 5, other deity aspects associated with Quetzalcoatl were

Tlahuizcalpantecuhtli, Venus as Morning Star; Xolotl, god of twins, Venus as Evening Star; Ce Acatl ("1 Reed") and Chiconahui Ehecatl ("9 Wind"), deities with date names; and Yacatecuhtli, "Nose-Lord," patron deity of the merchants, one of whose major centers was Cholula. Quetzalcoatl is also identified with Tezcatlipoca, his brother, as a creator deity and as one of the "suns." His parents were the deities Mixcoatl/Camaxtli/Totepeuh and ♀Chimalman/♀Coatlicue/♀Xochiquetzal. Also, the two priests who headed the sacerdotal hierarchy in Tenochtitlan were both given the title Quetzalcoatl.

Quetzalcoatl's attributes as both a mortal and a divine being in the postconquest accounts, as well as his other characteristics, all reinforce his function as a boundary marker. He was a twin, a creator deity opposed/united with Tezcatlipoca, a mediator who separated the cosmos into earth and sky. He thus appeared in the liminal time between the original creation and the peopling of the earth. As Venus, Morning and Evening Star, he appeared at the junction between night and day. And in the histories he was the first and last king of the Toltecs, appearing in the era that existed between the cosmogony and the age of the Aztecs.

In addition to these manifestations in the narrative traditions, Quetzalcoatl also appeared in zoomorphic form as a feathered serpent, the literal translation of his name. Serpents covered with feathers occur in Aztec art, sometimes paired with the date glyph 1 Reed and less frequently with 7 Reed, two dates that may refer to Venus as Morning and Evening Star (Saenz 1962:Fig. 7). The feathered serpent motif is actually more ancient and widespread than its appearance in Aztec culture, beginning perhaps as early as the Middle Formative period (c. 700 B.C.). The boundary-marking function of feathered serpents is also widespread. Undulating plumed serpents appear prominently in architecture as a border device found, for example, along the top edge of bas-reliefs, on stairway balustrades, on the entrance to temple doorways, and on the wall (coatepantli) around the ceremonial precinct (e.g., at Tenochtitlan, Teotihuacan, and Tula in central Mexico, and Chichen Itza in Yucatan). The antiquity and intercultural acceptance of this symbol may in part be a consequence of the logical relationship it expresses, as the union of sky (feathers) and earth (serpent) (Nicholson 1979:35).

Similarly, as a priest-ruler, Quetzalcoatl was the ultimate mediator, for he bridged the conceptual chasm between mortals and gods. The elite in Aztec society acted as human quetzalcoatls in their position as mediators between the common man and his deities, as eloquently expressed in a sixteenth-century discourse:

But, our lords,
they are those who guide us;
they govern us, they carry us on their backs and instruct us
    how our gods must be worshipped;
. . . those who received the title of Quetzalcoatl.
The experts, the knowers of speeches and orations,
    it is their obligation . . .
Those who observe the codices, those who recite them.
Those who noisily turn the pages of the illustrated manuscripts.
Those who have possession of the black and red ink and
    that which is pictured;
they lead us, they guide us, they tell us the way.
                                      (León-Portilla 1963:18–19)

This passage clearly links Quetzalcoatl with the elite, the literati who by virtue of their position owned and recited the books that contained knowledge, a symbol of their rulership over the people. The association between Quetzalcoatl and royal confirmation has already been alluded to in the discussion in Chapter 1 of the marriages arranged between intruding groups, such as the Mexica, and Culhua-Toltec royalty so that those groups could obtain the right to rule. The *Crónica Mexicayotl* (Tezozomoc 1975:43) even has Topiltzin Quetzalcoatl during his exile from Tollan mark the site where Tenochtitlan was later to be established, to more directly relate the legitimacy of the Tenochtitlan rulers to Quetzalcoatl.

Like the feathered serpent imagery, the relationship linking Quetzalcoatl to the legitimation of kingship and to ennobling Toltecs was not confined to Aztec culture but was a more generalized Mesoamerican phenomenon (e.g., D. Carrasco 1982:35; Cohodas 1978: 94). In the pre-Hispanic Mixtec pictographic documents, a personage named 9 Wind (Chiconahui Ehecatl in Nahuatl), similar to Aztec representations of Ehecatl, appears as a divine ancestor of the Mixtec royal dynasties (Furst 1978a:129; Furst 1986:58–63). A similar role is given to Nacxit, "dispenser of all legitimate authority" in Postclassic highland Maya beliefs (Nicholson 1957:255; see below), a name that is associated with Topiltzin Quetzalcoatl in the Aztec histories, who is called "Acxitl" in the *Memorial Breve* of Chimalpahin (Chapter 5). There is also a link in the Yucatecan historical traditions between Kukulcan ("Feathered Serpent" in Yucatec Maya) and the confirmation of kingship at the Early Postclassic Maya site of Chichen Itza in Yucatan (Cohodas 1978:94).

Because of its relationship to the founding or confirmation of dynasties, the Feathered Serpent is linked to the concepts of "Tollan," as the place of legitimacy and kingship, and "Toltecs," as the original civilized people. Although the Nahuatl word *Toltec* may be ultimately derived from the same root as Tollan, to refer to an inhabitant of Tollan, this was only its secondary meaning (Davies 1977:28) in the early colonial period. As used by the Aztecs, the word *toltec* referred instead to a skilled craftsman or artisan (Davies 1977:28; Molina 1977:29). Sahagún (1950–82:Bk. 10:165) elaborated on this meaning when he stated that the Toltecs had no real name for themselves and that their name was taken from their works, their crafts. In using the word *toltecayotl*, the Aztecs referred to the origin of all the arts (Sodi M. 1962:55). To be a Toltec was to be civilized, urban, knowledgeable in the arts and sciences, to live the legacy that had come down from ancient times (León-Portilla 1980:19), and thereby to have the legitimacy and authority of rulership.

As for *Tollan*, it literally means the "Place of Rushes" (water-dwelling plants), but the word also referred to a metropolis (Davies 1977:28). Many large cities were called Tollan, such as Tollan Teotihuacan, Tollan Chololan (Cholula), and Tollan Tenochtitlan (Davies 1977:32; Zantwijk 1985:35). Besides being an appellation of the major capitals, the name Tollan was used for the place where the gods reside (López Austin 1973:82) and was applied to mythical places of origin, like Chicomoztoc, the "Seven Caves" out of which the Mexica and other ethnic groups emerged (Davies 1977:37). Among the Maya this latter meaning of Tollan predominates, even though it was an intrusive Nahuatl word in the Maya area. As noted in Chapter 3, highland Maya texts indicate that Tollan was the doorway between the Upperworld and the Underworld that was used by the sun. They further state that Nacxit (a Nahuatl name associated with Quetzalcoatl, as noted above), was the ruler of the East who lived in Tollan, from whom the rulers received the investiture of authority (e.g., *Title of the Lords of Totonicapan* 1979:170).

Thus the words *Toltecs* and *Tollan* are related not simply from the derivation of Toltec as an inhabitant of Tollan but also from the fact that the terms refer to similar concepts: Toltecs as the inventors of knowledge, and Tollan as the place of origin for that knowledge. In some accounts the Toltecs were said to be the first people, or at least the first civilized people. They were responsible for inventing all the major attributes of civilization—religion, science, crafts, architecture, and calendrics (Sahagún 1950–82:Bk. 10:165–169). Hence, Tollan is fitting as the seat of Quetzalcoatl, the creator of all wisdom, the first king and the legitimator of future kings (D. Carrasco 1982:2, 4).

In effect, Tollan was the archetypal paramount sacred center from which all authority to rule was generated (D. Carrasco 1982:4, 104) and thus where the legitimacy of all later kings was confirmed (Cohodas 1978:94), a belief held by the Aztecs as well as the Maya (López Austin 1973:95). As such, Tollan was tied to related ideological notions of the "symbolism of the center, sacred genealogies, cosmogonic models, and hierocosmic symbols" (D. Carrasco 1982:3), as has been detailed in Chapters 3 and 5. Since the Toltecs were believed to have formed the first civilization, the Mexica Aztecs, like other Mesoamerican peoples, linked their own culture and right to rule to a Toltec origin in order to be endowed with a legitimating antiquity and ultimate truth.

With this understanding of presumed pre-Hispanic Aztec beliefs concerning Quetzalcoatl as a deity in his various aspects, Quetzalcoatl as a priestly title, and the role of Tollan and the Toltecs in the legitimation of ruling dynasties, one can analyze how the Topiltzin Quetzalcoatl epic developed after the conquest, recognizing at least in part the contributions of the Aztec and Spanish cultures. When the surviving texts that refer to him are examined in chronological order, they do not reveal a coherent story. Instead, the different elements—the hero's name, his rulership of Tollan, the fall of his city and his exile, and the prophecy of his return to unseat the Aztecs—vary from source to source and do not come together until the latter part of the sixteenth century. Even since that time the story of Quetzalcoatl has continued to be reworked as a reflection of Mexican national consciousness (see especially Keen 1971 and Lafaye 1976).

The first mention of the personage who would later be transformed into Topiltzin Quetzalcoatl has been attributed to Hernán Cortés (Nicholson 1957:126). In his Second Letter to Charles V of Spain, dated October 1520, Cortés included two speeches that he said were made by Motecuhzoma and that he included as direct quotations, although they had to have been translated first from Nahuatl to Maya by Cortés's native interpreter, Marina, and then from Maya to Spanish by the Maya-speaking Spaniard, Aguilar. These speeches contain the famous reference to the prophesied return of a ruler whom Motecuhzoma supposedly mistook Cortés to be. The first of them is given here in full to indicate not only what Cortés did say, but more to the point, what he did not say. The speeches do not actually mention Quetzalcoatl by name or refer to his attributes as a deity or a Toltec ruler. They do show that according to Cortés, Motecuhzoma believed Cortés to be the emissary of a great king, but not a king himself.

> "For a long time we have known from the writings of our ancestors that neither I, nor any of those who dwell in this land, are natives of it, but foreigners who came from very distant parts; and likewise we know that a chieftain, of whom they were all vassals, brought our people to this region. And he returned to his native land and after many years came again, by which time all those who had remained were married to native women and built villages and raised children. And when he wished to lead them away again they would not go nor even admit him as their chief; and so he departed. And we have always held that those who descended from him would come and conquer this land and take us as their vassals. So because of the place from which you claim to come, namely, from where the sun rises, and the things you tell us of the great lord or king who sent you here, we believe and are certain that he is our natural lord, especially as you say that he has known of us for some time. So be assured that we shall obey you and hold you as our lord in place of that great sovereign of whom you speak. . . ." (Cortés 1971:85–86)

The second speech, which Motecuhzoma is said to have made to the chiefs of the various cities (Cortés 1971:98), is nearly identical.

Both of these speeches have generally been taken at face value (Elliott 1967:51) to indicate a recognition on Motecuhzoma's part of both the legend of a returning lord and of Cortés or the Spanish king as that lord. They are said to "clinch the case" for the pre-Hispanic existence of the prophesied return of Quetzalcoatl and the role of this prophecy in the downfall of the Aztecs (Nicholson 1957: 126; see also D. Carrasco 1982:48). Other scholars who have scrutinized Cortés's letters, however, have concluded that these speeches are totally apocryphal (e.g., Cortés 1971:467; Elliott 1967:51; Frankl 1966; Lafaye 1976:150; Wagner 1944:188). Given the questionable character of Cortés and the dubious rectitude of his actions, many of which were patently illegal (Sotomayor 1979), this speech is seen as an attempt to legitimate his actions and ingratiate himself with the Spanish king, who had never given Cortés any authority to speak for him, by having the most powerful Indian leader hand over his dominion to Cortés as ambassador of the king. Motecuhzoma's "voluntary" submission to Cortés and the "legal transfer" of his empire to Charles V thereby could be used as well to justify the military actions against native "traitors" who refused to submit to their new lords. In fact, the Spaniards used a similar strategy in Peru in the 1570s, claiming that the Inca king was a usurper and had no right to rule (see Cortés 1971:468).

Cortés used his "very considerable reserve of imagination" (Elliott 1967:52) in composing all of his *Cartas de Relación*, as well as his equally considerable knowledge of legal precedent (Frankl 1966:10), as seen, for example, in the notion of a "natural lord," a Spanish term, in the speech above. His letters do not form a chronicle of the events of the conquest, as they purport to do; instead, they are a grouping of legal arguments in defense of his actions that directly contradicted the orders under which he was supposed to operate (Sotomayor 1979: 24). While these fabrications are acknowledged now, historians differ as to which aspects of the speech attributed to Motecuhzoma were Cortés's invention.

In particular, scholars have attempted to determine whether Cortés invented the story of the returning ruler or heard it somewhere. Some scholars believe he conceived the entire story, basing his phrasing and concepts on the Bible and legal documents, and that there was no such myth of a returning god or king (Frankl 1966:12; see Davies 1974:258). Others have suggested that the belief in the returning king did previously exist among the Aztecs, although no one can be sure how much of this idea Motecuhzoma accepted (D. Carrasco 1982:48; see Cortés 1971:xxviii; Wagner 1944:187). Some later colonial-period authors stated that Cortés picked up the story while he was in Tlaxcala (Wagner 1944:170) on his way to Tenochtitlan, probably based on Díaz del Castillo's (1970:158) account; or in the Antilles, where he lived for several years prior to his journey to the mainland (Elliott 1967:53; Sotomayor 1979:129); or elsewhere on the march to Tenochtitlan.

Although the writings of other conquistadores also mention a prophecy of a returning lord (e.g., Aguilar 1963; Díaz del Castillo

1970; Tapia 1963), these cannot confirm the veracity of Motecuhzoma's speech as recorded by Cortés, because all of these authors
relied on Cortés's Second Letter (Nicholson 1957:127), which had
been published in Spain as early as 1522. It is doubtful that they constitute eyewitness accounts of any of Motecuhzoma's speeches. Of
the conquest itself, only Cortés and perhaps Díaz del Castillo provided firsthand information, and both of their works were greatly
influenced by the bias of the authors, each of whom wrote to im-
press the king (Keen 1971:57–61; for other early accounts, see Keen
1971:56–61; Díaz del Castillo 1970:457; Wagner 1944:xiii–xxxiii).
The written accounts of both Cortés and Díaz del Castillo have been
heavily criticized by twentieth-century historians (e.g., Sotomayor
1979; Wagner 1944:xx), and Díaz del Castillo may not even have
been one of the original conquistadores, as he claimed to be, since
his name is not on the official list sent to Spain (Wagner 1944:xx;
see also Borah 1984:30).

In addition to the general presumption that Cortés's letters are
not to be believed, there is other negative evidence against a pre-
Hispanic prophecy concerning a ruler's return. The earliest postconquest and even preconquest (non-Aztec) documents do not mention
such a thing (Robertson 1959:30; Sotomayor 1979:100). Prophetic
history of this type was actually much more obvious in Maya than in
Aztec native traditions, and it is from his interactions with Maya individuals that Cortés may have conceived the notion of a returning
king, namely, from his own brief contacts in the Maya area (suggested in Cortés 1971:468) or from his two interpreters, Marina and
Aguilar, who had resided in Tabasco and Yucatan respectively. Nor
is there a known preconquest tradition that specifically refers to the
return (or antecedent departure) of Quetzalcoatl (Cortés 1971:467),
who was only a minor deity in Tenochtitlan religious ritual.

More significantly, there is no other contemporary confirmation
that when he first met Motecuhzoma, Cortés was believed to be
Quetzalcoatl. The speech imputed to Motecuhzoma in Cortés's Second Letter does not mention Quetzalcoatl by name, and it refers to a
man, not a god, who was supposed to return (Wagner [1944:187–188]
emphasized these points). Cortés's account of the Spanish occupation of Cholula, the center for the Quetzalcoatl cult, fails to mention
any association between the principal deity of that city and himself.
In fact, Cholula is notable as the scene of a great massacre carried
out by the Spaniards on their journey to Tenochtitlan.

Thus the supposition that with this speech Cortés discovered, and used to his own advantage, a belief in the return of Quetzalcoatl, who could unseat the powerful Motecuhzoma, is unfounded because the prophecy of the returning ruler may not have been an Aztec conception and because the speech is not associated with Quetzalcoatl. These details were added later as the story developed. On the other hand, certain details of this speech were never incorporated into the Topiltzin Quetzalcoatl epic. Cortés wrote that the ruler was a foreigner who led all the people known as the Aztecs into central Mexico and that he came to the region, left, came again, and left again. In the later accounts that mention Topiltzin Quetzalcoatl as a king, he was usually said to be a native of the area who came and left only once. Also, the speech by Motecuhzoma has him graciously welcome Cortés and thank the gods for his return, while later accounts show Motecuhzoma as fearful and anxious about his possible loss of power (Frankl 1966:11).

For the Spaniards, the account given in Cortés's letter fueled a story of their own making. They had already noticed the presence of the cross in the New World (López Austin 1973:13)—which they did not realize was an indigenous symbol (e.g., Séjourné 1960:116, 117, 122)—and many similarities in the religious practices of Christians and Aztecs. These indications, combined with their desire to believe that the Apostles had fulfilled Jesus' command to preach the gospel to all nations, stimulated the idea that not just any man had been to the New World before, and whose return was expected, but a religious man, possibly a saint who had somehow reached New Spain in biblical times. An opposing view that the devil, rather than a saint, had come to deceive the Indians with false degradations of Christian practices, was upheld by such notable clergy as Frs. Sahagún and Ríos (López Austin 1973:13), but this was a minority opinion and had little effect on the growing speculation during the sixteenth and seventeenth centuries concerning the identity of an Old World visitor.

The possibility of a saint's visit influenced not only Spanish questioning of the natives but also their interpretation of the responses obtained. As this notion gained momentum, a number of candidates were proposed for the proselytizer of the Indians, but the evidence favored St. Thomas the Apostle (see especially Keen 1971 and López Austin 1973). He was the only one of the original Apostles thought to have evangelized the Indies beyond the Ganges, perhaps even into

China. This supposition is based on the *Acts of Thomas* (Klijn 1962), one of the apocryphal texts whose stories had entered the histories of the Late Classical scholars (Barclay 1959:51). Many European authors of the time who wrote about the New World relied on the Apocrypha, which were widely known to the educated classes because of the many commentaries on the Bible (Huddleston 1967:40) and which exerted a profound influence on both doctrine and popular conceptions (Brown et al. 1978:243). St. Thomas's trips to India were easily stretched to reach as far as the new Indies discovered by Columbus.

A second reason for favoring St. Thomas was that his name was equivalent to Quetzalcoatl's, and Quetzalcoatl was now being identified with the early leader who had come, gone, and promised to return. Quetzalcoatl can be translated as "precious twin," and Thomas, whose second name was Didymus, had the same name: Thomas is the Hebrew word and Didymus is the Greek word for "twin" (López Austin 1973:21). The twinlike nature of Thomas is most apparent in the apocryphal *Acts of Thomas*, which refers to him as the "Twin of the Messiah," the twin brother of Christ (Klijn 1962:85). Thomas was thus the double of Christ, in a role equivalent to Quetzalcoatl as a twin or double, a transforming *nahual*, in various Aztec accounts. The Spanish friars of the colonial period seized on this similarity, pointing out as well that St. Thomas was a sculptor and Quetzalcoatl was said to be a creator of fine sculptures. This latter similarity was Durán's major point in arguing for the identification of Quetzalcoatl as St. Thomas (López Austin 1973:17).

The presence of a saint among the native Americans would allow for their incorporation among the people contacted in biblical times by the Apostles and would explain the similarities in religious beliefs and practices, while the supposed failure of the Aztecs to adhere to the precepts he taught would justify a new Spanish presence in the New World, both to punish them for their failings and to teach them again how Christians should live. In this convergence, Quetzalcoatl in his mortal manifestations as Topiltzin and Huemac became a chaste, monotheistic, peace-loving, monastic person who abhorred human sacrifice, in the European mold of a saint (Litvak King 1972:27).

These characteristics do not fit the "bloodthirsty" pre-Hispanic deity named Quetzalcoatl (D. Carrasco 1982:3) or the two high priests of the Aztecs given the title of Quetzalcoatl, priests dedicated to gods who demanded huge numbers of sacrificial victims. Nevertheless, for different reasons, the Aztecs, too, came to the conclusion that a very important visitor had come to Mexico long ago, and their concerns also had an impact on the shaping of the versions of the developing story of Topiltzin Quetzalcoatl. Quetzalcoatl was associated with sculptors and other artisans as part of the concept of *toltecayotl*—the origin of the civilized arts—in his aspect as a creator deity and his association with the Tollans, the centers of civilization and authority. As such, he was empowered to found new dynasties, whether it be a new Spanish dynasty or even a new Aztec dynasty to defeat the Spanish.

Thus the first foreign intrusion into the Aztec past by Cortés appeared against a backdrop of Aztec conceptions of cyclical time and of the role of the mediating deity associated with the origin-place of authority. For their part, the Spanish were intrigued by a possible previous visit to New Spain by an Old World missionary, and they also wanted to explain and justify the conquest, a desire they shared with the people they subjugated. In this setting were composed the first accounts in the native historical tradition that were to become part of the Topiltzin Quetzalcoatl story, and those which have survived date back to only a decade after the conquest.

The Developing Saga

Significantly, the earliest historical accounts detailing Topiltzin's activities were written by Franciscan friars, not by a native author. They are the two *Cano Relaciones* (the *Origen de los Mexicanos* [1941:261–263] and the *Relación de la Genealogía* [1941:241–243], written c. 1532), which tell the story of Topiltzin and his father, Totepeuh, the ruler of "old" Culhuacan who was killed by his brother-in-law, Atepanecatl/Apanecatl. Topiltzin became ruler of Culhuacan after killing his uncle, but later he took all the artisans (= *toltecs*) to Tollan. At Tollan the gods Huitzilopochtli and Tezcatlipoca ordered him to institute human sacrifice, something Topiltzin refused to do, so he left for Tlapallan, where he died. Huemac, who succeeded him in Tollan, ruled prosperously for many decades until an ugly phantasm appeared, which Huemac interpreted as a sign of the gods' displeasure. He then left Tollan for Chapultepec, where he hung himself. Thus the dynasty in Tollan begun by Topiltzin, who

had taken his people there from the origin-place, was ended by Huemac, his double, at Chapultepec, since the next ruler took the people
to the new Culhuacan in the Valley of Mexico.

Many important story elements are already present at this early
date: the entirely historical quality of the account, the name Topiltzin ("Our Prince") for the hero, his father Totepeuh, his rulership of
Tollan, the association with artisans, his opposition to the antagonist Tezcatlipoca/Huitzilopochtli, his refusal to sacrifice humans,
his exile in Tlapallan, and the succession of Huemac, who ended his
life in Chapultepec. The *Relación de la Genealogía* adds an additional significant detail concerning Topiltzin: his clothing was like
that of the Spaniards. This may be the first preserved mention of
the later lavishly embellished association between Topiltzin Quetzalcoatl and Cortés.

Even more interesting, however, are the murder of Topiltzin's
father and the usurpation of his throne in Culhuacan, resulting in
the founding of the Tollan dynasty. This episode never became part
of the later Topiltzin Quetzalcoatl story, but it is significant in that
it links Topiltzin to the episode of Achitometl's slaying of Acamapichtli the Elder in the "new" Culhuacan, an act that led to the
founding of the Tenochtitlan dynasty, as emphasized in these same
two documents. This is clear evidence of the cyclical nature of historical time, resulting in the repetition of events in the dynastic
histories pertaining to centers related to one another in an evolutionary sense, the Tollan dynasty preceding the Culhuacan dynasty,
which both presupposed and legitimated the Tenochtitlan dynasty.
Thus an important aspect of the creation of Tenochtitlan history—
projecting events in the Aztec era back to a prior, legitimating era—
is found in these early surviving examples of Aztec historiography,
linking the Aztec kings to their Toltec (really Culhua at this stage)
counterparts.

It should also be noted that other major elements of the later
Topiltzin Quetzalcoatl saga do *not* occur in these texts. First, the
name Quetzalcoatl itself is missing; instead, the hero is named only
Topiltzin, which is actually a royal title, an heir designation. Also,
the city of Tollan is deemphasized, appearing as a way station between the old and new Culhuacans, where the same event—the murder and usurpation by a relative—was repeated. Although the Culhua
are linked to the Toltecs, who are artisans, true to their name, the
dynastic history of Tollan is diminished to only two kings, who are
structurally equivalent.

The matter-of-fact, historical quality of these two parallel accounts is at variance with documents of an approximately contemporary date also written by Franciscans. The *Historia de los Mexicanos por sus Pinturas*, probably written by Fr. Andrés de Olmos (Wilkerson 1974) in about 1535, is much more cosmological in content, dealing with the creation and ordering of the universe by the gods and leading into the history of the different ethnic groups in the Valley of Mexico. This document adds two more personalities who would later be merged with Topiltzin Quetzalcoatl. One was Quetzalcoatl, the creator deity who played a prominent role in the cosmogony (*Historia de los Mexicanos por sus Pinturas* 1941:209–213), and in a separate context, Ce Acatl (1 Reed), a mortal, son of Camaxtli (1941:217–218).

Unlike the peaceful Ce Acatl Topiltzin Quetzalcoatl of the later transformations of the story, this Ce Acatl was a great warrior, although he also performed penances like a priest. The people of Tollan made him their first king because they admired his military prowess. Later Tezcatlipoca appeared to tell Ce Acatl that he was to go to Tlapallan. All the people of Tollan left with him, but they went only as far as Cholula, while Ce Acatl went on to Tlapallan, where he died. The story of Ce Acatl here is similar to the Topiltzin story of the two *Cano Relaciones* above, but with different names for the hero and his father. Huemac does not appear, Culhuacan is not mentioned, and as noted, Ce Acatl is much more warlike than the later Topiltzin Quetzalcoatl. Nevertheless, two important new details are apparent: Cholula, cult center of the god Quetzalcoatl, and Ce Acatl, a date name associated with the east and with Venus as Morning Star, an aspect of the deity Quetzalcoatl that further relates him to a Toltec king.

The combination of a ruler with a pre-Hispanic deity implied in the *Historia de los Mexicanos por sus Pinturas* can also be seen in documents dating from the 1540s, although these versions of the saga are extremely varied. The name Quetzalcoatl is used in a 1541 letter by Viceroy Mendoza (Nicholson 1957:132) for a ruler of the Mexica people (i.e., as a mortal rather than explicitly or exclusively as a god). This name also appears twice for both mortal and divine personages in a contemporary narrative account, the *Histoyre du Mechique* (1905:2), dated 1543, perhaps also written by Fr. Olmos. Like the *Historia de los Mexicanos por sus Pinturas*, this text deals with Quetzalcoatl as a cosmogonic agent under this name and the names of two of his deity aspects, Ehecatl and Xolotl. In addition, the name Quetzalcoatl is also given for the son of Camaxtli and ♀Chimalman. This is among the earliest known preserved accounts in which the name Quetzalcoatl is used for the Toltec ruler, as well as the first mention of the mother-earth goddess, ♀Chimalman, as his mother (see below for Fr. Motolinía's writings of approximately the same period).

In the *Histoyre du Mechique* (1905:34–38), as in the *Cano Relaciones*, there was a struggle between the hero and the murderers of his father, who here are Quetzalcoatl's brothers. Quetzalcoatl defeated them and ruled Tollan, where he was revered as a god. He was forced to leave his city by the god Tezcatlipoca, who stole the mirror used to control rain, and he traveled to other cities, including Culhuacan and Cholula. He later committed suicide and was transformed into Venus. This document thereby ties the earlier accounts about a ruler of Tollan, son of Camaxtli/Totepeuh, with Quetzalcoatl as Venus and a creator god who was opposed by his counterpart deity, Tezcatlipoca.

Another element added into this text is Huemac, who already appeared in the *Cano Relaciones* as the successor of Topiltzin to the throne in Tollan. Interestingly, in the *Histoyre du Mechique* (1905: 19) his story is separated from that of the god-king Quetzalcoatl. Huemac is referred to here as the ruler of the Culhua people after they had left (old) Culhuacan and were living in Tollan. Again, there is an emphasis on Culhuacan, rather than Tollan, as the homeland of the original civilized, legitimating pre-Aztec people, although they resided at one point in Tollan, which again serves as the doorway between the "Old" or "Divine" Culhuacan, in the realm of the gods, and the real Culhuacan south of Tenochtitlan. As in the *Cano Relaciones*, Huemac saw an apparition that frightened him into leading the people out of Tollan, but instead of fleeing to Chapultepec, he went on to found the new city of Culhuacan in the Valley of Mexico. In this respect the same text thus has two rulers who departed Tollan in separate contexts, Quetzalcoatl, who committed suicide (something Huemac is noted for in later texts), and Huemac, who continued the civilization of the Culhua-Toltecs by establishing their ultimate city. Already at this early date there is a structural equivalence of these two personages as part of the cyclical construction of the past.

The influence on the Topiltzin Quetzalcoatl story of the works by another Franciscan, Fr. Motolinía (1903:12–13; 1951:81–82) is difficult to assess strictly in chronological terms because his writings cannot be pinned down more specifically than the period 1536–43. His surviving accounts have many of the details presented above as well as some new slants on the story, including an emphasis on the hero as a chaste and penitent preacher. Quetzalcoatl is given as the son of ♀Chimalman and of Iztacmixcoatl (equivalent to Mixcoatl/Camaxtli/Totepeuh), after his marriage to ♀Ilancueitl as the father of all mankind (Chapter 3). Motolinía asserted that Quetzalcoatl was the ancestor of the Culhua people and that he was later deified as a god of the air (Ehecatl) in order to account for his quality in the Aztec histories as both mortal and divine. The notion that a pagan god had once been a man who was later apotheosized was common among the early Spanish historians because of the analogy with deities of classical Europe (Las Casas 1971:51).

In Motolinía's writings, which are thought to reflect the traditions of the Puebla area rather than the Valley of Mexico (Nicholson 1957: 76), the story of the exiled ruler of Tollan is missing, and Quetzalcoatl is still associated primarily with Culhuacan and with Cholula, a city near Puebla. His relationship with Cholula appears in a separate context (Motolinía 1951:137–138), where he is again described as the god of air, as the principal god of Cholula, and as a native of Tollan. Despite the omission of his rulership and exile, there is an important new element that would later appear in the developed Topiltzin Quetzalcoatl story: the linking of Quetzalcoatl, the god of the air, with a god who left and whose return was expected, a return supposedly associated with the arrival of the Spaniards. Here is the prophecy of the return, although it is not associated with a Toltec priest-ruler. Thus Motolinía has been credited with developing the legend of the return of Quetzalcoatl (Cortés 1971:467; Frankl 1966:13; Stenzel 1980:19–23; but see Wagner 1944:192) and with associating this return with the coming of the conquistadores.

The *Historia Tolteca-Chichimeca* (1976:133–135), written after 1544, is also from the Puebla area, but it belongs to the historical rather than cosmogonical side of this saga, recounting the fall of the Toltecs with Huemac, not Quetzalcoatl, as the ruler of Tollan who was tricked by the god Tezcatlipoca. He was killed at the cave of Cincalco, the first mention of this place in connection with Huemac since in an earlier text he had gone to Chapultepec (although these two locales became equivalent, especially as they are both associated with the boundaries in the west). Quetzalcoatl does appear in this document, but only as a deity—in fact, as the supreme deity, since he is addressed by the names Tloque Nauque and Ipalnemouani, names usually reserved for the supreme god, Ometeotl (León-Portilla 1974b:164). As in Motolinía's works, Quetzalcoatl is associated with Cholula rather than Tollan.

At about the same time, 1542 or 1543, the Spaniard Andrés de Tapia wrote an account of the conquest. He stated (Tapia 1963:34) that the principal god of Cholula, Quetzalcoatl, had once been a man who refused to allow human sacrifice and other violent acts, characteristics that appeared in Motolinía's writings as well. Tapia added that Quetzalcoatl wore a white tunic like a monk's cassock that was covered with red crosses, further associating him with a monastic, even Christian, figure. This tunic as described by Tapia is actually illustrated in the *Codex Ríos* drawing made several decades later of Quetzalcoatl, ruler of Tollan, in his guise as Ehecatl, the wind deity (Fig. 5.4a), although these crosses may have been a pre-Hispanic decorative motif. Tapia (1963:39) also summarized the speech from Cortés's letter, supposedly made by Motecuhzoma, but unlike Motolinía, he did not connect the statements about a returning ruler with the god of Cholula he had described.

Cortés's chaplain, Francisco López de Gómara (Wagner 1944:190), utilized the writings of Tapia and others to write a history of the conquest that has been called a political and military rationale for the actions of the Spanish (Frankl 1966:13). Writing in this same decade, López de Gómara did link Quetzalcoatl of Tollan with the sovereign who was to return and referred to him as a fair-skinned king (Stenzel 1980:26). It was Fr. Bartolomé de Las Casas (1971:53–55), however, who was the great propagator of the "white god" legend (López Austin 1973:15). Writing in 1555–59, Las Casas described Quetzalcoatl, the god of Cholula who, he said, had come from Yucatan, as a white man with large eyes, long black hair, and a large, round beard. Quetzalcoatl taught the Indians the art of silverworking, one of the Toltec arts, and prohibited human and animal sacrifice as well as any kind of violence. He left Cholula and went to the sea but told the people that his brothers, bearded white men like himself, would come back across the sea from the east. When he died, he was converted into a star. Las Casas added the information that in Tlaxcala he was worshiped under a different name, Camaxtli, or was the son of Camaxtli (a detail found in some of the Topiltzin Quetzalcoatl stories). Las Casas's work thus emphasizes the return of Quetzalcoatl and the identification of the Spaniards with the fulfillment of this prophecy, but he did not associate Quetzalcoatl with the other stories of the ruler of Tollan.

Contemporary with Las Casas's work is the *Leyenda de los Soles* (1975:124–125), written in 1558, a native-authored account in Nahuatl that is more like the earlier *Historia de los Mexicanos por sus Pinturas* and the *Histoyre du Mechique* in its cosmogonic aspects than its immediate predecessors in historical writing undertaken by Spaniards. In this text, a distinction is still maintained between the creator god, Quetzalcoatl, and the ruler of Tollan, son of Mixcoatl and ♀Chimalman, similar to Motolinía's history. The *Leyenda de los Soles* has the hero—named Ce Acatl, as in the *Historia de los Mexicanos por sus Pinturas*—traveling and making many conquests, going as far as Tlapallan, where he died. It does not refer to his rulership of Tollan except at his death, when his successor, Huemac, is mentioned. It is also only at this point in the document that the name Topiltzin is used instead of Ce Acatl. In other words, the author appears to refer to the several different existing storylines without actually connecting them himself in a systematic manner.

A Nahuatl poem, one of the *Cantares Mexicanos* (Census #GG 1019, see below in Appendix; Garibay K. 1964–68:III:1–2) possibly collected by Sahagún and dating from the period 1550–65, does refer to the exile of Topiltzin, here additionally named Nacxitl ("Four-Foot"), from Tollan and his death in Tlapallan. It does not give the name Quetzalcoatl or any reason for the exile. This text may reflect an ancient and widespread association between Nacxitl, legitimator of dynasties, and Tollan, that is also found in Maya historical traditions (see above).

The *Codex Ríos*, dating from c. 1566–89 but thought to be a copy of an earlier work, c. 1562–63, also provides information about Quetzalcoatl as ruler and deity, but again in separate contexts. According to the text of this document (*Codex Ríos* 1831:175–176), Quetzalcoatl lived during the fourth "sun." His divine character is marked by his miraculous conception within the womb of ♀Chimalman, and his father, so important in other accounts, has been eliminated. The parallels between this story and the conception of Jesus by the Virgin Mary are quite obvious. Quetzalcoatl again appears as the wind god and a creator god whose ceremony was celebrated on the date 1 Reed (*ce acatl*) in the town of Cholula, because this was the date he disappeared. Elsewhere in this account, where the various Aztec gods are described, Quetzalcoatl is named as the wind god (Ehecatl), the Morning Star (Tlahuizcalpantecuhtli, who has the 1 Reed sign), and as an actual feathered serpent. Tezcatlipoca also appears several times and is referred to as the one who tricked Quetzalcoatl, but this episode is not mentioned in the text relating the story of Quetzalcoatl. In all these aspects, Quetzalcoatl was clearly considered to be a deity.

Nevertheless, in the section on Quetzalcoatl's life during the fourth sun, the author stated that his other name was Topiltzin and that he, together with Xipe Totec, was a leader of the Toltec people. He led his people out of Tollan and populated the world with them, finally entering the "Red Sea" (Fig. 5.4a), a reference to Tlapallan ("Place of Red"), but this reference and other aspects of the story equate him with the biblical Moses. The text continues, saying that Quetzalcoatl told his people to expect his return, and because he was born in the year 1 Reed, the year the Spaniards came, the Indians believed Cortés was their returning god, who had foretold the arrival of a "bearded nation." In this section dealing with Toltec history, however, the illustrations depict Topiltzin Quetzalcoatl in the guise of Ehecatl, the wind deity, as noted above.

This document, which seems to deal with Quetzalcoatl the deity, thus identifies him with Topiltzin of Tollan, who went to Tlapallan, although the story takes place within a supernatural context during the time of the previous sun. The text fails to give other elements of the Topiltzin of Tollan story but does speak of the prophecy of his return and the belief that the Spaniards were at first identified with this god. Even at this late date, several decades after the conquest, the separate details of the saga of Topiltzin Quetzalcoatl had apparently not coalesced into that single story, often cited as having a historical reality, about a king of Tollan who left his city and went into exile.

The first synthesis fully to associate and elaborate Topiltzin Quetzalcoatl of Tollan (priest and ruler), Quetzalcoatl as a creator god, and Quetzalcoatl as the returning king for whom Motecuhzoma mistook Cortés has been credited to Fr. Sahagún (Elliott 1967:52; Frankl 1966:14; Stenzel 1980; Wagner 1944:192). Sahagún began writing his *General History* as early as 1547, but its most complete and final form, the *Florentine Codex*, was not written until 1575–80 (Glass and Robertson 1975:190). Interestingly, the synthesis, such as it is, is still separated into several different contexts in the twelve books of the *Florentine Codex* (Sahagún 1950–82; 1956). There is still no clear distinction between the mortal and the divine, since the most detailed account of Quetzalcoatl's fall and exile from Tollan is found in Book 3, "The Origin of the Gods," rather than Book 10, which deals with the Toltec people.

All but the first two chapters of Book 3 are taken up with Quetzalcoatl's problems in Tollan. This extensive coverage is due to the fact that the many different versions of the tricks played on Quetzalcoatl by the three "demons," who wanted him to leave his city, were arranged by Sahagún as separate chapters, as if they occurred in chronological order. Quetzalcoatl was eventually forced to leave Tollan and floated off to Tlapallan on a raft made of serpents (a serpent mat is illustrated in Book 11). The illustrations accompanying Book 3, like the *Codex Ríos* depictions, show Quetzalcoatl of Tollan in the guise of Ehecatl (Fig. 5.4b), and he is acknowledged in the text to have been the god of the air and the wind.

In this section of Sahagún's work, Quetzalcoatl was not the ruler of Tollan but its priest, while Huemac was the king. Elsewhere in the *Florentine Codex*, however, Sahagún (1950–82) provided other information about Quetzalcoatl. In the Appendix to Book 1, in Chapter 41 of Book 6, and in the Prologue to Book 8, Quetzalcoatl is named as the king, not the priest, of Tollan. Sahagún said in these latter contexts that his city was destroyed, its inhabitants went to Cholula, and Quetzalcoatl went to the east, to the city of the sun, called Tlapallan, but unlike the involved discussion in Book 3, he gave no explanation for his exile. Sahagún did note that because Quetzalcoatl went to the east, his return from that direction was expected in the past; hence his misidentification with Cortés and—an important point that weighed heavily on Sahagún's mind—the continued, though misguided, hope of the Indians that the real Quetzalcoatl would still come to deliver them, this time from their Spanish overlords.

It is in this context particularly that Sahagún's work has been said to show the influence of an Aztec nativistic or revitalization movement coming together with European Christian-millenarian conceptions (Frankl 1966:14; Stenzel 1980:47–48). Sahagún's real concern was that the Indians were deceiving themselves in believing in this messianic deity, who was really only a man (Motolinía's earlier argument), and hoping in vain that he would come and fulfill his prophecy (Sahagún 1950–82:Bk. 1:69). This text also reveals how the Quetzalcoatl story fit into the cyclical structuring of space-time: Quetzalcoatl belonged to the golden age of the Aztec past—as Sahagún (1950–82:Bk. 10:165) described it, to the first civilization in New Spain, an era of ethnic unity and harmony that immediately preceded the entry into the area of the diverse, disharmonious peoples, the Aculhua, Tepanecs, and Mexica (1950–82: Bk. 8:15)—and would reappear once more to deliver the Aztecs from the Spanish.

Sahagún's Toltecs are associated more with *toltecayotl*, the origin of the knowledge and skills of a civilized people, than with Tollan, since they possess all knowledge, and their god, Quetzalcoatl, was a symbol of knowledge (León-Portilla 1961:28). However, as Toltecs, and as the first people, they must have lived in a Tollan, the origin-place associated with the legitimacy of antiquity and of knowledge. In his "Book of the People," Sahagún (1950–82:Bk. 10:165–170) described the Toltec people, their knowledge of crafts, and their city of Tollan, the first city in New Spain. He said that the city was in ruins and that similar ruins were found in many other places because the Toltecs were widely dispersed when Topiltzin Quetzalcoatl, their god and priest, went to Tlapallan. Despite this generalizing tendency to treat all ancient sites as Toltec settlements, Sahagún was the first to link Tollan (in the native histories, a sacred and mythical locality) with an actual polity, most probably the place known today as Tula de Allende in the state of Hidalgo, northwest of the Valley of Mexico, which had an important pre-Aztec (Early Postclassic) occupation.

Tula de Allende was not a ruin during the Aztec era, however, but apparently was occupied, and was even ruled by members of the Tenochtitlan lineage (Barlow 1946a:426; Davies 1987:28). Mexica interest in this site is demonstrated by the fact that the sculptural decorations at Tenochtitlan's Templo Mayor were copied from earlier artworks that have since been recovered archaeologically at Tula (Davies 1987:29; Umberger 1987). Tula was actually visited by Sahagún in the 1550s (Nicolau d'Olwer and Cline 1973:187), which may explain his ability to describe the site's feathered-serpent columns in some detail in the *Florentine Codex* (1950–82:Bk. 10:165). They are also mentioned in the *Cantares Mexicanos* poem about Nacxitl cited above, although it is known archaeologically that these columns were mutilated and buried in late pre-Hispanic times. Despite the fact that scholars familiar with Sahagún's writings have cautioned against relying heavily on his work alone without confirmatory evidence from other sources (Nicolau d'Olwer and Cline 1973:189), the very common practice today of equating the Tollan of Topiltzin Quetzalcoatl with Tula (e.g., Diehl 1974, Diehl and Benfer 1975) is based virtually entirely on Sahagún's description of Tollan (Davies 1977: 40–41; Diehl 1983:57; Jiménez Moreno 1941). This identification has further fueled arguments in favor of the historicity of Topiltzin (see below).

Given Sahagún's concern with the Indians' faith in the prophecy of Quetzalcoatl's return, it is not surprising that he was also the source of the story (1950–82:Bk. 12:11–16) that Motecuhzoma II sent to Cortés the clothing and other accoutrements of the gods Quetzalcoatl, Tezcatlipoca, and Tlaloc in which Cortés was dressed (Wagner 1944:193). The fact that Motecuhzoma was supposed to have done so is often taken as evidence that he did indeed believe the Spaniards may have been gods, and especially that their leader was the god Quetzalcoatl. Nevertheless, this episode was not mentioned at all by Cortés, nor were these objects included in the list of items sent to Spain in Cortés's letters, as they should have been (1944:193). Actually, it was Juan de Grijalva, on an earlier exploratory trip to the Gulf Coast of Mexico in 1518, who had been given gifts, including some mosaic masks, to which Sahagún was probably referring (1944:193–194). There is no indication, however, that these masks were the vestments of Quetzalcoatl, and Sahagún's story of the initial mistaking of Cortés for Quetzalcoatl has been called "pure fancy" (1944:194). This judgment is too strong; in fact, this episode is entirely in keeping with the postconquest development of the Topiltzin Quetzalcoatl epic.

Like these "vestments of Quetzalcoatl," the fears and doubts of Motecuhzoma that supposedly rendered him incapable of fighting the Spaniards are considered a late postconquest elaboration (Sotomayor 1979:104–105), especially by Sahagún (1950–82:Bk. 12), as part of the story of the return of Quetzalcoatl. This view of Motecuhzoma's attitude toward the Spaniards is contrary to the statements attributed to him by Cortés in his Second Letter, which relates that Motecuhzoma welcomed Cortés as the ambassador of the returning king. The anguish suffered by Motecuzhoma at the thought of losing his empire to the returning god-king was said to result from many omens and other portents that heralded the coming defeat. Such omens are referred to as early as the 1536 inquisitional proceedings against Martín Ocelotl (Stenzel 1980:75). Motecuhzoma's anxiety was also noted in the works of Motolinía (1980:19), which date to about the same time. All these omens and signs must have been added to the histories after the conquest in order to show that it had been predicted (1980:77) as part of both the Aztec cyclical view of space-time and the traditional reactions of European Christians, especially the Franciscans, toward the approaching end of a world era (Frankl 1966:14), which they expected would be marked by such cosmic signs.

The first native-authored synthesis that combined the disparate elements of the Topiltzin Quetzalcoatl stories was the *Anales de Cuauhtitlan*, written in c. 1570, at about the same time as Sahagún's *Florentine Codex* and thus two generations after the conquest. Here Ce Acatl Topiltzin, the ruler of Tollan, is said to be the same person as Quetzalcoatl, giving him his full name, whose parts had referred to three separate individuals in earlier texts. This account most embellishes the story with such details as his miraculous conception from ♀Chimalman and his transformation into Venus. As in some other versions, the three demons, including Tezcatlipoca, tricked him into leaving his city, and he was succeeded by Huemac, who died in Cincalco at Chapultepec. This text thus provides virtually all the story elements that have come to be thought of as *the* Topiltzin Quetzalcoatl saga.

The culmination of the story in this form did not prevent further manipulation of this narrative, however. Subsequent accounts written toward the end of the sixteenth century by Mendieta, Durán, and Tovar (*Codex Ramirez*), and even later by Ixtlilxochitl, continued to separate and rejoin this multiple personality, distinguishing the ruler from the deity in a variety of ways. For Durán (1967:I:9–15, 61–65), writing in 1579–81, Topiltzin was the same as Huemac, a holy man, undoubtedly St. Thomas, while Quetzalcoatl was the god of Cholula and was actually Ehecatl. The two personages are connected in that both prophesied the coming of the Spanish (see also the *Codex Ramirez* [1980:77–82], from c. 1583–87, for a similar separation). In contrast, the Franciscan Fr. Mendieta (1945:88–89, 99–100), whose history is dated 1596, stated that it was the god Quetzalcoatl of Cholula who was fair and bearded, a holy man who prophesied his return, while the Quetzalcoatl who struggled with Tezcatlipoca and who went to Tlapallan was a deity, not a man. In Ixtlilxochitl's stories, dating from 1600–1640 (1975:265–282, 529–530; 1977:23–33), the elements are arranged quite differently: Topiltzin was the mortal ruler of Tollan, while Quetzalcoatl/Huemac was the saintly man who prophesied his return. Nevertheless, Ixtlilxochitl's fellow native and contemporary, Chimalpahin (1958:9–12; 1965:62) (who wrote during the period 1606–31 and who exhibited some of the clearest indications of the cyclical patterning of the Tenochtitlan dynasty), had only the one being, Topiltzin Quetzalcoatl, who left Tollan after its destruction and entered the sea but promised to return to reestablish his empire.

From this sketchy reconstruction of a portion of the postconquest dialogue between Europeans and Aztecs resurrected from the surviving documents in the native historical tradition, one can see that there was no straightforward development of the Topiltzin Quetzalcoatl saga. Instead, elements of different stories about a creator god and a culture hero are combined and recombined into new forms as part of the negotiation over Aztec history from the conquest through the first century of the colonial period. Although the documents have been presented in chronological order, as if they could represent a single conversation, in fact they were the product of many dialogues, and we cannot know to what degree a later text was a development out of one written at an earlier date. Only a very few portions of the dialogue are preserved in the texts we have, and other information on intensive cultural change during this period has not been presented here. Nevertheless, the processes by which the Aztecs and Spaniards created a new history to conform to their own cultural backgrounds and expectations do emerge.

To summarize, the Aztecs, for their part, brought to this creative undertaking the following elements that seem to be genuinely pre-Hispanic:

1. Quetzalcoatl literally as the feathered serpent: a boundary marker, representing the union between earth and sky, and a harbinger of the rainy season, paired/opposed to the fire serpent (*xiuhcoatl*), harbinger of the dry season, wielded by Huitzilopochtli, patron deity of Tenochtitlan. This identity is definitely pre-Aztec in date, as exemplified by the feathered-serpent imagery at Teotihuacan during the Early Classic period more than a millennium earlier and the feathered-serpent columns at both Tula in Hidalgo and Chichen Itza in Yucatan, which date from several centuries before the Aztec era. The serpent columns, with their heads on the ground and tails in the sky, have been described as "connecting upper and lower zones of the universe" (Kubler 1962:46) and served as the doorway

into temples on top of pyramids, the serpent once again acting as the threshold between the secular and sacred planes.

2. Quetzalcoatl as a deity: a primordial creator god who alternated with his double, particularly Tezcatlipoca, as the sun and who appeared in different manifestations as Ehecatl (god of air and wind), as Venus (the Morning Star, Tlahuizcalpantecuhtli) paired with Xolotl (the Evening Star), as Ce Acatl (1 Reed), as Yacatecuhtli, patron deity of merchants and of the mercantile center of Cholula in modern Puebla; and as patron deity of the *calmecac* while Tezcatlipoca was patron of the *telpochcalli*.

3. Quetzalcoatl as a priestly title for the two highest-ranking sacerdotes in the Aztec ecclesiastical hierarchy, at the head of the literati, keepers of knowledge in Aztec society, mediators between men and deities.

4. Quetzalcoatl and his equivalent aspects as the source and legitimator of kingship and dynasties (a pan-Mesoamerican concept) associated with the sacred locality, Tollan, the place of origin and investiture of authority, the epitome of civilization as opposed to barbarism.

5. *Toltecs*, creators of all the civilized skills, relics of a "golden age lost in the past" (Sodi M. 1962:63).

6. *Ce acatl*, 1 Reed, which corresponded to the year 1519, a date associated with the east, with dawn, with fertility, and with feathered serpents.

Cortés, who came from the east across the primeval water in the year 1519, by these very actions was associated in some ways with Quetzalcoatl (see Chapter 7). He also provided the story of a mortal man, a ruler who prophesied his return to take the throne of Motecuhzoma II. Many of the clergy added to this that the leader from the past was a holy man who had become apotheosized, a saint sent by God to proselytize the New World who was persecuted by false gods and demons and finally driven into exile by the devil. He foretold his return, which was the arrival of the Spaniards; hence he was given the attributes of European physiognomy and dress. With these actions, this Old World saint paved the way for the conquest and the subsequent events of the colonial period. The failure of the natives to accept his teachings justly condemned them to servitude under the Spanish.

The resulting combination of all these elements contributed by two alien cultures was the story of an apotheosized man who belonged to a past era, a civilizing creator, artist, and craftsman who was therefore a *toltec*. As a *toltec* and a leader of *toltecs*, as a ruler and a beginner of dynasties, he made his capital at Tollan, homeland of the Toltecs and origin of all that is most ancient and therefore most true, that which is civilized and legitimate, with himself as the first in a long line of kings ending with Motecuhzoma II. This deified hero was a man who eschewed violence and the abominating human sacrifices later practiced by the Aztecs, further revealing his non-Indian nature, and for this reason he was persecuted by his deity alter ego, Tezcatlipoca/Huitzilopochtli, most worshiped by the Mexica, with whom he alternated on the divine plane.

In terms of historical cycles, he was the first and last ruler of Tollan, its founder but also the man responsible for its downfall and the exodus of its people. This set the pattern for the rise and fall of the Aztecs, exemplifying the possibility of chaos at the end of a cycle that by 1521 the Aztecs had come to know too well. In keeping with his boundary-marking status, he not only predicted the end of the next cycle, that of the Mexica of the present, he also caused that end by returning to replace the current Mexica-Tenochca king, Motecuhzoma, the mortal embodiment of Huitzilopochtli, in the never-ending struggle for supremacy on the secular plane.

Furthermore, Topiltzin Quetzalcoatl was not the only historical figure created in this process. His identification with Motecuhzoma II, the Aztec boundary marker, was part of the process that gave rise to other Motecuhzomas of the past and future, one being the fifth *tlatoani* of Tenochtitlan, another the original ruler of the Mexica in the origin-place, and still others who would come and defeat the Spanish later. Another personage probably reshaped to conform to a conquest-era counterpart was Cuauhtlequetzqui, an early leader of the Mexica and god-bearer of Huitzilopochtli. According to a number of texts, especially the writings of Chimalpahin, he was the one who determined the actual location of the city of Tenochtitlan. His name has been translated as "Rising Eagle" (Chimalpahin 1965:305), and he may be the individual portrayed in the *Codex Telleriano-Remensis* (Fig. 2.10) at the top left of the page, sitting on a throne labeled with a glyph of an eagle with upraised footprints. His association with the eagle, and the reason for his name (or title), is that the sign Huitzilopochtli gave to mark the place where Tenochtitlan was to be built was an eagle on a cactus growing from a rock, with the eagle representing Huitzilopochtli himself as part of his solar aspect. Cuauhtlequetzqui's counterpart at the fall of the city of Tenochtitlan was, of course, Cuauhtemoc, "Descending Eagle," who surrendered to Cortés.

The Tenochtitlan dynastic modeling, including the change of Ilhuicamina's name to Motecuhzoma I and the repeating cycles of the dynasty, appears in the very earliest texts, dating from a decade after the conquest, while the most synthetic story of Topiltzin Quetzalcoatl in a structurally equivalent role was developed later, especially in the works of Sahagún and the *Anales de Cuauhtitlan* after the middle of the sixteenth century. The abrupt end of the dynasty with Motecuhzoma, which came about because of the intervention of the Spanish, set in motion the patterning for the entire dynasty, since royal genealogies compose a significant portion of historical traditions, and history had to be reshaped to account for this most unexpected event. The notion of Motecuhzoma as a boundary figure, as the last ruler of a native empire free from Europeans, thereby influenced the formation of Topiltzin Quetzalcoatl, a king of Tollan molded on the pre-Hispanic "Feathered Serpent," as a boundary figure projected back into the pre-Tenochtitlan past, to the age of the creators of civilization.

Of all the recreated traditions, the Topiltzin Quetzalcoatl saga was possibly the most elaborated and synthetic, both because the Spanish clergy had an intense interest in it and because the story that Cortés was a returning god-king whose replacement of the Aztec ruler had been foretold—a story that is Spanish as much as it is colonial Aztec—was of equally great interest to the Indians. They took on this belief in a prophecy fully realizing that Cortés was *not* the returning god. The "return" of Topiltzin Quetzalcoatl was part of a revitalization movement in which the native peoples looked to this new prophecy for hope that one of their own would rescue them from their Spanish oppressors, and they helped to flesh out the story of such a person in their past to fill this cyclically recurring role (the obvious candidate being someone associated with the legitimacy of kingship and the founding of native dynasties). In other words, the prophecy of the return was not a pre-Hispanic belief but became most important after the conquest.

As part of the development of the return of a post-Aztec Quetzalcoatl, the history of a pre-Aztec Quetzalcoatl was created in keeping with the cyclical view of time. To lay the groundwork for such a new god-king to defeat the Spanish and initiate a new Indian hegemony (a king perhaps named Motecuhzoma), as well as to explain the defeat of both the Aztecs (a known fact) and the Spanish (a future eventuality), the Toltec king also had to be understood as having been defeated in the distant past, resulting in his exile but thereby holding out the promise of a return. This was not entirely a native undertaking, because the influence of the Spanish, especially the Franciscans who wrote almost all of the earliest histories, was considerable. The stories of Motecuhzoma and Quetzalcoatl were formed and reformed from the combination of elements according to certain structuring principles used by both parties in a continuing dialectical process. Thus was history constructed and continually adjusted to explain to all, but especially to the Aztecs themselves, who the Aztecs were, how they came to be conquered, and what their ultimate destiny was to be in the new society that the Europeans and they were building together.

The Archaeologist-Ethnohistorian Dialogue: Reshaping Topiltzin Quetzalcoatl

The discussion of the creation of Topiltzin Quetzalcoatl of Tollan cannot be considered finished without some mention of the subsequent manipulations of this saga. It was noted at the beginning of this chapter that the stories of Quetzalcoatl created by both Europeans and Indians beginning in the sixteenth century have continued to be modified as conditions within Mexico changed, and indeed are still part of the Mexican national consciousness today. The work of modern scholars has also contributed to a new narrative starring Topiltzin Quetzalcoatl and the Toltecs. This twentieth-century version, like its sixteenth-century counterparts, is the result of a dialogue between two parties attempting to resolve a major conceptual problem. The modern dialogue involves archaeologists (relying on material objects from the past) and ethnohistorians (relying on the native historical traditions), and the problem is to reconstruct the actual events and processes of the pre-Hispanic past of Mesoamerica. Understanding the latest reworking of this story should help to illuminate the sixteenth and seventeenth-century reconstructions of the Aztec past, because archaeologists and ethnohistorians, like Aztecs and Spaniards before them, have manipulated various bits of data to compose a narrative of the past that conforms to their own expectations and organizational principles.

This reworking of Topiltzin Quetzalcoatl and the Toltecs began with the common assumption that a real man once did exist with the name—or more likely, the title—of Ce Acatl Topiltzin Quetzalcoatl, that he was the leader of the Toltecs, whose capital was Tula in Hidalgo, and that the Toltecs spread their influence throughout Mesoamerica, with resettlement as far away as Chichen Itza in Yucatan (D. Carrasco 1980:298; listing here just the major Toltec ethnohistorical studies: Davies 1977 especially; Jiménez Moreno 1941, 1956; Kirchhoff 1955; López Austin 1973; and Nicholson 1957, 1979. Stenzel [1980:87] thinks that the wind god was merged with an actual ruler of Tula). The Topiltzin Quetzalcoatl story as it has been preserved is recognized by these scholars as an amalgam of different traits, some of which are known to be Hispanic and therefore thought to be adulterations of a native version (Davies 1974: 258; López Austin 1973:15), while others are pre-Hispanic and relate to mythical beliefs as well as historical facts. Evidence of this real priest-ruler's activities has been sought not only in the postconquest documents of central Mexico that have just been analyzed but also in the oral histories of the Maya of Yucatan and highland Guatemala. Furthermore, archaeological remains have been thought to support, if not the existence of Topiltzin, at least the rule of the Toltecs at Tula and their movement into other parts of Mesoamerica during the Early Postclassic period (A.D. 900–1200).

Strong confirmation is thought to be present in the postconquest Maya histories in which the "Feathered Serpent" appears, translated as Gucumatz in the Quiche and Cakchiquel Maya languages, Cuchulchan in Tzeltal Maya, and Kukulcan in Yucatec Maya (Saenz 1962:30). Significantly, Toltecs can also be found in these histories, with their Nahuatl name, and the role they play is as founders of ruling lineages (Carmack 1968; Cohodas 1978:94; Davies 1977:191; López Austin 1973:95). In particular, the Quiche Maya document, the *Popol Vuh* (1971:4) has Gucumatz and Tepeu (the Nahuatl name Totepeuh, "Our Conqueror," elsewhere Topiltzin's father [Davies 1977:191]) as progenitors of the Quiche people, while ♀Chimalmat (the Nahuatl ♀Chimalman) is the mother-earth deity. The Yucatec Maya chronicles speak of Kukulcan, and even use one of his Nahuatl names, Nacxit Xochitl, in reference to his "sin" and downfall (*Chilam Balam of Chumayel* 1967:83, 169). Quetzalcoatl and Motecuhzoma both appear with their Nahuatl names at the fall of Mayapan, a major Maya capital, in another Yucatec historical tradition (*Chilam Balam of Maní* 1979:107, 127). As already noted, Tollan was considered a place of investiture for some Maya groups (López Austin 1973:95), again using its Nahuatl, not Maya, name. The most parsimonious way to account for these Nahuatl names in Maya oral histories is by postulating a strong central Mexican presence in the past, a Toltec infiltration or outright conquest of the Maya by which they imposed themselves as the new rulers.

In addition to the oral histories, a major confirmation of a Tula-Toltec presence in the Maya area has been assumed to be the archaeological site of Chichen Itza in Yucatan, which presents in its many architectural and sculptural details an almost exact replica of the same details at Tula in Hidalgo. The similarities between the two sites were noted in the 1880s by the French archaeologist-explorer Desiré Charnay (Cohodas 1978:xiv; Kubler 1962:176). In the early part of this century, however, Tula was dismissed as a candidate for the Tollan of the Aztecs in favor of Teotihuacan (Kubler 1962:43) because Tula did not live up to the grandeur and reputation of the great capital in the Aztec historical traditions. Their description of the Toltecs as builders of the first great city, inventors of all civilized crafts (especially in Sahagún's work), seemed to permit only the huge Classic Period city of Teotihuacan (c. A.D. 100–750) as a likely candidate, and thus scholars favored Teotihuacan over the "comparatively insignificant ruin" of Tula (Spinden 1928:169).

The question of whether Teotihuacan or Tula was the Tollan of Quetzalcoatl—whose resolution would influence acceptance of his historicity, the dating of the events of his life, and the search for the remains of the Toltec diaspora—was settled for most scholars in 1941. At that time Jiménez Moreno presented detailed evidence showing that the place-names Sahagún listed as being near Tollan or associated with that city could be found at or near Tula, not Teotihuacan (Jiménez Moreno 1941; see Davies 1977:40–43 for a summary of these arguments), even though this meant acknowledging that the Aztecs greatly exaggerated the grandeur of the city of the Toltecs. Part of Jiménez Moreno's reasoning in favor of Tula, however, was based on the already-noted characteristics it shared with the Maya site of Chichen Itza, said in Maya histories to have been ruled by an intruder named Kukulcan (Jiménez Moreno 1941:81–82).

Thus the archaeological evidence was combined with the documentary interpretation to create a historical episode in the past in order
to explain why the two sites, one in central Mexico and one in Yucatan, are so similar, as well as to confirm the historical veracity of
traditions recorded in both areas. Simply put, Topiltzin Quetzalcoatl
left Tula for the east and traveled to Chichen Itza, which he rebuilt
in the image of Tula and over which he presided with his Yucatec
name, Kukulcan.

This position required some accommodation, however. To this
time the Quetzalcoatl of the Aztec histories and the Kukulcan of
the Yucatec Maya histories were thought to have been separated
by several centuries, based on interpretations of the dates given in
the documents (e.g., *Chilam Balam of Chumayel* 1967:161; originally published 1933). In addition, the similarities between the sites
of Tula and Chichen Itza were thought to result from a movement
out of Yucatan into central Mexico, which is the opposite of what
Jiménez Moreno proposed. The notion that the "Feathered Serpent"
of Yucatan had traveled to Tula actually appeared centuries earlier
in the works of Mendieta (1945), Las Casas (1971), and the bishop in
the Maya area, Diego de Landa (1978), and it was accepted by archaeologists in the early twentieth century as well (e.g., Spinden 1928:
173). Having Chichen Itza as the progenitor of the Toltecs was also
in keeping with the undeniable fact that Chichen Itza is much larger
and grander than Tula.

Thus, Jiménez Moreno (1941) had to change the dates for Quetzalcoatl's life, adding two calendar rounds of fifty-two years each
to the previously accepted dates in the *Anales de Cuauhtitlan*, in
order for the two Feathered Serpents, one who left Tollan and one
who came to Chichen Itza, to become one person (Cohodas 1978:xv,
75–76, 88). This change was welcomed by the Maya archaeologist
J. Eric S. Thompson (1941:104–106) in order to fit his archaeological data in the Maya area within the developing scheme. Despite
Chichen Itza's impressiveness over its counterpart, Tula, the documentary interpretations were given priority over the archaeological
evidence (Margain 1971:75). Archaeologists divided the architecture
at Chichen Itza on stylistic grounds into earlier "Maya" and later
"Toltec" periods (Andrews IV 1965; Tozzer 1957). Battle scenes in
wall paintings and other art were interpreted as invading Toltecs
fighting Maya warriors (Tozzer 1957). In 1962 art historian George
Kubler admitted (although he did not believe it; see Kubler 1961) that

all scholars "now accept the thesis that Nahua-speaking Toltecs of highland origin lived as masters at Chichen Itza" (1962:176).

When Jiménez Moreno presented his arguments for Tula as Tollan, the site of Chichen Itza was being excavated and reconstructed by the Carnegie Institute of Washington. As a further contribution to the dialogue, based on this identification of Chichen Itza as a Toltec site, the archaeologist in charge of the Tula excavations in the 1940s, Jorge R. Acosta, purposely restored the ceremonial precinct at Tula to look like Chichen Itza (Molina-Montes 1982). Among other things, he added the staircase on Temple B of Tula to conform to the Temple of the Warriors at Chichen Itza and built the entire colonnade in front of Pyramid B and the Palacio Quemado modeled on the colonnade at Chichen Itza. Since that time, the similarities between Pyramid B at Tula and the Temple of the Warriors at Chichen Itza have often been offered as further proof that there was a strong connection between the two sites, but these are, of course, ex post facto: Tula's Pyramid B was "tailor-made to resemble the Temple of the Warriors" (1982:132).

Other archaeological work concentrated on finding evidence of the Toltecs and their leader outside of central Mexico, since the interpretation of the Aztec and Maya documents was that the "Feathered Serpent" led his people out of Tula and conquered other areas, in particular the Maya areas whose historical traditions include the Toltecs or Tollan as associated with conquest and the founding of dynasties. Evidence of the Toltec occupation of these other areas consists of traits deriving not just from the city of Tula but also from Chichen Itza, the second Toltec capital, and from other sites interpreted as coming under Toltec domination (e.g., Andrews IV 1965; Borhegyi 1965; Carmack 1968; Fox 1981; Ruz Lhuillier 1964; see Parsons 1969 for a discussion of the origins of these traits). Toltec sites were discovered not only in the highland Maya area of Guatemala and Chiapas but also in western and northwestern Mexico, Oaxaca, and Veracruz—that is, in virtually all areas of Postclassic Mesoamerican civilization (e.g., Weaver 1972:214–227). With the addition of these sites, the list of Toltec traits continued to increase, adding new characteristics found in each city.

Thus the Toltecs came to be considered the "dominant group" in Mesoamerica in the Early Postclassic period (Diehl, Lomas, and Wynn 1974:182). Jiménez Moreno (1966) described the extent of the Toltec Empire in Mesoamerica as stretching from Sinaloa to Yucatan. Because of their dominance, this pre-Aztec time span has come to be known as the "Toltec period" (Carmack 1968:57; Sanders, Parsons, and Santley 1979). Interestingly, the creation of this new Toltec empire necessitated even further accommodations to explain why many of the so-called Toltec traits either do not occur at Tula during the Early Postclassic period (e.g., there is a dearth of X Fine Orange pottery and metal objects, considered to be prime Toltec characteristics) or else do not have any priority at that site (as noted by Kubler 1961, 1962; Miller 1985; Parsons 1969). Thus the presence of many of these traits in the Maya area or elsewhere in Mesoamerica actually cannot be ascribed to incursions of people out of Tula on the basis of the archaeological evidence but only on the basis of the new saga as it has been recreated.

Another factor that has not fit well into this scheme is the improved dating of the two sites. The Tula archaeologist Acosta accepted Jiménez Moreno's date of A.D. 1170, based on documentary interpretations, for the collapse of Tula (Diehl 1983:160). More recent work at Tula using the radiocarbon method has shown that the city was abandoned perhaps a century earlier (1983:57, 160). Similarly, radiocarbon dating of the "Toltec" period constructions at Chichen Itza (Andrews V 1977:Table 1) turned out to be earlier than the date of entry of the Toltecs based on documentary interpretations. There the archaeologists simply pushed back the date of the Toltec incursions into Chichen Itza to a date earlier than the "customary" c. A.D. 1000 date (1977:8). Some investigations have shown that many of the "Mexican" traits that entered the Maya area were also much earlier than expected on the basis of the Toltec migration story (e.g., Borhegyi 1965; Ruz Lhuillier 1964), lending support to a renegotiated view allowing for early and sustained interaction between the two areas, so that the exile and movement of the "Feathered Serpent" mentioned in the Aztec and Maya histories was only one of many such Mexican penetrations. Furthermore, there could have been more than one person with the name or title of Quetzalcoatl, a modification that would resolve a number of contradictions both within the documents themselves and between the documents and the archaeological data (e.g., Davies 1977).

Although the new Topiltzin Quetzalcoatl epic, with its notion of a Toltec empire and Tula's primacy over Chichen Itza, was never universally accepted, especially by art historians (e.g., Cohodas 1978; Kubler 1961, 1962, 1984), it was a majority viewpoint and has begun to fall out of favor among archaeologists only recently as new data have emerged, especially from the Maya area (e.g., Morley, Brainerd, and Sharer 1983; Piña Chan 1980; compare Weaver 1981:378–381 to Weaver 1972:221–227). Thus the suggestion has been renewed that the similarities between the sites of Chichen Itza and Tula resulted from a movement from Yucatan to central Mexico (Morley, Brainerd, and Sharer 1983:164), not the other way around, or a series of interactions between these two areas (Kubler 1984:288–290). Given the lack of indisputable evidence for a migration out of Tula in the Early Postclassic, some scholars favor a return to Teotihuacan or the Mixtec culture as the source of the stories of an outward movement of Toltecs recorded in the oral traditions of the Maya (e.g., K. Brown 1980:72).

The story of the Toltecs therefore continues to evolve, with Topiltzin Quetzalcoatl becoming more and more insignificant in these new variations since prehistorians are more apt to work with entire cultures than with single individuals, although he was the focal point of the saga as it originally developed. Thus the use of this narrative belongs not only to the past, as the Aztecs and Spaniards understood it in the sixteenth century, but has also assumed a principal place in modern attempts at understanding Mesoamerican culture by reconstructing its history.

Attempts to find archaeologically verifiable facts in the historical traditions are becoming recognized as less than successful due to the growing realization that archaeology and documentary history "produce different forms or views of reality, each valid portrayals of the past" (Charlton 1981:155). A benefit to be gained from understanding why the Aztec historical traditions include many nonhistorical episodes or details that seem rearranged should be further pursuit of their symbolic meaning. This has often been done with the oral histories of other cultures, and it is the topic explored in the next chapter. Investigating the Aztec traditions from this perspective reveals that Aztec "history" is duplicated in the accounts preserved in other complex societies around the world, precisely because all these peoples constructed and utilized their past for the same purposes.

Chapter 7

Aztec Sacred History and Divine Kingship

If the Aztec histories are not "historical," what are they? The Topiltzin Quetzalcoatl saga in particular has been accepted by many as
mythicized history (López Austin 1973:10). Ironically, the more in-
tensely the historical Topiltzin Quetzalcoatl has been sought, the
more elusive he has become, because previously accepted factual
details are having to be discarded in the face of critical examination of the traditions (Davies 1980:xii; Nicholson 1979:39). There is
nevertheless a reluctance among ethnohistorians to deny the "rich
historical content" (Davies 1982:106) of the Aztec traditions. They
hold to the premise that the historically valid elements should continue to be distinguished from the mythical ones (Carmack 1972:
241) because they have the greatest value for understanding central
Mexican culture and history.

   This premise is perceived by its advocates as being opposed to
another school of thought that treats the Topiltzin Quetzalcoatl story
and other major aspects of the Aztec historical traditions as entirely
fictive astronomical myths or allegories created solely as a reflection
of native ideology (e.g., Bierhorst 1974:9; Brinton 1890a; Brundage
1979:111; Brundage 1982:273; Graulich 1981a, 1981b, 1983, 1984;
Krickeberg 1966:223–224). The dichotomy that exists between these
two positions is succinctly revealed in the opinion of a leading Aztec

ethnohistorian: "To reduce the basic Topiltzin narrative entirely to a 'dawn hero', lunar, or Venus myth, for example, as some have attempted to do, would constitute, in my view, an inadmissably radical position" (Nicholson 1979:39). From this perspective, Quetzalcoatl (or Huitzilopochtli, or other figures) are either historical personages who have become mythicized by various means (see López Austin 1973), or else they are little more than anthropomorphized astronomical bodies—the sun or Venus rising at dawn to slay its enemies, the moon and the stars.

Both of these viewpoints are inadequate for dealing with the native traditions, for they fail to consider that myth goes far beyond astral allegories and folk legends or the garbled mythicization of actual historical events. Valuing only the historical-sounding passages in the native traditions means "ignoring what anthropological hermeneutics outlaws: the use of sacred history as history" (Bharati 1985: 368). As the preceding chapters have detailed, European-style historicity was not the primary purpose for which the documents in the native historical tradition were created. Instead, the people we call the Aztecs kept "sacred histories," tales that incorporated historical events as they were cognized but for which historical accuracy (according to our perceptions) was not only an alien concept but an irrelevant one. Sacred history

> is exemplary, paradigmatic: not only does it relate how things came to be, it also lays the foundations for all human behavior and all social and cultural institutions. From the fact that man was created and civilized by Supernatural Beings, it follows that the sum of his behavior and activities belongs to sacred history; and this history must be carefully preserved and transmitted intact to succeeding generations. (Eliade 1958:x–xi)

The historical traditions that have survived say much about how the preconquest and conquest-era peoples of central Mexico viewed the workings of their complex society and cosmos. Their reality, as they conceived it, was acknowledged and understood as the outcome and hence the repetition of past events, by which it was endowed with the legitimacy of antiquity. At a deeper level—the level of underlying structural principles that ordered and hence gave meaning to both past and present—the historical traditions were a narrative form of symbolic classification (Needham 1979:36), revealing in the different episodes Aztec cultural categories and relationships and how they were transformed when they were put into operation. To dwell on the genuine historical details is thus to miss the full import of what has been preserved in these documents.

Much more specific information on Aztec and Spanish cultural categories and their transformation remains to be discerned from these texts. Here, two topics with potential for future study, which have already been introduced in the preceding chapters, are examined in greater detail. The first is the premise that Aztec history played an active role as a map or model for organizing social, economic, and political relationships in time and space in concert with the ceremonial calendar. The calendar, besides serving as a major time-keeping device, integrated the complex, heterogeneous community of greater Tenochtitlan by interrelating the various social units in coordination with the cyclical movement of space-time.

The second topic is the use of history to explicate certain philosophical problems dealing with the nature of rulership, problems that all complex societies have had to face. Comparing the Aztec traditions with those of other societies at a high level of sociocultural complexity reveals a near identity in their historical content that would be an astonishing coincidence if they were all literally true but in fact is totally expected given the role of sacred history in these cultures. Here particular emphasis is placed on the nature of kingship, the relationships that were conceived between the categories of "rulers" and "ruled," and how these concepts shaped the sacred history of the Tenochtitlan dynasty. These examples will begin to show how the Aztec past was much more meaningful to the people who told and performed it—and can be more meaningful to Aztec studies today—than mere history.

Sacred History and Calendar

Recently, an attempt has been made (Zantwijk 1985) to explain how the citizens of Tenochtitlan were organized in time and space in the spatial arrangement of their *calpoltin* (plural of *calpolli*, or ward) and the temporal rotation of services these *calpoltin* provided to the state. The *calpoltin* were especially coordinated in their obligations to the major and minor religious rites organized according to the ceremonial calendar of 18 months of 20 days. Aztec historical traditions have a place in this system, for many of the episodes mentioned as occurring in the distant past and in far-away places, are actually rituals performed every year in the calendrical ceremonies in places in or near the city of Tenochtitlan.

This aspect of the historical traditions is part of the aboriginal form of oral record keeping, in which even historical-sounding events were incorporated into prayers, songs, poems, and other types of verbal art obviously meant to be performed. The songs and discourses by which this history was recorded could not have been understood unless the audience already knew the traditions being acted out: "They must already know the tale so that they can enjoy the rendering of various episodes, appreciate the innovations, and anticipate the thrills still to come" (Vansina 1985:35).

The participation of the people in these rituals would have then confirmed the truth of their history. That is, the sacred histories "said" in words what the rituals "said" in action, both being symbolic constructions of the social order (following Leach 1965:13–14). By performing their history, the people of the present did the same things their predecessors did in the past. Thus they became their ancestors in order to give meaning to, and gain understanding of, their actions and to provide the continuity between past and present that was an axiom of Aztec thought (see Sahlins 1985:92 for a Hawaiian example of this).

It should therefore be possible to investigate the correlation between history and the ceremonial calendar to see how the ceremonies that interrelated groups in different parts of the city over a solar year can be tied to movements in space and time by the Mexica on their migration, as preserved in the accounts. It has previously been recognized that some episodes from the historical traditions were acted out during major ceremonies (e.g., B. Brown 1984 and D. Carrasco 1981; Matos Moctezuma 1987:48; also, see Chapter 3), usually based on the presumption that the rituals purposely recreated actual historical events, rather than the position adopted here, which is that the oral traditions were part of the ceremonial calendar that mapped social relations in space and time.

A well-known correlation between a historical episode and a calendrical ritual is the Panquetzaliztli ceremony, which gave its name to the fifteenth month in the Aztec solar year. This rite was dedicated to Huitzilopochtli and included a reenactment of the events at Coatepec at the major temple of Tenochtitlan, the Templo Mayor. The stories about what happened at Coatepec—the birth or rebirth

of Huitzilopochtli and the massacre of ♀Coyolxauhqui and the Centzonhuitznahua—often appear in the documents in the context of
Mexica history, but they are known to derive from the oral portion
of the performance of the Panquetzaliztli ritual (Sahagún 1950–82:
Bk. 3:3).

As Fr. Sahagún noted (1950–82:Bk. 2:175–176), the Templo
Mayor, with its twin temples dedicated to the worship of Huitzilopochtli and Tlaloc, was also known as the *coatepetl*, the "Hill of the
Serpent" (Coatepec), where Huitzilopochtli was born. The pyramid
on which the temples stood, which has been excavated in downtown
Mexico City, is still adorned with stone serpent heads, rendering it
literally a serpent hill. In the story, Huitzilopochtli dismembered his
sister, ♀Coyolxauhqui, with the *xiuhcoatl* (fire-serpent), a weapon
he is shown holding in later depictions of him within the temple
(e.g., in the *Codex Azcatitlan* and Sahagún's, Durán's, and Tovar's
illustrations). Significantly, a carved stone bearing the likeness of a
dismembered mother-earth deity identified as ♀Coyolxauhqui (León-
Portilla 1978) was recently found at the base of the Templo Mayor, a
further indication of this episode as sacred history incorporated into
actual ceremonial performances.

Huitzilopochtli's adversaries in the story were the Centzonhuitznahua; in the annual Panquetzaliztli ceremony, a battle took place
with the people of Huitznahua in which the latter were dispersed or
killed, and the fire serpent also appeared. In Sahagún's version of the
story (1950–82:Bk. 3:1–5), an ally of Huitzilopochtli was his older
brother Quauitlicac, who warned him of the approach of the others
to slay him; in the ceremony, the god image representing Huitzilopochtli was accompanied by his "elder brother," someone imperson-
ating Quauitlicac. There was also a sacrifice in the ballcourt, as in
the historical account (1950–82:Bk. 2:145–146).

More important to understanding the functioning of the sacred
history and its counterpart ritual is the fact that Huitznahua and
other place-names in the story were actual locations in and around
the city of Tenochtitlan and the Templo Mayor (Sahagún 1950–82:
Bk. 3:3). Huitznahua was a *calpolli* of Tenochtitlan located in the
southern part of the city, as its name implies (Zantwijk 1985). Thus
the events of the historical narrative were tied to actual places as part
of the integration of various *calpoltin* by their participation in different ceremonies (Zantwijk 1966), by the symbolic meaning attached
to the cardinal directions, and by the directional movement of ceremonial performers in their relationships to cosmological categories.

Furthermore, the ceremony of Panquetzaliztli occurred in association with the winter solstice (Broda 1976, 1982; although scholars
are not in agreement as to the timing of these ceremonies). The
sun was considered to come in close contact with the earth at this
time, resulting in an imbalance between the two and the threat of
conjunction (Hunt 1977:126–127). This was also the time when terrestrial waters were given more importance than celestial waters,
because irrigation canals were needed to grow a second crop (1977:
125). In the narrative accompanying the Panquetzaliztli ceremony,
the sacrifice of ♀Coyolxauhqui at Coatepec resulted in a drought, the
conjunction of the earth and sun, and Huitzilopochtli played the role
of master of terrestrial waters by building and destroying the lake
at Coatepec. Thus the annual cycles of the sun and the agricultural
seasons, whose origins were explained in the migration history, were
not simply reenacted but were invented anew each year by the ritual
experiences of the people.

Other ceremonies are also readily associated with events in the
historical traditions. As noted in Chapter 4, the ritual sacrifice of
♀Toci occurred during the eleventh month, Ochpaniztli (see also
B. Brown 1984), at the time of the fall equinox (Broda 1976, 1982).
Aspects of the ceremony that are also to be found in the historical
episode of the sacrifice of ♀Toci include the flaying of the skin of
the female impersonator of the goddess, the wearing of her skin by a
male impersonator, and mock combat (Sahagún 1950–82:Bk. 2:118–
126). The ♀Toci impersonator was called ♀Yaocihuatl, "Woman of
Discord" (B. Brown 1984:202), the name of the original Culhuacan
princess, who was sacrificed by the Mexica.

As part of this ritual, the ♀Toci impersonator went to Atempan, a
calpolli in the southern part of the city (Zantwijk 1985:87), whose
patron deity was the goddess ♀Toci (Chapter 5). This detail relates
the ceremony to a point in space in a particular direction—south,
where the Culhua people and the *chinampa* agricultural fields were
—and to a particular sociopolitical group, a *calpolli*. The linking of
♀Toci to Atempan further associates her with another mother-earth
goddess manifestation, ♀Cihuacoatl, whose secular counterpart, the
second to the king, was also called the *atempanecatl* and was said
to come from this *calpolli* (Chapter 5). Thus the ritual landscape
was equated with the political, and the actions of the gods were
firmly tied to their semidivine representatives on earth, the *tlatoani*
and the *cihuacoatl*, as well as to the commoners, organized in their
calpoltin.

Another historical episode that has a ceremonial counterpart is the sacrificial death of the young girl ♀Quetzalxochitl (also a manifestation of the mother-earth deity), who appeared in the past as the daughter of the Mexica leader Toxcuecuex (himself an aspect of Tlaloc). According to the migration account in the *Leyenda de los Soles*, this sacrifice instituted the rainy season. It appears in the ceremonial calendar of Tenochtitlan in the first month, Atlcaualo ("Ceasing of Water" = drought), just prior to the spring equinox (Broda 1976, 1982). As part of this ritual, seven children were sacrificed to the *tlaloques*, the rain gods, in order to "pay a debt" to them. The children's tears were said to bring the rain. Only one of these children was a female, and she was given the name ♀Quetzal-xochitl (Sahagún 1950–82:Bk. 2:43), the same as her counterpart in the histories given in sacrifice to the *tlaloques* in order to end the drought.

No such ritual is so obviously associated with the deaths of the daughters of Huitzilihuitl I, the fourth repetition in the historical traditions of the sacrifice of women. Nevertheless, in keeping with the pattern presented by the parallel episodes of mother-earth deity sacrifices, whose ceremonies occurred at or near the time of winter solstice and the two equinoxes—when the earth-sun relationship is most marked—this story may be associated with the summer solstice. The ceremony of the sixth month, Etzalcualiztli, when the summer solstice occurred (Broda 1976) or right before the solstice (Broda 1982), did not involve the prominent sacrificial death of a female but did incorporate two other aspects of the battle at Chapultepec. The priests in the ceremony were totally naked (the condition of Huitzilihuitl's daughters), which was an unusual occurrence, and a mock battle was conducted within the lake itself, which is how the battle of Chapultepec is depicted in some renderings (e.g., *Codex Azcatitlan*, *Tira de Tepechpan*).

Thus the sacrifices of the mother-earth goddesses as historical episodes, the recurring event that signaled both cosmological and political conjunctions and disjunctions in the narrative of the Mexica migrations, are associated in the calendrical round with the major seasonal changes at solstice and equinox, the points in the solar year marked by the alternating conjunctions and disjunctions of the sun (represented by Huitzilopochtli, the *tlatoani*) and the earth (represented by the mother deity, the recurring "queen," the *cihuacoatl*). The chronological sequencing of these episodes is a consequence of the story of the migration, of the movement of the Mexica through time and space, although this movement was also cyclical, since they periodically returned to the metaphorical sacred center at times of cyclical juncture. The migration began in the realm of the gods and moved slowly to the Valley of Mexico, the realm of the secular kings. It thereby recapitulated the cosmogony—the origin of the cosmos—within Mexica phylogeny—the development of society. The cycles of time in the past (history) were annually reproduced in the ceremonial calendar by which the different social groups reinvented their relationships with one another and with their universe. Thus, "social structure is the humanized form of cosmic order . . . [and the] final form of cosmic myth is current event" (Sahlins 1985:58).

Sacred History and Kingship

Besides recreating their history, the calendrical rituals disseminated and reiterated knowledge about other aspects of Aztec society. In particular, "people construct knowledge about kingship through rituals" (Feeley-Harnik 1985:293); hence the second aspect of the historical traditions to be dealt with here is their function in conceptualizing questions about the origin and nature of rulership, the categories and relations that separate and interrelate rulers and their subjects. For the Aztecs, as for other peoples, the origin of rulership lay in the primordial separation between people and gods. Rulers constituted a third category mediating between the first two and were considered both godlike and humanlike, depending on the context of the different situations in which these categories operated (see Sahlins 1985:103).

The Aztecs had a kind of divine kingship, although perhaps it is more accurately labeled "sacred" (e.g., Adler 1982:181; Young 1966: 136), since the *tlatoque* of Tenochtitlan, as represented in the historical traditions and ceremonies, failed to manifest all the characteristics of truly divine kings (given in Feeley-Harnik 1985 and Richards 1969). Nevertheless, as a principal mediator between the people and their gods, as a mortal representative of Huitzilopochtli, as a descendant of dynastic founders who had divine qualities, and as the steward of an ethnic historical tradition that was in fact a recapitulation of the cosmogony, the *tlatoani* was surely sacred, if not actually worshiped as a deity himself. It is not surprising, there-

fore, to find similarities in the conceptions of kingship between the
Aztecs and many other cultures with divine kings. These similarities are such that almost identical historical traditions exist among
these disparate cultures, for the simple reason that they all used
history to explicate their notions of rulership.

As noted in Chapter 6, there was a widespread belief in Postclassic Mesoamerica that the first king, legitimator of all subsequent
kings, was one of the creator deities who already mediated between
a supreme deity (Ometeotl to the Aztecs) and humans by being born
of the former and creating the latter, along with the world in which
they lived. The personified origin of kingly lines was associated with
the "Feathered Serpent," mediator par excellence between the celestial and terrestrial spheres. The place of his authority was Tollan, at
the threshold to the domain of the gods and hence the most powerful
locus accessible to mortals, the rightful place of mediating rulers.

In the Aztec versions of the origin myth of the legitimacy of kings
(and of the civilizations they ruled), as they were told after the conquest, Quetzalcoatl, the semidivine feathered serpent and creator
twin, established the kingship at Tollan. He merges with Ce Acatl,
1 Reed, a date tied to a specific direction (east, from which the sun
rises), and with Topiltzin, a noble prince and heir apparent. Quetzalcoatl, the man-god, the first ruler in Tollan, did not bequeath
the right to rule in a normal manner. Instead, he had to give up his
throne in order to open the position to ethnically diverse outsiders,
mortals who then competed for the claim to an office to which they,
unlike Quetzalcoatl, lacked an inherent right. Quetzalcoatl's loss of
power in the various versions of his saga was often a result of a
fault he or others committed, usually associated with *pulque*, the
intoxicating wine of the maguey plant.

That the Topiltzin Quetzalcoatl saga does not simply represent
the arbitrary mythicization of some long ago historical event but instead exemplifies the use of historical narratives to represent the origin and dynamics of sociocosmological categories is demonstrated
by the replication of the major elements of this story in the sacred
histories of other societies. (Recognizing this replication may actually help to reveal further the pre-Hispanic details of this saga.) Quetzalcoatl's story is paralleled in many details, for example, in the epic
of King Woot in Kuba (Bantu) myths in Central Africa (Heusch 1982:
101–102). Woot, the first Kuba king, was the inventor of all social
institutions and also of ironworking, while Quetzalcoatl and the Tol-

tecs were associated with the origin of the customs and crafts of civilization, including metallurgy. King Woot became drunk on palm wine, committed incest, and went into exile. On his journey away from his capital, he named the different people, animals, objects, and so forth, and gave the various ethnic groups their languages. Thus, out of the unity that had existed during his reign came a diversity that he created, a series of cultural discontinuities among men and other phenomena.

Similarly, Topiltzin Quetzalcoatl became drunk on *pulque*, or was otherwise associated with that beverage, committed indiscretions, including incest (in an interpretation of his actions with his sister in the *Anales de Cuauhtitlan* 1975:10), went into exile, and named the objects he encountered on his way to his ultimate end in the east, the same direction that was the destination of Woot. Woot is associated with the sun in Bantu thought; Quetzalcoatl is more often identified as Venus, companion to the sun. In the Bantu historical myths, after the fall of Woot came the migrations of the different wandering tribes, the same event that occurs in the Aztec histories when the Chichimec migrations into the Valley of Mexico follow immediately after the exile of Quetzalcoatl from Tollan.

It is also no coincidence that Quetzalcoatl's and Woot's downfalls were due to wine and drunkenness. Topiltzin Quetzalcoatl's associations with *pulque* are many and indicate that more than his "sin" of intoxication is at issue. Not only did he become drunk on the wine (as in Sahagún's account and the *Anales de Cuauhtitlan*), but as Ehecatl, one of his deity aspects, he discovered *pulque* for mankind (*Histoyre du Mechique* 1905:27–28). In Ixtlilxochitl's stories, he is the son of the inventor of *pulque* and is called Maeconetzin, "Son of Maguey."

The more general disjunctive function of *pulque* is revealed in a different context in a story told by Sahagún (1950–82:Bk. 10:193–194) about the early period in the history of mankind, before the different ethnic groups had separated. *Pulque* had just been invented, and all the leaders of the various groups partook of the beverage. However, the Huaxtec ruler drank, not the usual four bowls, but five bowls of *pulque*—just as Topiltzin Quetzalcoatl did in the *Anales de Cuauhtitlan* version—and so became drunk. While intoxicated, he took off his loincloth, exposing his genitals (an allusion to the sexual symbolism of *pulque*), and in shame all of the Huaxtecs abandoned the area and went to the Gulf Coast (where they were actually living in Aztec times). Following their departure, all the other ethnic groups separated as well, and so began a diaspora and the dispersal of the various peoples to their appointed places. Thus, this legend did not refer to a historical event associated with Topiltzin Quetzal-coatl of Tollan but was part of a more general connection linking drunkenness with exile, an eastern journey (Davies 1984:210), and the dispersal of ethnic groups across the Mesoamerican landscape.

The disjunctive aspect of *pulque* relates to an inherent charac-teristic of the beverage, not simply to the lack of moderation that results in drunkenness. *Pulque*, the fermented liquid from the heart of the maguey plant, belongs to the domain of rotten or putrefied foods that is often correlated with a disunion of otherwise related phenomena (Detienne 1977:95–97; Lévi-Strauss 1969:294). Simi-larly, many of the Central African myths involve palm wine as a cause of discord. For example, arguments over palm wine led to the separation of Bantu peoples, just as *pulque* resulted in the diaspora from origin-places associated with gods. Palm wine is categorized as lying between nature and culture, since the palm plant occurs readily in nature but must be processed by people to make wine, which is drunk only on culturally regulated occasions (Heusch 1982: 177–180). The same was true for *pulque*, a wild desert plant that produces a semenlike liquid associated with fertility. Nevertheless, in the myths of the "drunken king," the king drinks the beverage to excess and not within the usual social setting. He breaches the restrictions that had rendered the natural plant a cultural product so that "royalty rediscovers the natural order beyond culture" (1982: 180). This breach of the nature-culture distinction is characteristic of divine kings (see below).

The king's intoxication broke the original continuity between mankind and the gods—a continuity aptly symbolized by metaphori-cal replications of the biblical Tower of Babel, such as Coatepec and Tollan. This cosmological rupture began the age of cultural diversity, as just one of the culturally meaningful separations of phenomena begun by the king's exile since he gave objects and places their names on his journey to the east. Still, the subsequent kings, by virtue of the nature of their office, are the "more or less spurious" heirs of the original "drunken king" (Heusch 1982:102) who are capable of en-compassing the mortal and the divine, the natural and the cultural.

Because the ruler is conceptually different from the people he rules, he must be both above and beyond society. To explain the origin of this difference, the king is often considered to come from somewhere above or beyond, as a god or a stranger, or both: "In either event, royalty is the foreigner" (Sahlins 1985:78). The concept of the "stranger-king," to follow the usage in African and Polynesian examples (Feeley-Harnik 1985; Sahlins 1985), is very applicable to the Aztecs. The rulers of Tenochtitlan were considered originally to have been outsiders, from the periphery of their world, who gained legitimacy and ruled from the center.

The Tenochtitlan *tlatoani* was considered divine in the sense of being one with the god (Sahagún 1950–82:Bk. 6:52) and in his role as the living representative of Huitzilopochtli (Acosta Saignes 1946: 172). He was said to be responsible for the movement of the sun and was compared to the rising sun (Davies 1987:102). Thus the Aztec kings were different because they were unnatural, elevated to a level higher than that of ordinary men. Furthermore, they were different because in their historical traditions they persistently claimed to be foreigners from a far-distant place, the place of origin associated with the gods. That these notions are part of the general conceptions associated with kingship, rather than actual historical events unique to the Aztec case, is revealed in their appearance in the oral traditions of other societies with similar notions of kingship—for example, some Polynesian kingdoms:

> For the Hawaiians, the outside place—as the outer parts of the known world, or as the sea is to the inhabited land—is traditionally the site of ultrahuman powers. This distance in space is also a remove in time; the far-off is the homeland of the gods and thus the origin of cultural things. At the furthest horizon the ends of the earth meet the limits of the sky; hence 'Kahiki,' the distant foreign lands, are also above, 'heavenly.' That too is the status of ruling chiefs—*lani*, 'heavenly'—since tradition tells they came from foreign parts to impose by divine powers (*mana*) the separations (*tabus*) that constitute the cultural order. (Sahlins 1982:86)

In the Aztec histories, a number of different Chichimec groups were said to have wandered one after the other into the Valley of Mexico after the fall of Tollan, the primordial center of continuity with the gods. The people who called themselves Mexica, however, were more "foreign" than all the others. In the different versions that tell of the Mexica peregrination to the Valley of Mexico from the origin-place, they are always described as being the *last* of the various ethnic groups to leave Aztlan-Chicomoztoc. This means that not only did they have the most recent link to the place of origin (associated with the gods), but also they were the "most strange," the other groups having already become acculturated within the valley.

As the last group, they were the most distant, the most barbarian and least domesticated or acculturated, as they demonstrated by the barbarity of their actions—for example, the cutting off of the ears of their prisoners of war (*Anales de Tlatelolco* 1948:41) and the flaying of ♀Toci. To the established peoples in the valley, they were like wild animals, chaotic beings belonging to the primordial beginnings before culture was invented (in the same way that some African divine kings have been described; see, e.g., Feeley-Harnik 1985:281). Their response to the intruders was to band together and drive them out. Nevertheless, as the most different people, and simultaneously as the group most recently coming from the edge of the realm of the gods (Coatepec-Tollan), where their own tutelary deity was born, the Mexica were prime candidates for usurping the rule of the other peoples of the valley, an accomplishment they eventually achieved. Their patron deity and *tlatoani* were associated with the sun, whose path across the heavens had already been cleared by his elder brother, Venus (Quetzalcoatl, founder of kingship).

The first step in the transformation from barbarian stranger to legitimated king (necessary to explain the origin of de facto relationships among the elite and nonelite in Aztec society formulated as history), was the marriage to an autochthonous woman, a princess of the people with the original claim to the land and to rulership. In Aztec, as well as Indo-European, Polynesian, and African political legends, "[t]he king is an outsider, often an immigrant warrior prince . . . [who] takes power in another place, and *through a woman*: princess of the native people" (Sahlins 1985:82; emphasis in the original). In the Aztec histories, the autochthonous people were the Culhua, who not only claimed to be the lineal descendants of Toltec kings, and thus the link to the original power of rulership, but who also held the *chinampa* lands of the southern valley, representing agriculture and civilization. (In fact, the massive *chinampa* system of the southern lakeshore dates almost entirely to the 1400s and was built after the establishment of the Triple Alliance [Sanders, Parsons, and Santley 1979:281].)

In the traditions of societies adhering to the stranger-king concept, it is typical for the indigenous group to become wife-giver to the strangers—in the Aztec case, the Culhua gave their noblewomen to the Mexica—after which the dominant newcomers adopt the name of the indigenous people (Sahlins 1985:83). Thus the Mexica *tlatoani* took the title *culhuatecuhtli*, and his land was known as the land of the Culhua (which is how Cortés recorded it in his Second Letter; see Chapter 1). Other characteristics of this that the Aztecs shared with, for example, the Polynesians were the representation of the stranger-king or the tutelary god he incarnates as a virile young warrior and as the sun, while the autochthonous people were associated with feminism, the earth, the Underworld, and agriculture (1985:90). These are apt descriptions of Huitzilopochtli and ♀Toci, of Mixcoatl and ♀Chimalman, and of Acamapichtli and ♀Ilancueitl.

In addition to the generally parallel historical accounts of the Aztecs and Polynesians that reflect their shared conceptions of rulership, a Central African example shows how strong the similarities can be in fine details that are seemingly inconsequential and hence more likely to be considered truly factual. The marriage of the autochthonous woman (♀Ilancueitl) to the hunter-stranger, by which he received the right to rule, her marriage to her adopted son, and her sterility—story elements found in some versions of Aztec history (Chapter 2)—occur as well among the Lunda (Aruund), a Bantu people. Their oral historical traditions speak of ♀Lueji, daughter of a king who disinherited his son and left his kingdom to her instead (Heusch 1982:144–145). Queen ♀Lueji married a stranger and endowed him with the power to rule her people by giving him her bracelet, the symbol of office. Because she was sterile, her husband took a second wife to provide him with an heir. When he died, his son married ♀Lueji, his stepmother (in other words, when the son replaced his father, he married the older man's wife, his "mother," who had the original right to rule).

Like ♀Ilancueitl, ♀Lueji, the chthonic woman, is a queen who legitimates her stranger-husband, a hunter like the Chichimec Acamapichtli, and like ♀Ilancueitl she fails to have children by him in some versions of this tale. Also, as in the Aztec histories, this African queen marries her adoptive son, who becomes king. A final detail of similarity is the diversity in the Lunda accounts as to the question of ♀Lueji's inability to have children (Heusch 1982:152), the same situation as discussed for ♀Ilancueitl (in Chapter 2), who in the different accounts is sometimes fecund, sometimes childless, and sometimes a man. There are Lunda versions in which ♀Lueji is definitely sterile, others in which she has children, and an intermediate situation in which she first appears to be sterile but is cured and is then able to bear a child.

This Bantu example shows once again a point noted in Chapter 1: the autochthonous woman has the quality or power (here symbolized in a single object, a bracelet) to endow kings with the right to rule, and even though she was a ruler in her own right, she gave up this right to her husband upon marriage. The ennobling quality of the royal female, which is only implicit in the Aztec histories, is much more apparent in African societies for which modern ethnographic descriptions are available. In many of these cultures, "queen mothers" overtly transferred the royal relics that conferred kingship during accession rituals (e.g., Cohen 1977; Feeley-Harnik 1985:298; Packard 1981:44), relics that they guarded during the interregnum between the death of one king and the accession of the next. They thus played the crucial role of maintaining the continuity of the right of kingship so that it was uninterrupted by the deaths of mortal kings (Cohen 1977), especially because they were seen as ambivalent figures associated with nature and chaos (Packard 1981:45). Kingship was then symbolically reborn from these women, sometimes during the coronation itself in rituals that alluded to the biological rebirth of the king from the queen mother (see, e.g., Frankfort 1948: 43, 107–108, for ancient Egypt, and Packard 1981:45 for the Bashu of Zaire).

Despite these similarities with other cultures, Aztec conceptions differ from true divine kingship in that there is no evidence for the practice of ritual regicide, a key characteristic (Richards 1969:23). Regicide is an act inherent in the notion that the king was at one with the universe and its operation. It is his responsibility to maintain or reestablish "harmony in the natural and social orders, which are conceived as closely interdependent, if not identical" (P. Smith 1982:124–125). In some cases it was held that when the king weakened or failed in his obligations, endangering the order and functioning of both the cosmos and society, he had to be killed and replaced by a more vigorous successor (Richards 1969:23). Other aspects of regicidal acts had to do with the fact that the king is the victim par excellence for sacrifice since he belongs to both the mortal and divine realms. The king is the supreme sacrificial victim because he is the "closest to the divine" while at the same time the most perfect representative of the human species (Valeri 1985:140–142; see also Heusch 1985:213–214).

More often the death of the king was metaphorical or even feigned rather than real, and bona fide cases of regicide are rare (Young 1966: 135–136). Since the king is central to the periodic regeneration and revival of the world (Feeley-Harnik 1985:300) via his death and rebirth, ritual regicide was often associated with particular seasons and cyclical astronomical events—for example, at the summer solstice for the Swazi king (1985:281–282). In the Fijian case, the king was symbolically poisoned at his accession by drinking kava so that he would be killed as a "dangerous outsider" and reborn as a "domestic god" (Sahlins 1985:95).

Among the Mesoamerican cultures, the iconography of the Classic Period Maya (c. A.D. 300–900) reveals that they also engaged in acts of ritual regicide as part of the accession ceremony, involving the sacrificial death of a noble war captive (a "stranger") who served as a double for the king. The victim was carried on a raised scaffold under a thatched roof as part of the ceremony. At the appropriate time he was placed at the bottom of the scaffold, and his heart was removed. The new king then stepped on the victim's body, walked up the ladder, leaving his bloody footprints on it, and took the seat of the victim on the scaffold, now marked as a "cosmic realm" (Schele and Miller 1986:111, 216). The human object given in this sacrifice symbolizes the king on whose behalf it was performed (Valeri 1985: 63), as is most clearly revealed when the king takes the victim's place, thus uniting the king and the victim. With this sacrifice the king, like his victim, was incorporated into the god for whom the sacrifice was intended and became a divine king (1985:161, summarizing the similar Hawaiian case). The Maya kings also died a more literal slow death in sacrifice, as a part of their communing with divine forces, because of the heavy demands on them to draw their own blood on numerous occasions (Schele and Miller 1986:176).

For the Aztecs, however, there are no similar representations of regicide. The only *tlatoani* of pre-Hispanic Tenochtitlan said in a few texts to have been killed by his own people was Chimalpopoca, slain at the juncture between Tenochtitlan's period of subservience to Azcapotzalco and its overthrow of the Tepanecs, resulting in their independence. The Spanish also claimed that the people of Tenochtitlan killed Motecuhzoma II, though this is disputed as well (but see below). As for a metaphorical regicide in the context of human sacrifice, while the Aztecs put many war captives to death, and the *tlatoani* himself is said to have wielded the sacrificial knife, their large-scale sacrifices lack the more personal identity between victim and king that is known for the Classic Maya.

Thus, whereas elsewhere divine kingship often requires the death of the king—the "monstrous creature" who connects the social and natural worlds (Feeley-Harnik 1985:282)—for the Aztecs only the first king, Topiltzin Quetzalcoatl/Huemac, was required to leave his throne and die in order to begin the kingship. Nevertheless, another royal personage was consistently sacrificed, again symbolically, but this was not the king; it was the "queen" in her manifestations in Mexica history as the mother of gods and daughter of Chichimecs, the "woman of discord." This woman was sacrificed in order to bring about abrupt changes in Mexica settlements during their migration, regenerating their movement in the cycle from one representation of Tenochtitlan to the next. Her sacrifice also resulted in an alternation of relationships between the Chichimec-Mexica and the Toltec-Culhua, which would eventually endow the former with the legitimacy of rule when they reached the endpoint of their journey. Furthermore, the sacrifices established the correct balance of cosmological elements, setting the astral and terrestrial forces in their respective places, alternating with one another in diurnal and annual cycles. Hence the sacrificial episodes reappeared in the annual ceremonial calendar in association with the alternating relationships between the sun and the earth (at solstice and equinox).

In the Mexica histories, the "woman of discord," the incarnation of chaos and its tremendous power of generation, was literally put to death and reborn, but only up to the point of the establishment of the Tenochtitlan dynasty. Then the forces she represented were brought into balance via a marriage with their opposites, embodied by the stranger-king and his patron deity (unity in the context of kinship rather than sacrifice), which generated the dynasty of kings. Within this dynasty, the woman was no longer sacrificed, but her death is presupposed by the fact that she reappeared at patterned intervals when it was necessary to regenerate the legitimacy of kingship. Her subsequent manifestations guarded the right to rulership during the interregna following the deaths of the two kings named Motecuhzoma.

Similarly, the *cihuacoatl*, who in some incarnations, such as Tlacaelel, was a powerful "kingmaker" but never a king, fulfills the same function. He represents this key woman on the sociopolitical plane as the king's double, his "female twin," just as the Fijian chief is seen as "both invading male and . . . the female side of the native lineage" (Sahlins 1985:91), and it is in his ability to mediate such oppositions by incorporating them that his power lies (1985:90). The doubling of the king, a recurrent theme in divine kingship (Feeley-Harnik 1985:282), is expressed in the dual rulership of the Aztec *tlatoani* and *cihuacoatl*, as well as in the pairing of the "recycled king" with the "woman of discord."

The determination that the Aztecs held notions of sacred kingship quite similar in many details to those of other cultures around the world is based on an interpretation of their historical traditions. Examination of the rituals of accession, calendrical ceremonies in which the *tlatoani* played a major role, and other data pertaining to the political system should further elaborate this conception of kingship and how it was made operational. Nevertheless, it is clear that history was extremely important to the Aztecs themselves for elucidating the nature of the ruler, his role in the maintenance of society and the cosmos, and his relationships with the people who served him and the gods he served. Because the narrative of the past served these more general purposes, its constituent episodes—the "facts" and how they are woven together—are not unique to the Aztecs but are found in the historical traditions of many other people who made similar use of their pasts.

The *tlatoque* of Tenochtitlan were conceived as semidivine individuals of a distinctly different lineage, as emphasized in traditions of their torturous journey, a journey not through space but actually through the parallel evolution of cosmology, of kingship, and of their dynasty. As is often the case, the stories begin in the "otherworld" and "othertime," with a reversal of categories from their actual state. The stories tell how the Mexica were an intruding, usurping people from the farthest distant place and time (the emerging-place), barbarians and hunters, wanderers without land of their own—in fact, the antithesis of what they really were, which was civilized, urban agriculturalists who had probably lived in the area for some centuries (Zantwijk 1985:19).

As part of the story of their past, they perceived themselves to be strangers, upstarts, needing a valid claim to the power of rulership and to the agricultural land on which it was based. They believed that they achieved this power via marriage with women (who thereby married beneath their social standing) said inherently to possess not only this right but also the ability to bequeath it to men. The women represented the feminine earth deity in her relationship to her male counterpart, the masculine solar deity represented by the *tlatoani*. The union between the male intruder and the indigenous noblewoman, which generated the latest, and hence most powerful, dynasty in the valley, was incestuous because by his marriage the new *tlatoani* was "reborn" as the king from his wife.

Motecuhzoma and Cortés: The Dialectic of Structure and Event

With the demonstration that Aztec conceptions of rulership fit well with more general characteristics of sacred kings worldwide, it is interesting to see how these conceptions may have influenced the native reaction to the actual last group of intruding upstarts to come into the Valley of Mexico, the Spanish conquistadores led by Cortés. In particular, it is revealing to reexamine Motecuhzoma II's speech attributed to him by Cortés (Chapter 6), which, as noted, is usually considered either apocryphal or a reference to a pre-Hispanic prophecy of the return of Quetzalcoatl. Arguments have already been presented against the existence of such a prophecy prior to the Spanish *entrada* or to any reference to Quetzalcoatl in this speech, and it is unlikely that Motecuhzoma actually welcomed Cortés as a returning lord. Nevertheless, it is remarkable that Motecuhzoma is said to refer to himself and his people as foreigners from very distant parts who came to the valley, married the indigenous women, and thereby settled the land—all entirely native concepts referring to the "stranger-king" and the "autochthonous woman."

If Motecuhzoma II had been perturbed by Cortés's presence beyond any normal anxieties over unusual occurrences, it was not because he believed him to be the returning Quetzalcoatl. Instead, Cortés threatened Motecuhzoma's position because he was a stranger—the Spaniards were perhaps the strangest people the Aztecs had ever seen—from a place more distant than even Motecuhzoma thought his people had come. The conquistadores were the newest intruder group into the valley, from the east, the land of the rising sun across the primeval waters (the realm of the gods), in opposition to the Chichimec Mexica, who claimed to come from the west. Like the earlier Mexica, the Spaniards demonstrated their power over society by the most shocking disturbances of the cultural order, including the barbarous massacre of the people of Cholula.

By these and other characteristics, they held out the tremendous possibility of their rightfully usurping the rulership held by the kings of Tenochtitlan according to native concepts. The Spaniards' lust for the indigenous women, whom they were offered by chiefs on several occasions, and especially Cortés's liaisons with the daughters of Motecuhzoma, would have fit perfectly with Aztec conceptions of the establishment of the stranger-kings by their union with autochthonous women of the agricultural lands, although the Spanish king, Charles V, thought otherwise and never appointed Cortés his viceroy in New Spain.

In addition, Cortés managed to accomplish something often considered necessary for usurpation of the divine king's position: he imprisoned Motecuhzoma II. With divine kingship, the development of the cosmos is mirrored in the origin of the royal dynasty, and the king reproduces and incarnates the cosmos by mediating the natural and social orders.

> Since the king is identified with the cosmos, a fortiori he is identified with his kingdom, that is, with the land and its inhabitants. In fact, he personifies them; his kingdom is assimilated with his body. . . . By appropriating the king's body, it is thus possible to appropriate his realm. (Valeri 1985:146; see also Feeley-Harnik 1985:284)

The notion that possession of the king's body is a prerequisite for succession is also revealed in the Aztec stories of Topiltzin Quetzalcoatl, who carefully searched for the bones of his father, Mixcoatl/Camaxtli/Totepeuh, after the latter had been slain and installed them in a shrine, the Mixcoatepetl, prior to killing his father s murderers on top of that shrine and rightfully taking his father's throne (Chapter 5).

In agreeing to become Cortés's prisoner, Motecuhzoma may have signaled his own defeat (Davies 1974:264). Appearing to be weak and under Spanish control, he thereby threatened the welfare and autonomy of his kingdom, and may indeed have been killed by his own people, as some scholars believe (Davies 1974:269), in an act of regicide to regenerate the kingship with a young and stronger successor, Cuauhtemoc (Motecuhzoma's brother Cuitlahuac, his immedi-

ate successor, apparently lived only a short while). Cuauhtemoc was
also captured by Cortés, who kept him prisoner for several years before executing him during a march to Central America. The belief
that the kingdom was to have been regenerated by Cuauhtemoc appears in the later accounts of his marriage to ♀Tecuichpo, the final
manifestation of the dynastic genetrix, but simultaneously his inevitable defeat is indicated in his name or title as the "Descending
Eagle."

In the clash of conceptions resulting from the Spanish *entrada*,
Motecuhzoma II faced the same problems as did the Hawaiian king
Kaneoneo at the arrival of the Englishman, Captain Cook, in 1778.
According to the Hawaiian and Aztec conceptions of stranger-kings,
foreigners, especially those who are so foreign as possibly to constitute gods and who come from where the gods dwell, are the kings'
natural rivals (Sahlins 1985:140). The similarities between the Aztec
and Hawaiian cases of culture contact, the encounter between the
European explorer and the divine king, are many (Sahlins 1982:74).
In both situations, the alien natures of Cook and Cortés transformed
the native cultures because they failed to correspond to preexisting
indigenous categories.

Cook's voyage occurred at the time of the annual ceremonies
known as Makahiki, dedicated to the Hawaiian god Lono, and the
circumstances of his appearance coincided with certain aspects of
this god's attributes (Sahlins 1981, 1982, 1985). While it is clear that
of all the gods the Hawaiians knew, Cook was most like Lono, many
of the known coincidences between the Makahiki ritual and Cook's
voyage postdated that event, as a *result* of his presence. Because of
Cook's appearance and activities during his stay on the island, the
ceremonies dedicated to Lono were considerably modified in order
to conform to what Cook actually did: "Cook was not considered
a god because of empirical resemblances between the events of his
voyage and details of the Makahiki rites; rather, these rites were
latterly elaborated, primarily by [King] Kamehameha, *as an iconic
representation of Cook's voyage*" (Sahlins 1982:85; emphasis in the
original). In other words, what Cook did *became* the rites and beliefs associated with the god Lono, and thus this god was irrevocably
changed within the native pantheon (1985:31).

In the same way, the prophecy of the return of Quetzalcoatl was a
development based on what Cortés did, in the context of preexisting
beliefs and an entire pantheon of Aztec gods. It is impossible to deter-

mine exactly how soon after his coming to the Valley of Mexico Cortés came to be identified with Quetzalcoatl, since his letters are the only contemporary account of the conquest, and so the time frame for these developments is less well known than in the Hawaiian case. Nevertheless, some contributing factors can be put forward. It is incorrect to conclude that the Spaniards were thought to be gods; the natives knew that the Spaniards were mortal men rather than gods at the time of the meeting between Cortés and Motecuhzoma (Davies 1974:260). On the other hand, just as Motecuhzoma was the living representative of Huitzilopochtli, Cortés came to be identified with a deity, his tutelary with whom he was associated. In order to understand who he was and thereby better comprehend his actions, the Aztecs had to search their repertory of gods and heroes to match Cortés with one of them, just as the European clergy scanned their own histories to find an apostle who would fit Quetzalcoatl's characteristics as they came to perceive them. By his actions, Cortés was eventually identified with a particular Mesoamerican deity, and by that event the deity was necessarily transformed in his identification with both Cortés and St. Thomas.

It is known that Cortés came from the east across the sea in the year 1 Reed, a direction and date associated with feathered serpents, Venus as Morning Star, and Ehecatl (a deity with Gulf Coast origins). One can only speculate on the impact of the fact that Cortés's lieutenant, Pedro de Alvarado, because of his red hair, was called "Tonatiuh," which was the name of the sun deity, the younger companion of Venus. The Spaniards arrived on the Gulf Coast in the springtime just prior to the start of the rainy season, the season associated with the feathered serpent, as opposed to the fire serpent, the symbol of Huitzilopochtli. This too may have marked Cortés's presence as problematical for Motecuhzoma, the representative of Huitzilopochtli, especially since Cortés entered Tenochtitlan in November, at the beginning of the dry season (when the fire serpent was presumably especially prominent) and just before the month of Panquetzaliztli, when Huitzilopochtli was to be reborn. The Spanish leader's potential for usurping the throne as the latest and most distant "stranger" would also potentially place him on the side of legitimacy of rulership, and in Mesoamerican thought such legitimacy devolved as well on the anthropomorphic "Feathered Serpent."

Just as Lono was transformed by his association with Captain Cook, so Quetzalcoatl was changed by his identification with Cortés. Quetzalcoatl became a white-skinned, bearded god who wore European dress. The prophecy of his return to take Motecuhzoma's throne was also created based to some extent on Cortés's actions. It was developed in part by a nativistic movement in need of a messiah to deliver the Indians from the Spaniards and in part by the Spaniards, who wanted to think a European, possibly a saint, had visited the New World and paved the way for their conquest. The return was added to indigenous concepts of the exile of an original "drunken king" who founded the kingship and simultaneously initiated the diaspora from the origin-place, in order to conform to Aztec cultural categories and conceptions of cyclical time, in which the present must be continuous with the past and the future. Thus the dynamic nature of structural process, the transformation of cultural categories and relationships, is revealed in the creation of the static repetitiveness of sacred history, a history in which the past is modified so that it remains the same as the present in order to account for the actual and inevitable differences between the past and the present.

Appendix:
Documents Used in the Analysis

A. Primarily Prose Documents

Title	Census No.[a]	Date	Provenience	Language	References
Anales de Cuauhtitlan	GG 1033	c. 1570	Central Mexico	Nahuatl	Anales de Cuauhtitlan 1975
Anales de Tlatelolco	GR 230	c. 1528[b]	Tlatelolco	Nahuatl	Anales de Tlatelolco 1948
	GG 1073				
Cantares Mexicanos	GG 1019	16th century	Central Mexico	Nahuatl	Garibay K. 1964–68
Carta al Rey Don Felipe II of Pablo Nazareo of Xaltocan	GG 1075	1566	Xaltocan	Latin	Nazareo de Xaltocan 1940
Fragment de l'Histoire des Anciens Mexicains	GR 202	16th (?) century	Central Mexico	Nahuatl	Fragment de l'Histoire des Anciens Mexicains 1981
Leyenda de los Soles	GG 1055				
	GG 1111	c. 1558	Central Mexico	Nahuatl	Leyenda de los Soles 1975
Historia de Tlaxcala of Diego Muñoz Camargo	GG 1072	late 16th century	Tlaxcala	Spanish	Muñoz Camargo 1978
Historia Tolteca-Chichimeca	GR 359	after 1544	Cuauhtinchan, Puebla	Nahuatl	Historia Tolteca-Chichimeca 1976
	GG 1129				
Relaciones (Diferentes historias originales de los reynos de Culhuacan y México y de otras provincias) and Memorial Breve of Domingo Francisco de San Antón Muñón Chimalpahin Cuauhtlehuanitzin	GG 1027	c. 1606–31	Mexico City	Nahuatl	Chimalpahin 1958 (Memorial Breve), 1965, 1983 (Relaciones)
Anales Tepanecas of Chimalpahin	GG 1115	c. 1615	Mexico City	Nahuatl	Anales Tepanecas 1903
Crónica Mexicayotl (authored in part by Chimalpahin)	GG 1062	early 17th century	Mexico City	Nahuatl	Tezozomoc 1975

Title	Number	Date	Region	Language	Citation
Relaciones and *Historia Chichimeca* of Fernando de Alva Ixtlilxochitl	GG 1043, GG 1044	1600–1640	Teotihuacan-Texcoco	Spanish	Ixtlilxochitl 1975, 1977
"Crónica X" documents					
Historia de las Indias de Nueva España e Islas de Tierra Firme of Diego Durán	GR 114, GG 1036	c. 1579–81	Valley of Mexico	Spanish	Durán 1967
Crónica Mexicana of Hernando Alvarado Tezozomoc	GG 1012	c. 1598 or early 17th century	Central Mexico	Spanish	Tezozomoc 1980
Codex Ramirez and *Historia de la Benida de los Yndios Apoblar a México (Manuscrit de Tovar)* of Juan de Tovar	GR 365, GG 1131	c. 1583–87	Valley of Mexico	Spanish	*Codex Ramirez* 1980; Tovar 1972
Franciscan-authored documents					
"Cano Relaciones": *Relación de la Genealogía*	GG 1038	c. 1532	Central Mexico	Spanish	*Relación de la Genealogía* 1941
Origen de los Mexicanos	GG 1061	c. 1532	Central Mexico	Spanish	*Origen de los Mexicanos* 1941
Historia de los Mexicanos por sus Pinturas	GG 1060	c. 1535	Central Mexico	Spanish	*Historia de los Mexicanos por sus Pinturas* 1941
Histoyre du Mechique	GG 1049	c. 1543	Central Mexico	French (originally Spanish)	*Histoyre du Mechique* 1905

A. Primarily Prose Documents (Continued)

Title	Census No.[a]	Date	Provenience	Language	References
Historia de los Indios de la Nueva España and *Memoriales* of Toribio de Motolinía	GG 1070 GG 1071	c. 1536–43 or before 1552	Central Mexico	Spanish	Motolinía 1951, 1903
Historia Eclesiástica Indiana of Gerónimo de Mendieta	GG 1052	1596	Central Mexico	Spanish	Mendieta 1945
Historia General de las Cosas de Nueva España (*Florentine Codex*) (*Códices Matritenses*) of Bernardino de Sahagún	GR 274 GG 1104 GR 271 GG 1097	1575–80 c. 1559–75	Tlatelolco	Nahuatl and Spanish	Sahagún 1950–82 (*Florentine Codex*, Nahuatl text); Sahagún 1956 (*Florentine Codex*, Spanish text); Sahagún 1964

[a]Census # refers to the censuses compiled by Glass and Robertson (1975) for the primarily pictorial documents, and by Gibson and Glass (1975) for the prose manuscripts in the native historical tradition.
[b]The 1528 date is suspect because it is found only in a later (17th century?) copy of this manuscript, in a statement that the work was written in 1528 (see *Anales de Tlatelolco* 1948:31).

B. Primarily Pictorial Documents

Title	Census #	Date	Provenience	References
Anales de Tula	GR 369	16th century	Tula, Hidalgo	*Anales de Tula* 1949
Codex Aubin	GR 13 GG 1014	1576–96, 1587–1608	Mexico City	*Codex Aubin* 1963
Codex Azcatitlan	GR 20	16th century	Valley of Mexico	*Codex Azcatitlan* 1949
Codex Boturini	GR 34	16th century	Mexico City	*Codex Boturini* 1975

Codex Cozcatzin	GR 83	1572	Tenochtitlan-Tlatelolco area	Barlow 1946b, Robertson 1959
Codex de Huichapan	GR 142 GG 1042	late 16th–early 17th century	San Mateo Huichapan, Hidalgo	*Codex de Huichapan* 1976
Codex de Ixhuatepec	GR 167	18th century	Tenochtitlan-Tlatelolco area or San Juan Ixhuatepec	Zantwijk 1976
Codex en Cruz	GR 84	1553–69	Texcoco region	*Codex en Cruz* 1981
Codex García Granados (Techialoyan Q)	#715[a]	c. 1700–1743	Azcapotzalco?	Anonymous 1979; Barlow 1945a, 1946a, 1947
Codex Mendoza	GR 196 GG 1053	c. 1541–42	Mexico City	*Codex Mendoza* 1964
Codex Mexicanus	GR 207	1571–90	Valley of Mexico	*Codex Mexicanus* 1952
Codex Ríos (*Codex Vaticanus A*)	GR 270	c. 1566–89	Valley of Mexico	*Codex Ríos* 1831
Codex Telleriano-Remensis	GR 308	1562–63	Valley of Mexico	*Codex Telleriano-Remensis* 1899
Codex Xolotl	GR 412	16th century	Texcoco region	*Codex Xolotl* 1980
Genealogía de los Príncipes Mexicanos	GR 248	after 1544	San Cristóbal Ecátepec or Mexico City	*Genealogía de los Príncipes Mexicanos* 1958
Lienzo de Tlaxcala	GR 350	c. 1550	Tlaxcala	*Lienzo de Tlaxcala* 1964
Mapa Tlotzin	GR 356	before 1550	Texcoco	*Mapa Tlotzin* 1886, Radin 1920
Plano en Papel de Maguey	GR 189	c. 1557–62	Tenochtitlan-Tlatelolco area	*Plano en Papel de Maguey* 1910
Tira de Tepechpan	GR 317	1596	Tepechpan	*Tira de Tepechpan* n.d.

[a] The *Codex García Granados*, a Techialoyan document, is catalogued in Robertson 1975.

Bibliography

Abbreviations Used

ECN   *Estudios de Cultura Náhuatl*, Mexico City
HMAI *Handbook of Middle American Indians*, University of Texas
       Press, Austin
ICAP *International Congress of Americanists, Proceedings*
INAH Instituto Nacional de Antropología e Historia, Mexico City
JSAP   *Journal de la Société des Américanistes de Paris*
JLAL   *Journal of Latin American Lore*
MAMH *Memorias de la Academia Mexicana de la Historia*, Mexico City
MARI Middle American Research Institute, Tulane University
RMEA *Revista Mexicana de Estudios Antropológicos*, Mexico City
SEP   Secretaría de Educación Pública, Mexico City
UNAM Universidad Nacional Autónoma de México, Mexico City

Acosta, Fray Joseph de
1940   *Historia Natural y Moral de las Indias*. Edmundo O'Gorman, ed.
       Mexico City: Fondo de Cultura Económica. Originally published
       in 1590.
Acosta Saignes, Miguel
1946   Los Teopixque. *RMEA* 8(1–3): 147–205.
Adler, Alfred
1982   The Ritual Doubling of the Person of the King. In *Between Belief
       and Transgression: Structuralist Essays in Religion, History, and
       Myth*, Michel Izard and Pierre Smith, eds., 180–192. Chicago:
       University of Chicago Press.

238   *Bibliography*

Aguilar, Fray Francisco de
1963   The Chronicle of Fray Francisco de Aguilar. In *The
          Conquistadors: First-Person Accounts of the Conquest of Mexico*,
          Patricia de Fuentes, trans. and ed., 134–164. New York: Orion
          Press. Written in 1560.
Anales de Cuauhtitlan
1975   *Códice Chimalpopoca.* Primo Feliciano Velázquez, trans., 3–118.
          UNAM.
Anales de Tlatelolco
1948   *Anales de Tlatelolco: Unos Anales Históricos de la Nación
          Mexicana y Códice de Tlatelolco.* Heinrich Berlin and Robert
          Barlow, eds. Mexico City: Antigua Libreria Robredo de Porrúa e
          Hijos.
Anales de Tula
1949   Anales de Tula, Hidalgo, 1361–1521. Robert Barlow,
          commentator. *Tlalocan* 3(1): 2–13.
Anales Tepanecas
1903   Anales Mexicanos: México-Azcapotzalco, 1426–1589. F. Galicia
          Chimalpopoca, trans. *Anales del Museo Nacional de México*,
          epoca 1, 7:49–74.
Anderson, Arthur J. O.
1960   Sahagún's Nahuatl Texts as Indigenist Documents. *ECN* 2:31–42.
Andrews IV, E. Wyllys
1965   Archaeology and Prehistory in the Northern Maya Lowlands: An
          Introduction. In *HMAI*. Vol. 2, *Archaeology of Southern
          Mesoamerica*, pt. 1, Gordon R. Willey, ed., 288–330.
Andrews V, E. Wyllys
1977   Some Comments on Puuc Architecture of the Northern Yucatan
          Peninsula. In *The Puuc: New Perspectives*, Lawrence Mills, ed.,
          1–17. Pella, Ia.: Central College.
Annals of the Cakchiquels
1979   *The Annals of the Cakchiquels.* Adrián Recinos and Delia Goetz,
          trans., 1–159. Norman: University of Oklahoma Press.
Anonymous
1979   *Los Códices de México.* INAH.
Barclay, William
1959   *The Master's Men.* Nashville: Abingdon Press.
Barlow, Robert H.
1945a   Los Caciques Precortesianos de Tlatelolco en el Códice García
          Granados (Techialoyan Q). *MAMH* 4(4): 467–483.
1945b   Some Remarks on the Term "Aztec Empire." *Americas* 1:345–349.
1946a   El Reverso del Códice García Granados. *MAMH* 5(4): 422–438.
1946b   Los Caciques de Tlatelolco en el Códice Cozcatzin. *MAMH* 5(4):
          416–421.
1947   Otros Caciques Coloniales de Tlatelolco, 1567–1623. *MAMH* 6(2):
          189–192.
1949   The Extent of the Empire of the Culhua Mexica. *Ibero-Americana*
          28. Berkeley: University of California Press.

Berdan, Frances F.

1982   *The Aztecs of Central Mexico: An Imperial Society.* New York: Holt, Rinehart and Winston.

Bharati, Agehananda

1985   Pattini: The Anthropological Consummation of a Goddess. *American Anthropologist* 87:364–369.

Bierhorst, John

1974   *Four Masterworks of American Indian Literature.* New York: Farrar, Straus and Giroux.

Bixler, Ray H.

1982   Comment on the Incidence and Purpose of Royal Sibling Incest. *American Ethnologist* 9:580–582.

Bohannan, Laura

1952   A Genealogical Charter. *Africa* 22:301–315.

Borah, Woodrow

1984   Some Problems of Sources. In *Explorations in Ethnohistory: Indians of Central Mexico in the Sixteenth Century,* H. R. Harvey and Hanns J. Prem, eds., 23–39. Albuquerque: University of New Mexico Press.

Borhegyi, Stephan F. de

1965   Archaeological Synthesis of the Guatemalan Highlands. In *HMAI.* Vol. 2, *Archaeology of Southern Mesoamerica,* pt. 1, Gordon R. Willey, ed., 3–58.

Brady, Ivan

1982   Les Îles Marquises: Ethnography from Another Beachhead. *American Ethnologist* 9:185–190.

Bricker, Victoria Reifler

1981   *The Indian Christ, the Indian King: The Historical Substrate of Maya Myth and Ritual.* Austin: University of Texas Press.

Brinton, Daniel G.

1890a   *Essays of an Americanist.* Philadelphia: Porter and Coates.
1890b   *Rig Veda Americanus.* Philadelphia: D. G. Brinton.

Broda, Johanna

1970   Tlacaxipeualiztli: A Reconstruction of an Aztec Calendar Festival from 16th Century Sources. *Revista Española de Antropología Americana* 5:197–274.
1975   Algunas Notas Sobre Critica de Fuentes del México Antiguo: Relaciones Entre las Crónicas de Olmos, Motolinía, Las Casas, Mendieta y Torquemada. *Revista de Indias* 25(139–142): 123–165.
1976   Los Estamentos en el Ceremonial Mexica. In *Estratificación Social en la Mesoamérica Prehispánica,* Pedro Carrasco and Johanna Broda, eds., 37–66. INAH.
1982   Astronomy, *Cosmovisión,* and Ideology in Pre-Hispanic Mesoamerica. In *Ethnoastronomy and Archaeoastronomy in the American Tropics,* Anthony F. Aveni and Gary Urton, eds. Annals of the New York Academy of Sciences 385:81–110.

Brown, Betty Ann

1984   Ochpaniztli in Historical Perspective. In *Ritual Human Sacrifice in Mesoamerica*, Elizabeth H. Boone, ed., 195–210. Washington, D.C.: Dumbarton Oaks.

Brown, Kenneth L.
1980 Archaeology in the Quiche Basin, Guatemala. *Mexicon* 2:72–73.

Brown, Raymond E., Karl P. Donfried, Joseph A. Fitzmyer, and John Reumann, eds.
1978 *Mary in the New Testament: A Collaborative Assessment by Protestant and Roman Catholic Scholars*. Philadelphia: Fortress Press.

Brundage, Burr Cartwright
1979 *The Fifth Sun: Aztec Gods, Aztec World*. Austin: University of Texas Press.
1982 *The Phoenix of the Western World: Quetzalcoatl and the Sky Religion*. Norman: University of Oklahoma Press.

Bucher, Bernadette
1981 *Icon and Conquest: A Structural Analysis of the Illustrations of de Bry's Great Voyages*. Basia Miller Gulati, trans. Chicago: University of Chicago Press.

Calnek, Edward B.
1973 The Historical Validity of the Codex Xolotl. *American Antiquity* 38:423–427.
1978 The Analysis of Prehispanic Central Mexican Historical Texts. *ECN* 13:239–266.

Carlson, John B.
1980 On Classic Maya Monumental Recorded History. In *Third Palenque Round Table*, 1978, pt. 2. Merle Greene Robertson, ed., 199–203. The Palenque Round Table Series, vol. 5. Austin: University of Texas Press.

Carmack, Robert M.
1968 Toltec Influence on the Postclassic Culture History of Highland Guatemala. *MARI Publication* 26:49–92.
1972 Ethnohistory: A Review of Its Development, Definition, Methods, and Aims. *Annual Review of Anthropology* 1:227–246.

Carrasco, Davíd
1980 Quetzalcoatl's Revenge: Primordium and Application in Aztec Religion. *History of Religions* 19:296–320.
1981 Templo Mayor: The Aztec Vision of Place. *Religion* 11:275–297.
1982 *Quetzalcoatl and the Irony of Empire: Myths and Prophecies in the Aztec Tradition*. Chicago: University of Chicago Press.

Carrasco, Pedro
1966a La Etnohistoria en Meso-américa. 36th *ICAP*, 1964, Barcelona 2: 109–110.
1966b Sobre Algunos Términos de Parentesco en el Náhuatl Clásico. *ECN* 6:149–166.
1976 La Sociedad Mexicana Antes de la Conquista. In *Historia General de México* 1:165–288. Mexico City: El Colegio de México.
1984 Royal Marriages in Ancient Mexico. In *Explorations in*

Ethnohistory: Indians of Central Mexico in the Sixteenth Century. H. R. Harvey and Hanns J. Prem, eds. Albuquerque: University of New Mexico Press.

Caso, Alfonso
1953   *El Pueblo del Sol.* Mexico City: Fondo de Cultura Económica.

Charlton, Thomas H.
1981   Archaeology, Ethnohistory and Ethnology: Interpretive Interfaces. In *Advances in Archaeological Method and Theory* 4:129–174. New York: Academic Press.

Chavero, Alfredo
n.d.   *México a Través de los Siglos.* Vol. 1, *Historia Antigua y de la Conquista.* Vicente Riva Palacio, ed. Mexico City. Published c. 1887.

Chilam Balam of Chumayel
1967   *The Book of Chilam Balam of Chumayel.* Ralph Roys, trans. Norman: University of Oklahoma Press. Originally published 1933.

Chilam Balam of Maní
1979   *The Codex Pérez and The Book of the Chilam Balam of Maní.* Eugene R. Craine and Reginald C. Reindorp, trans. Norman: University of Oklahoma Press.

Chimalpahin Cuauhtlehuanitzin, Domingo Francisco de San Antón Muñón
1958   *Das "Memorial Breve Acerca de la Fundación de la Ciudad de Culhuacán."* Walter Lehmann and Gerdt Kutscher, trans. and eds. Quellenwerke zur Alten Geschichte Amerikas aufgezeichnet in den Sprachen der Eingeborenen, vol. 7. Stuttgart.
1965   *Relaciones Originales de Chalco Amaquemeca.* Silvia Rendón, trans. Mexico City: Fondo de Cultura Económica.
1983   *Octava Relación.* José Rubén Romero Galván, trans. UNAM.

Clavijero, Padre Francisco Javier
1976   *Historia Antigua de México.* 5th ed. Mexico City: Editorial Porrúa.

Cline, Howard F.
1971   Missing and Variant Prologues and Dedications in Sahagún's *Historia General:* Texts and English Translations. *ECN* 9: 237–252.
1972   Introduction: Reflections on Ethnohistory. In *HMAI.* Vol. 12, *Guide to Ethnohistorical Sources,* pt. 1, Howard F. Cline, ed., 3–16.

Codex Aubin
1963   *Historia de la Nación Mexicana: Reproducción del Códice de 1576 (Códice Aubin).* Charles E. Dibble, trans. and ed. Madrid: José Porrúa Turanzas.

Codex Azcatitlan
1949   *El Códice Azcatitlan.* Robert Barlow, commentator. *JSAP* 38: 101–135.

Codex Boturini
1975   *Códice Boturini.* Colección de Documentos Conmemorativos del DCL Aniversario de la Fundación de Tenochtitlan, no. 1. SEP.

Codex de Huichapan
1976   *El Códice de Huichapan. Pt. 1, Relato Otomí del México Prehispánico y Colonial.* Manuel Alvarado Guinchard, trans. INAH Colección Científica, no. 48.

Codex en Cruz
1981   *Codex en Cruz.* 2 vols. Charles E. Dibble, ed. Salt Lake City: University of Utah Press.

Codex Mendoza
1964   *Antigüedades de México Basadas en la Recopilación de Lord Kingsborough.* José Corona Núñez, ed. Vol. 1. Mexico City: Secretaría de Hacienda y Crédito Público.

Codex Mexicanus
1952   Commentaire du Codex Mexicanus Nos. 23–24 de la Bibliothèque Nationale de Paris. Ernest Mengin, commentator. *JSAP* 41: 287–498.

Codex Ramirez
1980   *Códice Ramirez: Relación del Origen de los Indios que Habitan esta Nueva España, Según sus Historias.* Manuel Orozco y Berra, ed., 9–149. 3d ed. Mexico City: Editorial Porrúa.

Codex Ríos
1831   *Antiquities of Mexico, Comprising Facsimiles of Ancient Mexican Paintings and Hieroglyphs.* Lord Kingsborough, comp. Vol. 6. London.

Codex Telleriano-Remensis
1899   *Codex Telleriano-Remensis: Manuscrit Mexicain No. 385 a la Bibliothèque Nationale.* E.-T. Hamy, commentator. Paris.

Codex Xolotl
1980   *Códice Xolotl.* Charles E. Dibble, ed. 2 vols. 2d ed. UNAM.

Cohen, Ronald
1977   Oedipus Rex and Regina: The Queen Mother in Africa. *Africa* 47: 14–30.

Cohodas, Marvin
1978   *The Great Ball Court at Chichén Itzá, Yucatan, Mexico.* New York: Garland Publishing.

Cortés, Hernán
1971   *Letters from Mexico.* Introduction by J. H. Elliott. A. R. Pagden, trans. New York: Orion Press.

Davies, Nigel
1973   *Los Mexicas: Primeros Pasos Hacia el Imperio.* UNAM.
1974   *The Aztecs: A History.* New York: G. P. Putnam's Sons.
1977   *The Toltecs Until the Fall of Tula.* Norman: University of Oklahoma Press.
1979   Mixcoatl: Man and God. 42d *ICAP*, 1976, Paris, 6:19–26.
1980   *The Toltec Heritage from the Fall of Tula to the Rise of Tenochtitlan.* Norman: University of Oklahoma Press.

1982   Tula Revisited. *Mexicon* 3:104–107.
1984   The Aztec Concept of History: Teotihuacan and Tula. In *The Native Sources and the History of the Valley of Mexico,* Jacqueline de Durand-Forest, ed., 207–214. BAR International Series 204. Oxford.
1987   *The Aztec Empire: The Toltec Resurgence.* Norman: University of Oklahoma Press.
Detienne, Marcel
1977   *The Gardens of Adonis: Spices in Greek Mythology.* Janet Lloyd, trans. Atlantic Highlands, N.J.: Humanities Press.
Díaz del Castillo, Bernal
1970   *The Discovery and Conquest of Mexico, 1517–1521.* A. P. Maudslay, trans. New York: Octagon Books.
Dibble, Charles E.
1960   Spanish Influence on the Aztec Writing System. In *Homenaje a Rafael García Granados,* 171–177. INAH.
1971   Writing in Central Mexico. In *HMAI.* Vol. 10, *Archaeology of Northern Mesoamerica,* pt. 1, Gordon F. Ekholm and Ignacio Bernal, eds., 322–331.
1974   The Nahuatlization of Christianity. In *Sixteenth-Century Mexico: The Work of Sahagún,* Munro S. Edmonson, ed., 225–234. Albuquerque: University of New Mexico Press.
Diehl, Richard A.
1974   *Studies of Ancient Tollan: A Report of the University of Missouri Tula Archaeological Project.* Richard A. Diehl, ed. University of Missouri Monographs in Anthropology, no. 1.
1981   Tula. In *Supplement to the HMAI.* Vol. 1, *Archaeology,* Jeremy A. Sabloff, ed., 227–295.
1983   *Tula: The Toltec Capital of Ancient Mexico.* London: Thames and Hudson.
Diehl, Richard A., and Robert A. Benfer
1975   Tollan: The Toltec Capital. *Archaeology* 28(2): 112–124.
Diehl, Richard A., Roger Lomas, and Jack T. Wynn
1974   Toltec Trade with Central America: New Light and Evidence. *Archaeology* 27(3): 182–187.
Dorson, Richard M.
1961   Ethnohistory and Ethnic Folklore. *Ethnohistory* 8:12–30.
Durán, Fray Diego
1967   *Historia de las Indias de Nueva España e Islas de la Tierra Firme.* Angel Ma. Garibay K., ed. 2 vols. Mexico City: Editorial Porrúa.
Duverger, Christian
1983   *L'Origine des Aztèques.* Paris: Editions du Seuil.
Eliade, Mircea
1958   *Birth and Rebirth: The Religious Meanings of Initiation in Human Culture.* New York: Harper Bros.
1961   *Images and Symbols: Studies in Religious Symbolism.* New York: Sheed and Ward.
1969   *The Two and the One.* New York: Harper and Row.

Elliott, J. H.
1967   The Mental World of Hernán Cortés. *Transactions of the Royal Historical Society*, 5th ser., 17:41–58.

Elzey, Wayne
1976a   The Nahua Myth of the Suns: History and Cosmology in Pre-Hispanic Mexican Religions. *Numen* 23(2): 114–135.
1976b   Some Remarks on the Space and Time of the "Center" in Aztec Religion. *ECN* 12:315–334.

Feeley-Harnik, Gillian
1985   Issues in Divine Kingship. *Annual Review of Anthropology* 14: 273–313.

Feldman, Lawrence H.
1966   Conflict in Historical Interpretation of the Aztec State, Society and Culture. *ECN* 6:167–175.

Fernández de Oviedo y Valdés, Gonzalo
1945   *Historia General y Natural de las Indias, Islas y Tierra-Firme del Mar Océano*. Vol. 10. Asunción: Editorial Guaranía. Originally published in the 1550s.

Fox, John W.
1981   The Late Postclassic Eastern Frontier of Mesoamerica: Cultural Innovation Along the Periphery. *Current Anthropology* 22: 321–346.

Fragment de l'Histoire des Anciens Mexicains
1981   *Geschichte der Azteken: Codex Aubin und vewandte Dokumente*. Walter Lehmann and Gerdt Kutscher, trans. and eds. Quellenwerke zur Alten Geschichte Amerikas aufgezeichnet in den Sprachen der Eingeborenen, vol. 13. Berlin: Gebr. Mann Verlag.

Frankfort, Henri
1948   *Kingship and the Gods: A Study of Ancient Near Eastern Religion as the Integration of Society and Nature*. Chicago: University of Chicago Press.

Frankl, Victor
1966   Die "Cartas de Relación" des Hernán Cortés und der Mythos der Wiederkehr des Quetzalcoatl. *ADEVA*. Mitteilungen 10:7–17. Graz.

Furst, Jill Leslie
1978a   *Codex Vindobonensis Mexicanus I: A Commentary*. State University of New York at Albany, Institute for Mesoamerican Studies, Publication 4.
1978b   The Year 1 Reed, Day 1 Alligator: A Mixtec Metaphor. *JLAL* 4: 93–128.
1986   The Lords of "Place of the Ascending Serpent": Dynastic Succession on the Nuttall Obverse. In *Symbol and Meaning Beyond the Closed Community: Essays in Mesoamerican Ideas*, Gary H. Gossen, ed., 57–68. State University of New York at Albany, Institute for Mesoamerican Studies, Studies on Culture and Society, vol. 1.

Gardner, Brant
1981   A Structural and Semantic Analysis of Classical Náhuatl Kinship
          Terminology. *ECN* 15:89–124.
Garibay K., Angel María
1954   *Historia de la Literatura Náhuatl.* 2 vols. Mexico City: Editorial
          Porrúa.
1964–68 *Poesía Náhuatl.* Vols. 2 and 3, *Cantares Mexicanos.* Manuscrito
          de la Biblioteca Nacional de México. UNAM.
Geertz, Clifford
1973   *The Interpretation of Cultures.* New York: Basic Books.
Genealogía de los Príncipes Mexicanos.
1958   Fragmento de Genealogia de los Príncipes Mexicanos. Alfonso
          Caso, ed. *JSAP* 47:21–31.
Gibson, Charles
1952   *Tlaxcala in the Sixteenth Century.* New Haven, Conn.: Yale
          University Press.
1964   *The Aztecs Under Spanish Rule.* Stanford, Calif.: Stanford
          University Press.
1971   Structure of the Aztec Empire. In *HMAI.* Vol. 10, *Archaeology of
          Northern Mesoamerica,* pt. 1, Gordon F. Ekholm and Ignacio
          Bernal, eds., 376–394.
1975   Prose Sources in the Native Historical Tradition. In *HMAI.* Vol.
          15, *Guide to Ethnohistorical Sources,* pt. 4, Howard F. Cline, ed.,
          311–321.
Gibson, Charles, and John B. Glass
1975   A Census of Middle American Prose Manuscripts in the Native
          Historical Tradition. In *HMAI.* Vol. 15, *Guide to Ethnohistorical
          Sources,* pt. 4, Howard F. Cline, ed., 322–400.
Gillespie, Susan D.
n.d.   Ballgames and Boundaries. Paper presented at the International
          Symposium on the Mesoamerican Ballgame and Ballcourts in the
          New World, Tucson, 1985.
Gillmor, Frances
1964   *The King Danced in the Market Place.* Tucson: University of
          Arizona Press.
Glass, John B.
1975   A Survey of Native Middle American Pictorial Manuscripts. In
          HMAI. Vol. 14, *Guide to Ethnohistorical Sources,* pt. 3, Howard F.
          Cline, ed., 3–80.
Glass, John B., and Donald Robertson
1975   A Census of Native Middle American Pictorial Manuscripts. In
          HMAI. Vol. 14, *Guide to Ethnohistorical Sources,* pt. 3, Howard F.
          Cline, ed., 81–252.
Goody, Jack, and Ian Watt
1962–63 The Consequences of Literacy. *Comparative Studies in Society
          and History* 5:304–345.
Gossen, Gary H.
1972   Temporal and Spatial Equivalents in Chamula Ritual Symbolism.

In *Reader in Comparative Religion: An Anthropological Approach*, 3d ed., William A. Lessa and Evon Z. Vogt, eds., 135–149. New York: Harper and Row.

1977   Translating Cuscat's War: Understanding Maya Oral History. *JLAL* 3:249–278.

Graulich, Michel

1981a   The Metaphor of the Day in Ancient Mexican Myth and Ritual. *Current Anthropology* 22:45–60.

1981b   More on the Day and Ancient Mexican Myth. *Current Anthropology* 22:438–439.

1983   Myths of Paradise Lost in Pre-Hispanic Central Mexico. *Current Anthropology* 24:575–588.

1984   Aspects Mythiques des Peregrinations Mexicas. In *The Native Sources and the History of the Valley of Mexico*, Jacqueline de Durand-Forest, ed., 24–75. BAR International Series 204. Oxford.

Grove, David C.

1983   Review of *The Art and Iconography of Late Post-Classic Central Mexico*, Elizabeth Hill Boone, ed. *American Antiquity* 48: 871–872.

Harvey, H. R., and Hanns J. Prem

1984   Introduction to *Explorations in Ethnohistory: Indians of Central Mexico in the Sixteenth Century*, H. R. Harvey and Hanns J. Prem, eds., 1–21. Albuquerque: University of New Mexico Press.

Heusch, Luc de

1982   *The Drunken King; or, The Origin of the State*. Roy Willis, trans. Bloomington: Indiana University Press.

1985   *Sacrifice in Africa: A Structuralist Approach*. Linda O'Brien and Alice Morton, trans. Bloomington: Indiana University Press.

Historia de los Mexicanos por sus Pinturas

1941   *Nueva Colección de Documentos para la Historia de México*. Joaquín García Icazbalceta, ed., 3:209–240. Mexico City: Editorial Chavez Hayhoe.

Historia Tolteca-Chichimeca

1976   *Historia Tolteca-Chichimeca*. Paul Kirchhoff, Lina Odena Güemes, and Luis Reyes García, eds. and trans. INAH.

Histoyre du Mechique

1905   Histoyre du Mechique. Edouard de Jonghe, ed. *JSAP* 2:1–41.

Huddleston, Lee Eldridge

1967   *Origins of the American Indians: European Concepts, 1492–1729*. Austin: University of Texas Press.

Hudson, Charles

1966   Folk History and Ethnohistory. *Ethnohistory* 13:52–70.

Hunt, Eva

1977   *The Transformation of the Hummingbird: Cultural Roots in a Zinacantan Mythical Poem*. Ithaca: Cornell University Press.

Ichon, Alain

1973   *La Religión de los Totonacas de la Sierra*. José Arenas, trans. SEP.

Ixtlilxochitl, Fernando de Alva
1975   *Obras Históricas.* Vol. 1. Edmundo O'Gorman, ed. UNAM.
1977   *Obras Históricas.* Vol. 2. Edmundo O'Gorman, ed. UNAM.
Jiménez Moreno, Wigberto
1941   Tula y los Toltecas Según las Fuentes Históricas. *RMEA* 5:79–83.
1956   *Notas Sobre Historia Antigua de México.* Mexico City: Ediciones S.A.E.N.A.H.
1966   Mesoamerica before the Toltecs. In *Ancient Oaxaca,* John Paddock, ed., 1–82. Stanford, Calif.: Stanford University Press.
Joyce, Rosemary A.
1981   Classic Maya Kinship and Descent: An Alternative Suggestion. *Journal of the Steward Anthropological Society* 13(1): 45–57.
Karttunen, Frances
1983   *An Analytical Dictionary of Nahuatl.* Austin: University of Texas Press.
Keen, Benjamin
1971   *The Aztec Image in Western Thought.* New Brunswick, N.J.: Rutgers University Press.
Kirchhoff, Paul
1954–55 Composición Etnica y Organización Política de Chalco Según las Relaciones de Chimalpahin. *RMEA* 14(pt. 2): 297–298.
1955   Quetzalcoatl, Huémac y el Fin de Tula. *Cuadernos Americanos* 84(6): 163–196.
Klein, Cecilia F.
1975   Post-Classic Mexican Death Imagery as a Sign of Cyclic Completion. In *Death and the Afterlife in Pre-Columbian America,* Elizabeth P. Benson, ed., 69–85. Washington, D.C.: Dumbarton Oaks.
1980   Who Was Tlaloc? *JLAL* 6:155–204.
Klijn, A.F.J.
1962   *The Acts of Thomas.* Leiden: E. J. Brill.
Krickeberg, Walter
1966   El Juego de Pelota Mesoamericano y su Simbolismo Religioso. *Traducciones Mesoamericanistas* 1:191–313. Sociedad Mexicana de Antropología.
Kubler, George A.
1961   Chichen-Itza y Tula. *Estudios de Cultura Maya* 1:47–80.
1962   *The Art and Architecture of Ancient America: The Mexican, Maya, and Andean Peoples.* Harmondsworth, Eng.: Penguin Books.
1972a La Evidencia Intrínseca y la Analogía Etnológica en el Estudio de las Religiones Mesoamericanas. In *Religión en Mesoamerica,* Jaime Litvak King and Noemí Castillo Tejero, eds., 1–24. 12th Mesa Redonda, Sociedad Mexicana de Antropología.
1972b *Mexican Architecture of the Sixteenth Century.* 2 vols. Westport, Conn.: Greenwood Press.
1984   *The Art and Architecture of Ancient America: The Mexican, Maya and Andean Peoples.* 3d ed. New York: Penguin Books.

Kurtz, Donald V.
1982   The Virgin of Guadalupe and the Politics of Becoming Human.
        Journal of Anthropological Research 38:194–210.
Lafaye, Jacques
1972   Mexico According to Quetzalcoatl: An Essay of Intra-History.
        Diogenes 78:18–37.
1976   *Quetzalcóatl and Guadalupe: The Formation of Mexican
        National Consciousness, 1531–1813.* Benjamin Keen, trans.
        Chicago: University of Chicago Press.
Landa, Fray Diego de
1978   *Yucatan Before and After the Conquest.* William Gates, trans.
        New York: Dover Publications.
Las Casas, Fray Bartolomé de
1971   *Los Indios de México y Nueva España: Antología.* Edmundo
        O'Gorman, ed. 2d ed. Mexico City: Editorial Porrúa.
Leach, Sir Edmund
1964   Animal Categories and Verbal Abuse. In *New Directions in the
        Study of Language,* Eric H. Lenneberg, ed., 23–63. Cambridge,
        Mass.: MIT Press.
1965   *Political Systems of Highland Burma.* Boston: Beacon Press.
1967   Genesis as Myth. In *Myth and Cosmos: Readings in Mythology
        and Symbolism,* John Middleton, ed., 1–13. Garden City, N.J.:
        Natural History Press.
1969   *Genesis as Myth and Other Essays.* London: Jonathan Cape.
1970   *Claude Lévi-Strauss.* New York: Viking Press.
1976   *Culture and Communication: The Logic by Which Symbols Are
        Connected.* Cambridge: Cambridge University Press.
1983   *Structuralist Interpretations of Biblical Myth.* Cambridge:
        Cambridge University Press.
León-Portilla, Miguel
1961   *Los Antiguos Mexicanos a Través de Sus Crónicas y Cantares.*
        Mexico City: Fondo de Cultura Económica.
1963   *Aztec Thought and Culture: A Study of the Ancient Nahuatl
        Mind.* Jack Emory Davis, trans. Norman: University of Oklahoma
        Press.
1974a   *El Reverso de la Conquista: Relaciones Aztecas, Mayas e Incas.*
        Mexico City: Editorial Joaquín Mortiz.
1974b   *La Filosofía Náhuatl: Estudiada en sus Fuentes.* 4th ed. UNAM.
1978   *México-Tenochtitlan: Su Espacio y Tiempo Sagrados.* INAH.
1980   *Toltecáyotl: Aspectos de la Cultura Náhuatl.* Mexico City: Fondo
        de Cultura Económica.
1983   Cuícatl y Tlahtolli: Las Formas de Expresión en Náhuatl. *ECN* 16:
        13–108.
Lévi-Strauss, Claude
1963   *Structural Anthropology.* Vol. 1. Claire Jacobson and Brooke
        Grundfest Schoepf, trans. New York: Basic Books.
1966   *The Savage Mind.* Chicago: University of Chicago Press.

1969   *The Raw and the Cooked.* John and Doreen Weightman, trans. New York: Harper and Row.

1973   *From Honey to Ashes.* John and Doreen Weightman, trans. New York: Harper and Row.

1979   *The Origin of Table Manners.* John and Doreen Weightman, trans. New York: Harper and Row.

1981   *The Naked Man.* John and Doreen Weightman, trans. New York: Harper and Row.

Leyenda de los Soles

1975   *Códice Chimalpopoca.* Primo Feliciano Velázquez, trans., 119–142. UNAM.

Lienzo de Tlaxcala

1964   *Lienzo de Tlaxcala.* Alfredo Chavero, ed. Artes de México 11, no. 51–52.

Linnekin, Jocelyn S.

1983   Defining Tradition: Variations on the Hawaiian Identity. *American Ethnologist* 10:241–252.

Litvak King, Jaime

1972   La Introducción Posthispánica de Elementos a las Religiones Prehispánicas: Un Problema de Aculturación Retroactiva. In *Religión en Mesoamerica*, Jaime Litvak King and Noemí Castillo Tejero, eds., 25–29. 12th Mesa Redonda, Sociedad Mexicana de Antropología.

López Austin, Alfredo

1973   *Hombre-Díos: Religión y Política en el Mundo Náhuatl.* UNAM.

1974   The Research Method of Fray Bernardino de Sahagún: The Questionnaires. In *Sixteenth-Century Mexico: The Work of Sahagún*, Munro S. Edmonson, ed., 111–150. Albuquerque: University of New Mexico Press.

López de Meneses, Amada

1948   Tecuichpochtzin, Hija de Moteczuma (¿1510?–1550). *Revista de Indias* 9:471–496.

Lord, Albert B.

1964   *The Singer of Tales.* Cambridge, Mass.: Harvard University Press.

Mapa Tlotzin

1886   Mapa Tlotzin: Historia de los Reyes y de los Estados Soberanos de Acolhuacan. J.M.A. Aubin, commentator. *Anales del Museo Nacional de México*, epoca 1, 3:304–320.

Maranda, Elli Köngäs

1972   Theory and Practice of Riddle Analysis. In *Toward New Perspectives in Folklore*, Americo Paredes and Richard Bauman, eds., 51–61. Austin: University of Texas Press.

Margain, Carlos R.

1971   Pre-Columbian Architecture of Central Mexico. In *HMAI*. Vol. 10, *Archaeology of Northern Mesoamerica*, pt. 1. Gordon F. Ekholm and Ignacio Bernal, eds., 45–91.

Matos Moctezuma, Eduardo
1987   The Templo Mayor of Tenochtitlan: History and Interpretation. In *The Great Temple of Tenochtitlan: Center and Periphery in the Aztec World*, Johanna Broda, Davíd Carrasco, and Eduardo Matos Moctezuma, eds., 15–60. Berkeley: University of California Press.

Mendieta, Fray Gerónimo de
1945   *Historia Eclesiástica Indiana*. Mexico City: Editorial Salvador Chavez Hayhoe.

Métraux, Alfred
1946   Twin Heroes in South American Mythology. *Journal of American Folklore* 59:114–123.

Middleton, John
1967   Introduction to *Myth and Cosmos: Readings in Mythology and Symbolism*, John Middleton, ed., ix–xi. Garden City, N.J.: Natural History Press.

Miller, Mary Ellen
1985   A Re-examination of the Mesoamerican Chacmool. *The Art Bulletin* 67(1): 7–17.

Molina, Fray Alonso de
1977   *Vocabulario en Lengua Castellana y Mexicana y Mexicana y Castellana*. Mexico City: Editorial Porrúa.

Molina-Montes, Augusto
1982   Archaeological Buildings: Restoration or Misrepresentation. In *Falsifications and Misreconstructions of Pre-Columbian Art*, Elizabeth H. Boone, ed., 125–141. Washington, D.C.: Dumbarton Oaks.

Morley, Sylvanus G., and George W. Brainerd. Rev. by Robert J. Sharer
1983   *The Ancient Maya*. 4th ed. Stanford, Calif.: Stanford University Press.

Motolinía, Fray Toribio de
1903   *Memoriales*. Mexico City: Luis García Pimentel.
1951   *Motolinía's History of the Indians of New Spain*. Francis Borgia Steck, trans. and ed. Washington, D.C.: Academy of American Franciscan History.

Muñoz Camargo, Diego
1978   *Historia de Tlaxcala (Crónica del Siglo XVI)*. Alfredo Chavero, ed. 2d ed. Mexico City: Editorial Innovación.

Muría, José María
1973   *Sociedad Prehispánica y Pensamiento Europeo*. SEP.

Nazareo de Xaltocan, Pablo
1940   Carta al Rey Don Felipe II. In *Epistolario de Nueva España, 1505–1818*. Vol. 10, *1564–1569*, Francisco Paso y Troncoso, ed., 109–129. Mexico City: Antigua Libreria Robredo de Jose Porrúa e Hijos.

Needham, Rodney
1979   *Symbolic Classification*. Santa Monica, Calif.: Goodyear Publishing Co.

Nicholson, H. B.
1957   Topiltzin Quetzalcoatl of Tollan: A Problem in Mesoamerican
          Ethnohistory. Ph.D. diss., Department of Anthropology, Harvard
          University.
1971a   Major Sculpture in Pre-Hispanic Central Mexico. In *HMAI*. Vol.
          10, *Archaeology of Northern Mesoamerica*, pt. 1, Gordon F.
          Ekholm and Ignacio Bernal, eds., 92–134.
1971b   Religion in Pre-Hispanic Central Mexico. In *HMAI*. Vol. 10,
          Archaeology of Northern Mesoamerica, pt. 1, Gordon F. Ekholm
          and Ignacio Bernal, eds., 395–446.
1974   Tepepolco, the Locale of the First Stage of Fr. Bernardino de
          Sahagún's Great Ethnographic Project: Historical and Cultural
          Notes. In *Mesoamerican Archaeology: New Approaches*, Norman
          Hammond, ed., 145–154. Austin: University of Texas Press.
1975   Middle American Ethnohistory: An Overview. In *HMAI*. Vol. 15,
          Guide to Ethnohistorical Sources, pt. 4, Howard F. Cline, ed.,
          487–505.
1979   Ehecatl Quetzalcoatl vs. Topiltzin Quetzalcoatl of Tollan: A
          Problem in Mesoamerican Religion and History. 42d *ICAP* 1976,
          Paris, 6:35–47.
Nicolau d'Olwer, Luis, and Howard F. Cline
1973   Bernardino de Sahagún, 1499–1590. In *HMAI*. Vol. 13, *Guide to
          Ethnohistorical Sources*, pt. 2, Howard F. Cline and John B. Glass,
          eds., 186–207.
Offner, Jerome A.
1983   *Law and Politics in Aztec Texcoco.* Cambridge: Cambridge
          University Press.
Origen de los Mexicanos
1941   *Nueva Colección de Documentos para la Historia de México.*
          Joaquín García Icazbalceta, ed., 3:256–280. Mexico City: Editorial
          Chavez Hayhoe.
Packard, Randall M.
1981   *Chiefship and Cosmology: An Historical Study of Political
          Competition.* Bloomington: Indiana University Press.
Parsons, Lee A.
1969   *Bilbao, Guatemala: An Archaeological Study of the Pacific Coast
          Cotzumalhuapa Region.* Vol. 2. Milwaukee Public Museum
          Publications in Anthropology, no. 12.
Pasztory, Esther
1983   *Aztec Art.* New York: Harry N. Abrams.
Phelan, John Leddy
1970   *The Millennial Kingdom of the Franciscans in the New World: A
          Study in the Writing of Gerónimo de Mendieta, 1525–1604.* 2d ed.
          Berkeley: University of California Press.
Pickands, Martin
1986   The Hero Myth in Maya Folklore. In *Symbol and Meaning Beyond
          the Closed Community: Essays in Mesoamerican Ideas*, Gary H.

Gossen, ed., 101–123. State University of New York at Albany, Institute for Mesoamerican Studies, Studies on Culture and Society, vol. 1.

Piña Chan, Román
1980   *Chichén Itzá: La Ciudad de los Brujos del Agua*. Mexico City: Fondo de Cultura Económica.

Plano en Papel de Maguey
1910   Facsimile. In *The True History of the Conquest of New Spain by Bernal Díaz, One of Its Conquerors*. Vol. 3. Alfred Percival Maudslay, trans. Hakluyt Society, ser. 2, vol. 25. London.

Popol Vuh
1971   *The Book of Counsel: The Popol Vuh of the Quiche Maya of Guatemala*. Munro S. Edmonson, trans. *MARI Publication* 35.

Prem, Hanns J.
1984a   Die Herrscherfolge von Colhuacan. *Mexicon* 6:86–88.
1984b   The Chronological Dilemma. In *The Native Sources and the History of the Valley of Mexico*, Jacqueline de Durand-Forest, ed., 5–24. BAR International Series 204. Oxford.

Radin, Paul
1920   The Sources and Authenticity of the History of the Ancient Mexicans. *University of California Publications in American Archaeology and Ethnology* 17(1): 1–150.

Relación de la Genealogía
1941   *Nueva Colección de Documentos para la Historia de México*. Joaquín García Icazbalceta, ed., 3:240–256. Mexico City: Editorial Chavez Hayhoe.

Richards, Audrey I.
1960   Social Mechanisms for the Transfer of Political Rights in Some African Tribes. *Journal of the Royal Anthropological Institute of Great Britain and Ireland* 90:175–190.
1969   Keeping the King Divine. *Proceedings of the Royal Anthropological Institute* 1968, 23–35.

Robertson, Donald
1959   *Mexican Manuscript Painting of the Early Colonial Period: The Metropolitan Schools*. New Haven: Yale University Press.
1974   The Treatment of Architecture in the Florentine Codex of Sahagún. In *Sixteenth-Century Mexico: The Work of Sahagún*, Munro S. Edmonson, ed., 151–164. Albuquerque: University of New Mexico Press.
1975   Techialoyan Manuscripts and Paintings, with a Catalog. In *HMAI*. Vol. 14, *Guide to Ethnohistorical Sources*, pt. 3, Howard F. Cline, ed., 253–280.

Rodriguez, Gustavo A.
1935   *Doña Marina*. Mexico City: Secretaría de Relaciones Exteriores.

Ruz Lhuillier, Alberto
1964   Influencias Mexicanas en las Tierras Altas y Bajas del Área Maya. 35th *ICAP* 1962, Mexico City, 1:225–243.

Saenz, Cesar A.
1962   *Quetzalcóatl.* INAH.
Sahagún, Fray Bernardino de
1950–82 *Florentine Codex: General History of the Things of New Spain.*
        12 vols. Charles E. Dibble and Arthur J. O. Anderson, eds. and
        trans. Santa Fe: School of American Research and the University
        of Utah.
1956   *Historia General de las Cosas de Nueva España.* 4 vols. Angel
        María Garibay K., ed. Mexico City: Editorial Porrúa.
1964   *Códices Matritenses de la Historia General de las Cosas de la
        Nueva España.* Manuel Ballesteros-Gaibrois, ed. 2 pts. Madrid:
        Ediciones Jose Porrúa Turanzas.
Sahlins, Marshall
1981   *Historical Metaphors and Mythical Realities: Structure in the
        Early History of the Sandwich Islands Kingdom.* Ann Arbor:
        University of Michigan Press.
1982   The Apotheosis of Captain Cook. In *Between Belief and
        Transgression: Structuralist Essays in Religion, History, and
        Myth,* Michel Izard and Pierre Smith, eds.; John Leavitt, trans.;
        73–102. Chicago: University of Chicago Press.
1985   *Islands of History.* Chicago: University of Chicago Press.
Sanders, William T., Jeffrey R. Parsons, and Robert S. Santley
1979   *The Basin of Mexico: Ecological Processes in the Evolution of a
        Civilization.* New York: Academic Press.
Sandstrom, Alan R., and Pamela Effrein Sandstrom
1986   *Traditional Papermaking and Paper Cult Figures of Mexico.*
        Norman: University of Oklahoma Press.
Schele, Linda, and Mary Ellen Miller
1986   *The Blood of Kings: Dynasty and Ritual in Maya Art.* Fort Worth:
        Kimbell Art Museum.
Séjourné, Laurette
1960   *Burning Water: Thought and Religion in Ancient Mexico.* New
        York: Grove Press.
Seler, Eduard
1902–23 *Gesammelte Abhandlungen zur Amerikanischen Sprach-und
        Altertumskunde.* 5 vols. Berlin.
Smith, Mary Elizabeth
1973   *Picture Writing from Ancient Southern Mexico: Mixtec Place
        Signs and Maps.* Norman: University of Oklahoma Press.
Smith, Pierre
1982   Aspects of the Organization of Rites. In *Between Belief and
        Transgression: Structuralist Essays in Religion, History, and
        Myth,* Michel Izard and Pierre Smith, eds.; John Leavitt, trans.;
        103–128. Chicago: University of Chicago Press.
Sodi M., Demetrio
1962   Consideraciones Sobre el Origen de la Toltecáyotl. *ECN* 3:55–73.

Sotomayor, Arturo
1979   *Cortés Según Cortés.* Mexico City: Editorial Extemporaneos.
Soustelle, Jacques
1959   *Pensamiento Cosmológico de los Antiguos Mexicanos
         (Representación del Mundo y del Espacio).* María Elena Landa A.,
         trans. Puebla, Mex.: Federación Estudiantil Poblana 1959–1960.
1970   *Daily Life of the Aztecs on the Eve of the Spanish Conquest.*
         Patrick O'Brien, trans. Stanford, Calif.: Stanford University Press.
Spinden, Herbert J.
1928   *Ancient Civilizations of Mexico and Central America.* 3d ed.
         American Museum of Natural History, Handbook Series, no. 3.
         New York.
Spranz, Bodo
1973   *Los Dioses en los Códices Mexicanos del Groupo Borgia: Una
         Investigación Iconográfica.* María Martínez Peñaloza, trans.
         Mexico City: Fondo de Cultura Económica.
Stenzel, Werner
1980   *Quetzalcoatl von Tula: Die Mythogenese einer Postkortesischen
         Legende.* Zeitschrift fur Lateinamerika-Wien, no. 18.
Sturtevant, William C.
1966   Anthropology, History, and Ethnohistory. *Ethnohistory* 13:1–51.
Sullivan, Thelma D.
1982   Tlazolteotl-Ixcuina: The Great Spinner and Weaver. In *The Art
         and Iconography of Late Post-Classic Central Mexico,* Elizabeth
         Hill Boone, ed., 7–35. Washington, D.C.: Dumbarton Oaks.
Tapia, Andrés de
1963   Relation of Some of the Things That Happened to the Very
         Illustrious Don Hernando Cortés, Marques del Valle. In *The
         Conquistadors: First-person Accounts of the Conquest of Mexico,*
         Patricia de Fuentes, ed. and trans., 19–48. New York: Orion Press.
         Written in the 16th century.
Tezozomoc, Hernando Alvarado
1975   *Crónica Mexicayotl.* Adrián León, trans. UNAM.
1980   *Crónica Mexicana.* (Preceded by the *Códice Ramirez.*) Manuel
         Orozco y Berra, ed., 151–701. 3d ed. Mexico City: Editorial
         Porrúa.
Thompson, J. Eric S.
1941   A Coordination of the History of Chichen Itza with Ceramic
         Sequences in Central Mexico. *RMEA* 5:97–111.
1970   *Maya History and Religion.* Norman: University of Oklahoma
         Press.
Tira de Tepechpan
n.d.   *Tepechpan Codex. Principal Events in Mexican Annals Between
         the Years 1298–1596.* Chicago: Julius Wisotzki.
Title of the Lords of Totonicapan
1979   *Title of the Lords of Totonicapan.* (Preceded by *The Annals of the
         Cakchiquels.*) Dionisio José Chonay and Delia Goetz, trans.,
         160–196. Norman: University of Oklahoma Press.

Todorov, Tzvetan
1984   *The Conquest of America: The Question of the Other.* Richard
        Howard, trans. New York: Harper and Row.
Torquemada, Fray Juan de
1975   *Monarquía Indiana.* Vol. 1. UNAM.
Tovar, Fray Juan de
1972   *Manuscrit Tovar: Origenes et Croyances des Indiens du Mexique.*
        Jacques Lafaye, ed. From the Manuscript of Phillips of the John
        Carter Brown Library. Graz.
Townsend, Richard Fraser
1979   *State and Cosmos in the Art of Tenochtitlan.* Dumbarton Oaks
        Studies in Pre-Columbian Art and Archaeology, no. 20.
Tozzer, Alfred M.
1957   *Chichén Itzá and Its Cenote of Sacrifice: A Comparative Study of
        Contemporaneous Maya and Toltec.* Memoirs of the Peabody
        Museum of Archaeology and Ethnology, vols. 11–12.
Trautmann, Thomas R.
1981   *Dravidian Kinship.* New York: Cambridge University Press.
Turner, Victor W.
1972   Betwixt and Between: The Liminal Period in *Rites de Passage.* In
        Reader in Comparative Religion: An Anthropological Approach,
        3d ed., William A. Lessa and Evon Z. Vogt, eds., 338–347. New
        York: Harper and Row.
Uchmany, Eva Alexandra
1980   Cambios Religiosos en la Conquista de México. *RMEA* 26:1–57.
Umberger, Emily
1982   The Structure of Aztec History. *Archaeoastronomy* 4(4): 10–17.
1987   Antiques, Revivals, and References to the Past in Aztec Art. *Res*
        13:62–105.
Valeri, Valerio
1985   *Kingship and Sacrifice: Ritual and Society in Ancient Hawaii.*
        Paula Wissing, trans. Chicago: University of Chicago Press.
Vansina, Jan
1973   *Oral Tradition: A Study in Historical Methodology.*
        Harmondsworth, Eng.: Penguin Books.
1985   *Oral Tradition as History.* Madison: University of Wisconsin
        Press.
Vargas Ugarte, Rubén
1947   *Historia del Culto de María en Iberoamérica.* Vol. 1. Buenos
        Aires: Editorial Harpes.
Veytia, Mariano Fernández de Echeverría y
1944   *Historia Antigua de México.* 2 vols. Mexico City: Editorial
        Leyenda.
Wagner, Henry Raup
1944   *The Rise of Fernando Cortés.* Los Angeles: Cortés Society.
Watts, Alan W.
1963   *The Two Hands of God: The Myths of Polarity.* New York: George
        Braziller.

Weaver, Muriel Porter
1972   *The Aztecs, Maya and Their Predecessors: Archaeology of Mesoamerica*. New York: Seminar Press.
1981   *The Aztecs, Maya and Their Predecessors: Archaeology of Mesoamerica*. 2d ed. New York: Academic Press.
Weitlaner, Roberto J., and Irmgard Weitlaner de Johnson
1943   Acatlán y Hueycantenango, Guerrero. *El México Antiguo* 6: 140–204.
Wilkerson, S. Jeffrey K.
1974   The Ethnographic Works of Andrés de Olmos, Precursor and Contemporary of Sahagún. In *Sixteenth-Century Mexico: The Work of Sahagún*, Munro S. Edmonson, ed., 27–78. Albuquerque: University of New Mexico Press.
Young, Michael W.
1966   The Divine Kingship of the Jukun: A Re-Evaluation of Some Theories. *Africa* 36:135–152.
Zantwijk, Rudolf A. M. van
1957   Aztec Hymns as the Expression of the Mexican Philosophy of Life. *International Archives of Ethnography* 48(1): 67–118.
1963   Principios Organizadores de los Mexicas: Una Introducción al Estudio del Sistema Interno del Régimen Azteca. *ECN* 4:187–220.
1966   Los Seis Barrios Sirvientes de Huitzilopochtli. *ECN* 6:177–185.
1976   La Organización Social de la México-Tenochtitlan Naciente: Una Interpretación de la Primera Pintura del Códice Mendocino. 41st *ICAP* 1974, Mexico City, 2:188–208.
1978   Iquehuacatzin, un Drama Real Azteca. *ECN* 13:89–96.
1981   La Entronización de Acamapichtli de Tenochtitlan y las Características de su Gobierno. *ECN* 15:17–26.
1985   *The Aztec Arrangement: The Social History of Pre-Spanish Mexico*. Norman: University of Oklahoma Press.
Zuidema, R. T.
1962   Reflections on Inca Historical Conceptions. 34th *ICAP* 1960, Vienna, 718–721.
1977   The Inca Kinship System: A New Theoretical View. In *Andean Kinship and Marriage*, Ralph Bolton and Enrique Mayer, eds., 240–281. American Anthropological Association Special Publication no. 7.
1978   Mito e Historia en el Antiguo Perú. *Allpanchis* 11:15–52. Cuzco.

Index

Note: Italicized numbers refer to entries in figures and tables. Women and goddesses are identified by the biological sign ♀.

Abocaci, 112, *113*

Acacitli, 70, 72, 73, 170

Acamapichtli (1st king), 5, 8, 13, *14*, 15, 17, *19*, 27, 29, 30, *33*, 36, 37, 40, *41*, 49, 63, 69, 84, *100–101*, 129, 130, 164; ancestry/parentage of, 21, 22, 25, 26–28, 32–34, 35, 36, 37, 38, 39, 46, 48–49, 50, 85, 94; arrows of, 7; and ♀Atotoztli, 25, 26–28, 32, 34, 35, 46, 49, 50, 85, 94; children of, 101; Coatlichan associated with, 32, 34, 37, 38, 39–41, 93; as Culhua descendant, 21, 22, 36, 37–38; ennobled, 25, 39, 50; generation-jumping marriage of, 36, 37; and ♀Ilancueitl, *19*, 20, 21, 25, 26, 29, 30, 32, 34, 35–42, 43, 44, 48–49, 50, 85, 94, 114; as nomad/hunter, 31; as progenitor, not first king, 38, 42, 102; sun associated with, 93; Topiltzin Quetzalcoatl linked with, 145, 146; wife of, *19*, 20, 21, 22, 26, 29, 32, 34, 35–42, 43, 49, 50, 85, 94, 114

Acamapichtli the Elder (Huehue Acamapichtli), 27, *27*, 28, *33*, 34, 35, 37, 38, 39, 46, 47, 146, 186

Achitometl (Huehue Achitometl), 29, 30, 36, 37, 74; as father of ♀Atotoztli/ ♀Ilancueitl, 28, 29, 31, 59–60; killed Huehue Acamapichtli, 38, 39, 146, 186; as ruler of Culhuacan, 32, 35, 37

Acolmiztli: as father of ♀Atotoztli/ ♀Ilancueitl, 35, 43; as ruler of Coatlichan, 27, 34, 43, 44; as Underworld deity, 44, 93

Acolnahuacatl, 70, *71*

Acosta, Jorge R., 205, 206

Acosta, Fr. Joseph de, xxxix, 114

Acts of Thomas, 184

Aculhua, 4, 5, 20, 28–31, 32, 50, 51, 140; cities of (*see* Coatlichan; Texcoco); historian of (*see* Ixtlilxochitl)

Acxitl, 177. *See also* Topiltzin Quetzalcoatl

Acxocuauhtli, 36, 37

African legends, 6, 52; compared to Aztec, 17, 216–17, 218, 220, 221–22

Quetzalcoatl *(continued)*
with, 175, 176, 187, 189, 190, 191;
Cortés mistaken for, 159, 161, 164,
180, 186, 192, 193, 195, 198, 226,
228–30; Cortés not taken for, 182;
crafts associated with, 184, 185, 190;
as creator deity, 147, 176, 191; Culhuacan associated with, 189; cult of,
175, 176, 187; as Ehecatl (wind god),
143, *144*, 175, 187, 189, 191, 192,
193, 198, 229; and feathered serpent,
143, 176, 192, 193, 197; as fertility
god, 147, 151; fourth sun associated
with, 191, 192; as god who left and
would return, 159, 189, 190, 192,
226; Huemac associated with, 153–
54, *161*; Huitzilopochtli linked with,
145, 155; and ♀Ilancueitl, 189; legitimates kingship, 177–78, 198, 224;
as mediator, 176–77; as patron deity,
154; rainy season associated with,
151; as supreme deity, 190; and Tezcatlipoca, 145, 146–48, 149, 153–54,
159, 161, 176, 192, 198; Tlapallan
associated with, 192, 193; Tollan associated with, 179, 192, 193, 198, 216;
Topiltzin Quetzalcoatl merged with,
146–48, 149, 176, 187, 192, 198, 216
(see also Topiltzin Quetzalcoatl); as
Venus/Morning Star, 137, 143, 148,
154, 176, 192, 198; as Xolotl, 176,
187; Year 1 Reed associated with, 191,
192, 216
Quetzalmachoncatl, 125, *126*, 127
♀Quetzalxochitl, 141–42, *142*; ances-
try/parentage of, 79, 80, 171, 214;
♀Chimalaxochitl linked with, 81, *82*;
♀Coyolxauhqui linked with, 81, *82*; as
mother-earth goddess, 120; sacrificed,
79, *82*, 84, 89, 90, *91*, 151, 214
Quiche Maya, 202
♀Quilaztli, 62, 138
Quisteil rebellion, 166

Radiocarbon dating, 206
Rain god, 86, 88, 89, 154, 212, 214
Rainy season, 88–89, 151
Reed. *See* Year, 1 Reed, 2 Reed, 7 Reed
Regicide, 16, 17, 222, 223–24, 227, 228
Relación de la Genealogía, 10, *14*, 145–
46, 148, 150, 151, 185, 186
Richards, Audrey I., xxiii, xxv, 6

Ritual, 118, 229; agricultural, 213; as
boundary marker, 23; calendar for,
xxiii, xxiv, 210–11, 212; fire, 23, 68,
92; history transmitted by, xxvi, 211–
15, 216; kingship explained by, 215;
political relationships confirmed by,
213; regicide, 222, 223–24, 227, 228;
sacrifice, 92–93, 213, 214
Rwanda, 17

Sacrifice: to change seasons/bring rain,
79, 89, 90, *91*, 151, 213–14, 224; at
Chapultepec, 89; of ♀Coyolxauhqui,
63, 64, *65*, 65, 67, 68, 78, 79, 80, *82*,
84, 88, 90, *91*, 212, 213; discontinuity
in, 84; ends cycle, 23, 68, 79, 80, 89,
90, *91*, 94; forces Mexica migration,
68, 78–79, 80, *82*, 85, 90, 94, 224; gods
demand, *65*, 68, 79, *82*, 83, 84, 88,
158, 185, 214; heart, *65*, 67, 79, 80,
82, 84, 89, *91*, 223; of Huitzilihuitl
the Elder and his daughters, 69–70,
70, 72, 74, 75, 76, 90, *91*, 92, 170–71;
of king, 222–23; kingship regenerated
by, 224, 227, 228; mutilation in, *65*,
84, *91*; places for, 67–68, 89; political relationships confirmed by, *91*,
224; Quetzalcoatl prohibited, 190; of
♀Quetzalxochitl, 79, *82*, 84, 89, 90, *91*,
151, 214; ritual, 92–93, 118, 213, 214;
of ♀Toci, 67–68, 78, 80, *82*, 84, 92–93,
118, 213; as unifying, 80; of women,
xl–xli, 58, *65*, 68, 69, 74–75, 76, 77–
78, 79, 80, 81, *82*, 84, 85, 89, 90, *91*,
92–93, 94, 141, 170, 171, 213–14, 224;
of ♀Yaocihuatl, 213
Sahagún, Fr. Bernardino de, xxxi, xxxii,
xxxiii, *10*, 63, *65*, 67, 86, 88, 148, 158,
203, 212; on Cortés as Quetzalcoatl,
195; on Toltecs, 83, 178, 194–95; on
Topiltzin Quetzalcoatl saga, 135, 150,
192–95, 217
Sahlins, Marshall, xxxviii, 219
Seasons: dry, 79, 88–89, 151, 213; Huitzilopochtli and, 88–89; Quetzalcoatl
and, 151; rainy, 88–89, 151; sacrifice ends/begins, 79, 89, 90, *91*, 151,
213–14, 224
Serpent: ♀Coatlicue and, 87; feathered
(see Feathered serpent); fire, 63, 66,
197, 212, 229; hill *(see* Coatepec);
Itzcoatl and, 7; as mediator, 87, 216

202; as real man, 174, 202; son of, 29; Spanish-authored texts on, 135, 138–40, 143, 145, 147–48, 150, 151–52, 171–72, 174, 175, 176, 179–85, 185–201, 217; Spanish dress worn by, 190; Tenochtitlan associated with, 177; Tezcatlipoca linked with, 145, 146–48, 149, 151, 152, 153–54, 159, 161, 176, 185, 188, 192, 196, 198, 199; Tlapallan associated with, 185, 186, 187, 191, 192, 193; Tollan associated with, 29, 29, 135, 136, 143, 147–48, 164, 174, 179, 185, 187, 188, 191, 192, 193, 196, 198, 199, 216; as *toltec*, 199; as Topiltzin, 185–86; twinned/doubled, 136, 143–45, 154, 156, 161, 176, 184; as Venus, 148, 192; at water's edge, 157, 162; wife of, 189; Xipe Totec and, 152–53, 159, 192; Year 1 Reed associated with, 140, 141, 150, 191, 192, 216

Torquemada, Fr. Juan de, xxxi, xxxix, 43, 46, 48, 130, 132

Totepeuh, *142*, 143, 149, 202; as Mixcoatl's equivalent, 136–37, 146, 176, 185, 186, 189, 227 (*see also* Mixcoatl)

Tovar, Fr. Juan de, *10*, 14, 114, 196. See also *Codex Ramirez*

Toxcuecuex, 69, 79, 80, 141, 153, 171, 214

♀Toxochipantzin, 29, 29, 74

♀Toxpanxochitl, 70, 70, 71, 72–73, 74, 75, 75, 76, 77, 78, 82

Toxpanxochitl, 72

Triple Alliance, 3, 6, 63, 100, 132, 161

Tula de Allende, xii, xiii, xiv, 206; Chichen Itza similar to, 197, 203, 204, 205, 207; as Tollan, xiv, 194–95, 203, 204, 205, 207

Turner, Victor, 163

Twins, 225; creator, 133; god of (*see* Xolotl); of Motecuhzoma I, 15, 128, 131–34, 156–57, 161; mother of, 131; of Topiltzin Quetzalcoatl, 136, 143–45, 147, 154, 156, 161, 176, 184

Tzacualtitlan Tenanco Amaquemecan, 46

Tzimpan, 170

Uex, Francisco, 166
Underworld, 88; deities, 44, 71, 93;

entrance to, 89–90, 162 (*see also* Xicococ)

Valeri, Valerio, xxxvi, 227

Valley of Mexcio, xvii, xx, 3, 4, 20, 68–69, 90

Vansina, Jan, xxvi

Venus: as Evening Star (Xolotl), 154, 155, 176, 187, 198; as Morning Star (Quetzalcoatl), 133, 137, 143, 148, 154, 176, 192, 198, 229; Topiltzin Quetzalcoatl and, 148, 192

Veracruz, 205

Veytia, Mariano, xxxix

Virgin Mary, 97, 116, 117–19, 165

Virgin of Guadalupe, 116–17, 118, 119

Water, 78, 88, 213

Water-bird, 18, 29

Water's edge, 156, 157, 162, 164

White Heads, 166

Wind. *See* Ehecatl

Woman: of discord, xiv, xli, 59–60, 117, 129, 130, 213, 214 (*see also* Queens); earth/agriculture associated with, 222 (*see also* Mother-earth goddess); end/begin cycles, 17–18, 68, 79, 80, 89, 90, 91, 93, 94, 96, 97, 105, 114, 115, 119, 120; ennoble kings (*see* Ennoblement, power of); gender ambiguity of, 74; merging of kinship roles of, 19, 20, 21, 22, 25, 34, 35–42, 48–50, 54, 54–55, 59, 60–61, 62, 74, 75, 85, 93, 94, 114, 116, 117–18, 130, 141; more than one kinship role, 12, 21, 22, 25, 26–28, 32, 34, 35, 46, 49–50, 85, 94; sacrificed, xl–xli, 58, 65, 68, 69, 74–75, 76, 77–78, 79, 80, 81, 82, 84, 85, 89, 90, 91, 92–93, 94, 141, 170, 171, 213–14, 224

Woot, King, of Kuba, 216–17

Writing, xvii, xix–xx. See also History

Xicco, 148

Xicococ, 89–90, 138, *139*, 148

Xicocotitlan, 148

Xihuitl Temoc, 36, *37*

Xipe Totec, 147, 152–53, 158–59, 192

Xiuhtemoc, 29

Xochimilco, 62

♀Xochiquetzal, 62, 89, 137, 141, 153, 176. *See also* ♀Chimalman; Mother-earth goddess

ABOUT THE AUTHOR

SUSAN D. GILLESPIE is Research Associate in the Department of Anthropology at the University of Illinois at Urbana-Champaign, where she received a Ph.D. in 1983. The 1980 Komchen archaeological project in Yucatan introduced her to fieldwork in Mexico, and she has since directed excavations at Charco Redondo, on the coast of Oaxaca, and at Llano del Jícaro, an Olmec monument workshop in Veracruz. Her interest in archaeological theory led her to reexamine the popular story of Quetzalcoatl and the Toltecs in Mesoamerican prehistory in order to determine why archaeologists retained their faith in this ambiguous episode from postconquest historical traditions rather than trust their own archaeological data, which often contradicted it. This book resulted from that inquiry. Among her other publications on pre-Hispanic Mesoamerican ideology and iconography are "Ballgames and Boundaries," in *The Mesoamerican Ballgame*, edited by Vernon L. Scarborough and David R. Wilcox (University of Arizona Press, 1991).